Contents

Accounting, 20e
or
Financial Accounting, 8e

Warren • Reeve • Fess

Prepared by

Carl S. Warren
University of Georgia, Athens

James M. Reeve
University of Tennessee, Knoxville

SOUTH-WESTERN
™
THOMSON LEARNING

Australia · Canada · Mexico · Singapore · Spain · United Kingdom · United States

Study Guide, Chapters 1–16, to accompany ACCOUNTING, 20e
by Warren, Reeve, and Fess

Team Director: Dave Shaut
Senior Acquisitions Editor: Sharon Oblinger
Senior Developmental Editor: Ken Martin
Senior Marketing Manager: Dan Silverburg
Production Editor: Heather Mann
Manufacturing Coordinator: Doug Wilke
Production Services: Mary Hartkemeyer
Printer: Globus Printing, Inc.

Printed in the United States of America
1 2 3 4 5   04 03 02 01

For more information contact South-Western College Publishing, 5101 Madison Road, Cincinnati, Ohio, 45227 or find us on the Internet at http://www.swcollege.com.

For permission to use material from this text or product, contact us by
• **telephone: 1-800-730-2214**
• **fax: 1-800-730-2215**
• **web: http://www.thomsonrights.com**

ISBN: 0-324-05193-X

This book is printed on acid-free paper.

Introduction to Accounting and Business

QUIZ AND TEST HINTS

The following hints may be helpful to you in preparing for a quiz or a test over the material covered in Chapter 1.

1. Terminology is important in this chapter. Do the Matching Exercise on pages 23–24. Expect multiple-choice, true/false, or matching questions to include the terms introduced throughout the chapter. For example, you should be able to distinguish between the different types of business organizations, identify business stakeholders, and distinguish between financial and managerial accounting. Pay special attention to the terms beginning on page 10 to the end of the chapter. These terms will be used frequently throughout the remainder of the text.

2. Know the accounting equation: Assets = Liabilities + Owner's Equity. Be able to compute one amount when given the other two. For example, if assets equal $100,000 and liabilities equal $60,000, owner's equity must equal $40,000. Be able to determine the effect of change in the basic elements on one another. For example, if assets increase by $10,000 and liabilities decrease by $5,000, owner's equity must increase by $15,000.

3. Be able to record business transactions within the framework of the accounting equation. Use the illustration on pages 12–15 as a basis for review and study. Pay particular attention to items that are increased and decreased by transactions a through h. Note the introduction of new terms such as account payable, account receivable, revenue, and expense. These new terms are highlighted in color in the text.

4. Be able to describe each of the financial statements listed on page 17. You may be required to prepare a short income statement, statement of owner's equity, and balance sheet. You will probably not be required to prepare a statement of cash flows.

5. Review the summary data for NetSolutions on page 16. Trace the numbers into the statements shown in Exhibit 4 on page 17. Know the format of each statement such as the number of columns and placement of dollar signs. Some of the numbers in Exhibit 4 appear on more than one statement. Sometimes a quiz or a test question will provide partially completed statements, and you will be required to complete the statements. Recognizing amounts that appear on more than one statement will aid you in answering this type of question.

FILL IN THE BLANK—Part A

Instructions: Answer the following questions or complete the statements by writing the appropriate words or amounts in the answer blanks.

1. An organization in which basic resources (inputs), such as materials and labor, are assembled and processed to provide goods or services (outputs) to customers is a(n) _____.

2. A business organized under state or federal statutes as a separate legal entity is a(n) _____.

3. A person or entity that has an interest in the economic performance of a business is called a(n) _____ _____.

4. An information system that provides reports to stakeholders about the economic activities and condition of a business is _____.

5. Moral principles that guide the conduct of individuals are called _____.

6. A specialized field of accounting that uses estimated data to aid management in running day-to-day operations and in planning future operations is called _____ accounting.

7. A concept of accounting that requires that economic data be recorded in dollars is the _____ _____ _____ concept.

8. The resources owned by a business are called _____.

9. The rights of the owners are called _____ _____.

10. Assets = Liabilities + Owner's Equity is the _____ _____.

11. Carson offered for sale at $75,000 land that had been purchased for $45,000. If Zimmer paid Carson $70,000 for the land, the amount that Zimmer would record for the purchase of the land in the accounting records is _____.

12. The liability created by a purchase on account is referred to as a(n) _____ _____.

13. If liabilities are $85,000 and owner's equity is $45,000, the amount of the assets is _____.

14. If assets are $375,000 and owner's equity is $295,000, the amount of the liabilities is _____.

15. The amount a business earns by selling goods or services to its customers is called _____.

16. If operations for an accounting period resulted in cash sales of $60,000, sales on account of $150,000, and expenses paid in cash of $195,000, the net income or (net loss) for the period is _____.

17. A summary of the changes in the owner's equity that have occurred *during a specific period of time*, such as a month or a year, is the

_____ _____ _____ _____.

18. The owner's equity at the beginning of the period was $19,000; at the end of the period, assets were $98,000 and liabilities were $41,000. The owner made no additional investments or withdrawals during the period. The net income or (net loss) for the period is _____.

19. The form of balance sheet that resembles the basic format of the accounting equation, with assets on the left side and the liabilities and owner's equity sections on the right side, is called the _____ form.

20. If total assets increased by $85,000 and liabilities decreased by $9,000 during the period, the amount and direction (increase or decrease) of the period's change in owner's equity was _____.

FILL IN THE BLANK—Part B

Instructions: Answer the following questions or complete the statements by writing the appropriate words or amounts in the answer blanks.

1. A type of business that changes basic inputs into products that are sold to individual customers is a(n) _____ business.

2. A type of business that purchases products from other businesses and sells them to customers is a(n) _____ business.

3. A business owned by one individual is called a(n) _____.

4. Individuals whom the owners have authorized to operate the business are called _____.

5. A specialized field of accounting primarily concerned with the recording and reporting of economic data and activities to stakeholders outside the business is called _____ accounting.

6. The authoritative body that has the primary responsibility for developing accounting principles is the _____ _____

_____ _____.

7. A concept of accounting that limits the economic data in the accounting system to data related directly to the activities of the business is the _____ _____ concept.

8. The rights of creditors that represent debts of the business are called

_____.

9. An economic event or condition that directly changes an entity's financial condition or directly affects its results of operations is called a(n)

_____ _____.

10. Items such as supplies that will be used in the business in the future are called _____ _____.

11. A claim against the customer is called a(n) _____ _____.

12. If owner's equity is $46,000 and liabilities are $34,000, the amount of assets is _____.

13. If assets are $98,000 and liabilities are $32,500, the amount of owner's equity is _____.

14. The amounts used in the process of earning revenue are _____.

15. A summary of the revenue and expenses *for a specific period of time*, such as a month or a year, is called a(n) _____ _____.

16. If operations for an accounting period resulted in cash sales of $90,000, sales on account of $40,000, and expenses paid in cash of $135,000, the net income or (net loss) for the period is _____.

17. A list of the assets, liabilities, and owner's equity *as of a specific date*, usually at the close of the last day of a month or a year, is called a(n) _____ _____.

18. If total assets increased by $21,500 and owner's equity increased by $8,000 during a period, the amount and direction (increase or decrease) of the period's change in total liabilities was _____.

19. A summary of the cash receipts and cash payments *for a specific period of time*, such as a month or a year, is called a(n) _____ _____ _____.

20. The owner's equity at the beginning of the period was $46,000; at the end of the period, assets were $99,000 and liabilities were $22,000. If the owner made an additional investment of $10,000 and withdrew $8,000 during the period, the net income or (net loss) for the period is _____.

MULTIPLE CHOICE

Instructions: Circle the best answer for each of the following questions.

1. Accountants employed by a particular business firm or not-for-profit organization, perhaps as chief accountant, controller, or financial vice-president, are said to be engaged in:

   a. general accounting

   b. public accounting

   c. independent accounting

   d. private accounting

2. A type of business that changes basic inputs into products that are sold to individual customers.

   a. service business

   b. manufacturing business

   c. merchandising business

   d. proprietorship business

3. The accounting concept that requires economic data be recorded in dollars.

   a. cost concept

   b. objectivity concept

   c. business entity concept

   d. unit of measure concept

4. The amounts for recording properties and services purchased by a business are determined using the:

   a. business entity concept

   b. cost concept

   c. matching principle

   d. proprietorship principle

5. Another way of writing the accounting equation is:

   a. Assets + Liabilities = Owner's Equity

   b. Owner's Equity + Assets = Liabilities

   c. Assets = Owner's Equity − Liabilities

   d. Assets − Liabilities = Owner's Equity

6. If total liabilities increased by $20,000 during a period of time and owner's equity increased by $5,000 during the same period, the amount and direction (increase or decrease) of the period's change in total assets is:

   a. $20,000 increase

   b. $20,000 decrease

   c. $25,000 decrease

   d. $25,000 increase

7. A business paid $6,000 to a creditor in payment of an amount owed. The effect of the transaction on the accounting equation was:

   a. an increase in an asset and a decrease in another asset

   b. a decrease in an asset and an increase in a liability

   c. a decrease in an asset and a decrease in a liability

   d. an increase in an asset and an increase in owner's equity

8. The total assets and the total liabilities of a particular business enterprise at the beginning and at the end of the year are stated below. During the year, the owner had withdrawn $30,000 for personal use and had made an additional investment in the enterprise of $25,000.

	Assets	Liabilities
Beginning of year	$290,000	$190,000
End of year	355,000	220,000

   The amount of net income for the year was:

   a. $5,000

   b. $25,000

   c. $30,000

   d. $40,000

9. If revenue was $70,000, expenses were $59,000, and the owner's withdrawals were $25,000, the amount of net income or net loss was:

   a. net income of $11,000

   b. net income of $36,000

   c. net loss of $59,000

   d. net income of $70,000

10. Which of the following is not one of the major sections of the statement of cash flows?

    a. cash flows from marketing activities

    b. cash flows from investing activities

    c. cash flows from financing activities

    d. cash flows from operating activities

TRUE/FALSE

Instructions: Indicate whether each of the following statements is true or false by placing a check mark in the appropriate column.

		True	False
1.	Accounting is often characterized as the "language of business."	___	___
2.	Accountants who render accounting services on a fee basis and staff accountants employed by them are said to be engaged in private accounting.	___	___
3.	Managerial accounting uses estimated data instead of financial accounting data to run day-to-day operations.	___	___
4.	The concept that expenses incurred in generating revenue should be matched against the revenue in determining net income or net loss is called the cost concept.	___	___
5.	The financing activities section of the statement of cash flows includes cash transactions that enter into the determination of net income.	___	___
6.	The debts of a business are called its accounts receivable.	___	___
7.	A partnership is owned by not less than four individuals.	___	___
8.	A business transaction is the occurrence of an event or of a condition that must be recorded.	___	___
9.	A summary of the changes in the owner's equity of a business entity that have occurred during a specific period of time, such as a month or a year, is called a statement of cash flows.	___	___
10.	A claim against a customer for sales made on credit is an account payable.	___	___

EXERCISE 1-1

Instructions: Some typical transactions of Clem's Laundry Service are presented below. For each transaction, indicate the increase (+), the decrease (−), or no change (0) in the assets (A), liabilities (L), and owner's equity (OE) by placing the appropriate sign(s) in the appropriate column(s). More than one sign may have to be placed in the A, L, or OE column for a given transaction.

	A	L	OE
1. Received cash from owner as an additional investment	___	___	___
2. Purchased supplies on account	___	___	___
3. Charged customers for services sold on account	___	___	___
4. Received cash from cash customers	___	___	___
5. Paid cash for rent on building	___	___	___
6. Collected an account receivable in full	___	___	___
7. Paid cash for supplies	___	___	___
8. Returned supplies purchased on account and not yet paid for	___	___	___
9. Paid cash to creditors on account	___	___	___
10. Paid cash to owner for personal use	___	___	___

PROBLEM 1-1

Instructions: The assets, liabilities, and owner's equity of Ed Casey, who operates a small repair shop, are expressed in equation form below. Following the equation are ten transactions completed by Casey. On each of the numbered lines, show by addition or subtraction the effect of each of the transactions on the equation. For each transaction, identify the changes in owner's equity by placing the letter R (revenue), E (expense), D (drawing), or I (investment) at the right of each increase or decrease in owner's equity. On the lines labeled "Bal.," show the new equation resulting from the transaction.

	Assets	=	Liabilities	+	Owner's Equity
	Cash + Supplies + Land	=	Accounts Payable	+	Ed Casey, Capital

1. Casey started a repair shop and deposited $40,000 cash in the bank for use by the business.............................. (1) _____

2. Casey purchased $2,000 of supplies on account. .... (2) _____

   Bal. _____

3. Casey purchased land for a future building site for $14,000 cash. .... (3) _____

   Bal. _____

4. Casey paid creditors $1,800 on account. .... (4) _____

   Bal. _____

5. Casey withdrew $2,000 for personal use. .... (5) _____

   Bal. _____

6. Casey paid $2,800 for building and equipment rent for the month............................. (6) _____

   Bal. _____

7. During the month, another $900 of expenses were incurred on account by the business............................... (7) _____

   Bal. _____

8. During the month, Casey deposited another $10,000 of personal funds in the business bank account................ (8) _____

   Bal. _____

9. Casey received $500 for a cash service call. .... (9) _____

   Bal. _____

10. Casey used $600 worth of supplies............................... (10) _____

   Bal. _____

PROBLEM 1-2

The amounts of the assets and liabilities of Tom's Painting Service at December 31 of the current year, and the revenues and expenses for the year are as follows:

Cash	$10,050
Accounts receivable	8,950
Supplies	4,000
Accounts payable	4,450
Sales	27,450
Supplies expense	5,450
Advertising expense	4,825
Truck rental expense	1,525
Utilities expense	700
Miscellaneous expense	1,400

The capital of Tom Wallace, owner, was $4,000 at the beginning of the current year. During the year, Wallace withdrew $1,000 and made an additional investment of $2,000.

Instructions: Using the forms provided, prepare the following:

(1) An income statement for the year ended December 31, 20--.

(2) A statement of owner's equity for the year ended December 31, 20--.

(3) A balance sheet as of December 31, 20--.

(1)

Tom's Painting Service

Income Statement

For Year Ended December 31, 20--

(2)   *Tom's Painting Service*

Statement of Owner's Equity

For Year Ended December 31, 20--

(3)   *Tom's Painting Service*

Balance Sheet

December 31, 20--

2

Analyzing Transactions

QUIZ AND TEST HINTS

The following hints may be helpful to you in preparing for a quiz or a test over the material covered in Chapter 2.

1. Terminology is important in this chapter. Do the Matching Exercise on pages 78–79. Pay special attention to major account classifications discussed on pages 46–47 of the text.

2. Memorize the "Rules of Debit and Credit" and the "Normal Balances of Accounts." All instructors will ask questions to test your knowledge of these items.

3. Be able to prepare general journal entries for the types of transactions presented in this chapter. Review the illustration beginning on page 49, and be sure you understand each entry. Be especially careful not to confuse debits and credits. Remember that a credit is indented slightly to the right when preparing a general journal entry. A good review is to rework the Illustrative Problem.

4. You should be familiar with the process of posting accounts for working assigned problems. However, you will probably not be required to post accounts on an examination.

5. You may be required to prepare a trial balance from a list of accounts with normal balances.

6. You might expect one or two questions on how to correct errors. These types of questions may require you to prepare a correcting journal entry. Review the section of the chapter and illustration containing this information.

FILL IN THE BLANK—Part A

Instructions: Answer the following questions or complete the statements by writing the appropriate words or amounts in the answer blanks.

1. An accounting form that is used to record the increases and decreases in each financial statement item is the _____.

2. A list of the accounts in the ledger is called the _____ _____ _____.

3. Increases in owner's equity as a result of selling services or products to customers is called _____.

4. The simplest form of an account is the _____.

5. Amounts entered on the left side of an account are _____.

6. An increase in Accounts Receivable is recorded by a _____ entry in the account.

7. An increase in Ken Lindgren, Capital is recorded by a _____ entry in the account.

8. A decrease in Accounts Payable is recorded by a _____ entry in the account.

9. A decrease in Salaries Expense is recorded by a _____ entry in the account.

10. Unearned Revenue is a(n) _____ account.

11. A decrease in Cash is recorded by a _____ entry in the account.

12. The normal balance of the supplies account is a _____ balance.

13. The normal balance of Lisa Jones, Capital is a _____ balance.

14. The initial record in which the effects of a transaction are recorded is the _____.

15. The process of recording a transaction in the journal is called _____.

16. The _____-_____ _____ is a system of accounting for recording transactions, based on recording increases and decreases in accounts so that debits equal credits.

17. The process of transferring the debits and credits from the journal entries to the accounts is called _____.

18. An all-purpose journal is the _____-_____ _____.

19. The _____ concept of accounting implies that the error may be treated in the easiest possible way.

20. An error in which the order of the digits is changed mistakenly, such as writing $542 as $452 or $524, is called a(n) _____.

FILL IN THE BLANK—Part B

Instructions: Answer the following questions or complete the statements by writing the appropriate words or amounts in the answer blanks.

1. A group of accounts for a business is called a(n) _____.

2. Resources that are owned by the business are called _____.

3. Debts owed to outsiders (creditors) are _____ of the business.

4. The owner's right to the assets of the business is the _____ _____.

5. Assets used up or services consumed in the process of generating revenues are reported as _____.

6. Amounts entered on the right side of an account are _____.

7. The amount of the difference between the debits and the credits that have been entered into an account is the _____ of the account.

8. The recording of a transaction in a journal is called _____.

9. The _____ account is used to record amounts withdrawn by an owner of a proprietorship.

10. _____ _____ is the liability created by receiving the revenue in advance.

11. A decrease in Notes Payable is recorded by a _____ entry in the account.

12. An increase in J.B. Moore, Drawing, is recorded by a _____ entry in the account.

13. A decrease in Accounts Receivable is recorded by a _____ entry in the account.

14. _____ analysis compares an item in a current statement with the same item in prior statements.

15. Wages Payable is a(n) _____ account.

16. Patent Rights is a(n) _____ account.

17. The normal balance of the prepaid insurance account is a _____ balance.

18. The normal balance of the fees earned account is a _____ balance.

19. A summary listing the titles and balances of accounts in the general ledger is called a(n) _____ _____.

20. An error in which the entire number is mistakenly moved one or more spaces to the right or the left, such as writing $542.00 as $54.20 or $5,420.00, is called a(n) _____.

MULTIPLE CHOICE

Instructions: Circle the best answer for each of the following questions.

1. The receipt of cash from customers in payment of their accounts would be recorded by a:
    a. debit to Cash and a credit to Accounts Payable
    b. debit to Cash and a credit to Accounts Receivable
    c. debit to Cash and a credit to Fees Earned
    d. debit to Cash and a credit to Fees Expense

2. The first step in recording a transaction in a two-column journal is to:
    a. list the account to be credited
    b. list the amount to be credited
    c. list the amount to be debited
    d. list the account to be debited

3. The drawing account of a sole proprietorship is debited when:
    a. the owner invests cash
    b. the owner withdraws cash
    c. a liability is paid
    d. an expense is paid

4. The equality of debits and credits in the ledger should be verified at the end of each accounting period by preparing a(n):
    a. accounting statement
    b. balance report
    c. trial balance
    d. account verification report

5. Of the following errors, the one that will cause an inequality in the trial balance totals is:
    a. incorrectly computing an account balance
    b. failure to record a transaction
    c. recording the same transaction more than once
    d. posting a transaction to the wrong account

6. Credits to cash result in:
    a. an increase in owner's equity
    b. a decrease in assets
    c. an increase in liabilities
    d. an increase in revenue

7. Debits to expense accounts signify:
   a. increases in owner's capital
   b. decreases in owner's capital
   c. increases in assets
   d. increases in liabilities

8. When rent is prepaid for several months in advance, the debit is to:
   a. an expense account
   b. a capital account
   c. a liability account
   d. an asset account

9. When an asset is purchased on account, the credit is to:
   a. a capital account
   b. a revenue account
   c. a liability account
   d. an expense account

10. When a payment is made to a supplier for goods previously purchased on account, the debit is to:
    a. an asset account
    b. a liability account
    c. a capital account
    d. an expense account

TRUE/FALSE

Instructions: Indicate whether each of the following statements is true or false by placing a check mark in the appropriate column.

		True	False
1.	Amounts entered on the left side of an account, regardless of the account title, are called credits or charges to the account.	____	____
2.	The difference between the total debits and the total credits posted to an account yields a figure called the balance of the account.	____	____
3.	Accounting systems provide information on business transactions for use by management in directing operations and preparing financial statements.	____	____
4.	The income statement accounts are listed first in the chart of accounts followed by the balance sheet accounts.	____	____
5.	The residual claim against the assets of a business after the total liabilities are deducted is called owner's equity.	____	____
6.	Every business transaction affects a minimum of one account.	____	____
7.	The process of recording a transaction in a journal is called posting.	____	____
8.	A group of accounts for a business entity is called a journal.	____	____
9.	A listing of the accounts in a ledger is called a chart of accounts.	____	____
10.	A recording error caused by the erroneous rearrangement of digits, such as writing $627 as $672, is called a slide.	____	____

EXERCISE 2-1

Eight transactions are recorded in the following T accounts:

Cash			
(1)	20,000	(5)	2,500
(7)	2,000	(8)	3,500

Machinery	
(2)	6,300

Ann Moran, Drawing	
(8)	3,500

Accounts Receivable			
(4)	5,000	(7)	2,000

Accounts Payable			
(5)	2,500	(2)	6,300
		(3)	820
		(6)	1,600

Service Revenue		
	(4)	5,000

Supplies	
(3)	820

Alan Moran, Capital		
	(1)	20,000

Operating Expenses	
(6)	1,600

Instructions: For each debit and each credit, indicate in the following form the type of account affected (asset, liability, owner's equity, revenue, or expense) and whether the account was increased (+) or decreased (−).

Transaction	Account Debited		Account Credited	
	Type	Effect	Type	Effect
(1)				
(2)				
(3)				
(4)				
(5)				
(6)				
(7)				
(8)				

PROBLEM 2-1

During June of the current year, Joan Star started Star Service Company.

Instructions:

(1) Record the following transactions in the two-column journal given below.

June   1.   Invested $5,000 in cash, equipment valued at $14,500, and a van worth $21,000.

16.   Purchased additional equipment on account, $5,500.

28.   Purchased supplies on account, $500.

30.   Paid $2,100 to creditors on account.

(2) Post to the appropriate ledger accounts on the following pages.

(3) Prepare a trial balance of the ledger accounts of Star Service Company as of June 30 of the current year, using the form that follows the ledger accounts.

(1)   **JOURNAL**   PAGE *1*

	DATE	DESCRIPTION	POST. REF.	DEBIT	CREDIT	
1						1
2						2
3						3
4						4
5						5
6						6
7						7
8						8
9						9
10						10
11						11
12						12
13						13
14						14
15						15
16						16
17						17
18						18
19						19
20						20
21						21
22						22
23						23

(2)   **LEDGER ACCOUNTS**

ACCOUNT   *Cash*   ACCOUNT NO.   *11*

DATE	ITEM	POST. REF.	DEBIT	CREDIT	BALANCE	
					DEBIT	CREDIT

ACCOUNT   *Supplies*   ACCOUNT NO.   *12*

DATE	ITEM	POST. REF.	DEBIT	CREDIT	BALANCE	
					DEBIT	CREDIT

ACCOUNT   *Equipment*   ACCOUNT NO.   *18*

DATE	ITEM	POST. REF.	DEBIT	CREDIT	BALANCE	
					DEBIT	CREDIT

ACCOUNT   *Vehicles*   ACCOUNT NO.   *19*

DATE	ITEM	POST. REF.	DEBIT	CREDIT	BALANCE	
					DEBIT	CREDIT

ACCOUNT   *Accounts Payable*   ACCOUNT NO.   *21*

DATE	ITEM	POST. REF.	DEBIT	CREDIT	BALANCE	
					DEBIT	CREDIT

ACCOUNT   *Joan Star, Capital*   ACCOUNT NO.   *31*

DATE	ITEM	POST. REF.	DEBIT	CREDIT	BALANCE	
					DEBIT	CREDIT

(3)

PROBLEM 2-2

On January 2, 20--, Judy Turner, an attorney, opened a law office. The following transactions were completed during the month.

a. Invested $20,000 cash and $13,200 worth of office equipment in the business.

b. Paid a month's rent of $2,500.

c. Paid $1,000 for office supplies.

d. Collected legal fees of $19,600.

e. Paid secretary a salary of $1,100.

f. Purchased $200 worth of office supplies on account.

g. Bought an auto for business use. It cost $13,000. Turner paid $2,600 down and charged the balance.

h. Withdrew $5,000 from the firm for personal use.

i. Paid $800 for auto repairs and maintenance.

j. Received a $240 telephone bill.

k. Paid the $240 telephone bill.

l. Paid premiums of $1,700 on property insurance.

m. Paid $2,000 on accounts payable.

n. Paid $5,000 cash for books for the law library.

o. Paid $500 cash for janitor service.

Instructions:

(1) Record the transactions in the T accounts that follow.

(2) Prepare a trial balance, using the form on the following page.

Cash		Office Supplies		Office Equipment

| Prepaid Insurance | | Auto |

| Library | | Accounts Payable |

Judy Turner, Capital

Rent Expense

Auto Repairs &
Maintenance Expense

Judy Turner, Drawing

Salary Expense

Janitor Expense

Legal Fees

Telephone Expense

(2)

PROBLEM 2-3

The following errors were made in journalizing and posting transactions:

a. A $1,000 premium paid for insurance was debited to Prepaid Rent and credited to Cash.

b. A $200 purchase of supplies on account was recorded as a debit to Supplies and a credit to Accounts Receivable.

c. A withdrawal of $1,500 by the owner was debited to Cash and credited to the drawing account.

Instructions: Prepare entries in the two-column journal provided below to correct these errors.

JOURNAL PAGE

	DATE	DESCRIPTION	POST. REF.	DEBIT	CREDIT	
1						1
2						2
3						3
4						4
5						5
6						6
7						7
8						8
9						9
10						10
11						11
12						12
13						13
14						14
15						15
16						16
17						17
18						18
19						19
20						20
21						21
22						22
23						23
24						24
25						25
26						26

3

The Matching Concept and the Adjusting Process

QUIZ AND TEST HINTS

The following hints may be helpful to you in preparing for a quiz or a test over the material covered in Chapter 3.

1. Terminology is important in this chapter. Do the Matching Exercise on pages 118–119 in the text.

2. The major focus of this chapter is the adjusting process. You should be able to prepare adjusting entries for each of the four types of adjustments: deferred expenses, deferred revenues, accrued expenses, and accrued revenues. You should also be able to prepare the adjusting entry for depreciation. Review the illustrations in the chapter, especially Exhibit 5, and the adjusting entries required in the Illustrative Problem.

3. Some instructors may give you an unadjusted trial balance and adjusted trial balance and require you to figure out what the adjusting entries must have been. This would be similar to Exercises 3-26 and 3-27 and Problems 3-3A and 3-3B. To review for this type of problem, cover up the "Effect of Adjusting Entry" column in Exhibit 8 and see if you can figure out what the adjusting entries must have been.

FILL IN THE BLANK—Part A

Instructions: Answer the following questions or complete the statements by writing the appropriate words or amounts in the answer blanks.

1. The _____ _____ concept assumes that the economic life of the business can be divided into time periods.

2. Under the _____ basis of accounting, revenues and expenses are reported in the income statement in the period in which cash is received or paid.

3. The _____ _____ concept supports reporting revenues when the services are provided to customers.

4. _____ journal entries bring the accounts up to date at the end of the accounting period.

5. Items that have been initially recorded as assets but are expected to become expenses over time or through the normal operations of the business are called _____ _____.

6. Expenses that have been incurred *but have not been recorded* in the accounts are called _____ _____.

7. The _____ _____ account is debited for the amount of prepaid advertising expense expired during the period.

8. The _____ _____ — _____ account is credited for the amount of depreciation of equipment during the period.

9. The _____ _____ account is debited for the amount of unearned fees that have been earned during the period.

10. The _____ _____ account is credited for taxes accrued at the end of the period.

11. If the adjusting entry to record depreciation expense on equipment is omitted, the net income for the period will be _____.

12. If the adjusting entry to record accrued fees earned at the end of the period is omitted, the owner's equity will be _____ on the balance sheet.

13. If the adjusting entry to record accrued wages expense at the end of the period is omitted, the liabilities will be _____ on the balance sheet.

14. If the balance of the supplies account on January 1 is $2,500, supplies purchased during the year were $10,000, and the supplies on hand at December 31 were $1,800, the amount for the appropriate adjusting entry at December 31 is _____.

15. The prepaid insurance account has a debit balance of $1,200 at the end of the year. If unexpired insurance at the end of the year is $800, the amount of prepaid insurance that should be reported on the end-of-year balance sheet is _____.

16. Physical resources that are owned and used by a business and are permanent or have a long life are called _____ _____.

17. The portion of the cost of a fixed asset that is recorded as an expense each year of its useful life is called _____.

18. The difference between the cost of a fixed asset and its accumulated depreciation is called the _____ _____ of the asset.

19. The net income reported on the income statement is $90,000. However, adjusting entries have not been made at the end of the period for insurance expense of $550 and accrued salaries of $750. The correct net income should have been _____.

20. The _____ trial balance is prepared after all the adjusting entries have been posted.

FILL IN THE BLANK—Part B

Instructions: Answer the following questions or complete the statements by writing the appropriate words or amounts in the answer blanks.

1. Under the _____ basis of accounting, revenues are reported in the income statement in the period in which they are earned.

2. The _____ concept supports the reporting of revenues and the related expenses in the same period.

3. An analysis and updating of the accounts when financial statements are prepared is called the _____ process.

4. Items that have been initially recorded as liabilities but are expected to become revenues over time or through the normal operations of the business are called _____ _____.

5. Revenues that have been earned *but have not been recorded* in the accounts are called _____ _____.

6. The decrease in the ability of a fixed asset to provide useful services is called _____.

7. The _____ _____ account is credited when recording depreciation of a fixed asset.

8. If the adjusting entry to record accrued interest revenue is omitted, the total assets will be _____ on the balance sheet.

9. If the adjusting entry to record the amount of prepaid insurance that has expired during the period is omitted, the owner's equity will be _____ on the balance sheet.

10. The _____ _____ account is debited for the amount of accrued interest expense at the end of the period.

11. The _____ _____ account is credited for the amount of prepaid rent that has expired during the period.

12. The _____ _____ account is debited for the amount of depreciation on equipment during the period.

13. The _____ _____ account is credited for the amount of accrued fees at the end of the period.

14. _____ analysis compares each item in a current statement with a total amount within the same statement.

15. If the debit amount of an adjusting entry adjusts an income statement account, the credit amount of the adjusting entry must adjust a(n) _____ _____ account.

16. If the credit amount of an adjusting entry adjusts an asset account, the debit amount of the adjusting entry must adjust a(n) _____ account.

17. If the adjusting entry to record the amount of prepaid insurance that has expired during the period is omitted, the net income for the period will be

    _____ .

18. If the adjusting entry to record depreciation on equipment for the period is omitted, total assets will be _____ on the balance sheet.

19. If the balance of the supplies account on January 1 was $500, supplies purchased during the year were $1,750, and the supplies on hand at December 31 were $300, the amount for the appropriate adjusting entry at December 31 is _____ .

20. The prepaid insurance account has a debit balance of $3,600 at the end of the year. If unexpired insurance at the end of the year is $2,800, the amount of insurance expense that should be reported on the income statement is _____ .

MULTIPLE CHOICE

Instructions: Circle the best answer for each of the following questions.

1. Entries required at the end of an accounting period to bring the accounts up to date and to assure the proper matching of revenues and expenses are called:
   a. matching entries
   b. adjusting entries
   c. contra entries
   d. correcting entries

2. The amount of accrued but unpaid expenses at the end of the fiscal period is both an expense and a(n):
   a. liability
   b. asset
   c. deferral
   d. revenue

3. If the effect of the debit portion of an adjusting entry is to increase the balance of an expense account, which of the following describes the effect of the credit portion of the entry?
   a. Decreases the balance of a contra asset account
   b. Increases the balance of an asset account
   c. Decreases the balance of an asset account
   d. Increases the balance of an expense account

4. If the effect of the credit portion of an adjusting entry is to increase the balance of a liability account, which of the following describes the effect of the debit portion of the entry?
   a. Increases the balance of a contra asset account
   b. Increases the balance of an asset account
   c. Decreases the balance of an asset account
   d. Increases the balance of an expense account

5. The balance in the prepaid rent account before adjustment at the end of the year is $12,000, which represents three months' rent paid on December 1. The adjusting entry required on December 31 is:
   a. debit Prepaid Rent, $4,000; credit Rent Expense, $4,000
   b. debit Rent Expense, $4,000; credit Prepaid Rent, $4,000
   c. debit Prepaid Rent, $8,000; credit Rent Expense, $8,000
   d. debit Rent Expense, $8,000; credit Prepaid Rent, $8,000

6. At the end of the preceding fiscal year, the usual adjusting entry for accrued salaries owed to employees was omitted. The error was not corrected, but the accrued salaries were included in the first salary payment in the current fiscal year. Which of the following statements is true?

    a. Salary Expense was overstated and net income was understated for the current year.

    b. Salaries Payable is understated at the end of the current fiscal year.

    c. Salary Expense was overstated and net income was understated for the preceding year.

    d. Salary Expense and Salaries Payable were overstated for the preceding year.

7. The decrease in usefulness of fixed assets as time passes is called:

    a. consumption

    b. deterioration

    c. depreciation

    d. contra asset

8. The difference between the fixed asset account and the related accumulated depreciation account is called the:

    a. book value of the asset

    b. fair market value of the asset

    c. net cost of the asset

    d. contra account balance of the asset

9. If a $250 adjustment for depreciation is not recorded, which of the following financial statement errors will occur?

    a. expenses will be overstated

    b. net income will be understated

    c. assets will be understated

    d. owner's equity will be overstated

10. The net income reported on the income statement is $50,000. However, adjusting entries have not been made at the end of the period for supplies expense of $500 and accrued salaries of $1,300. Net income, as corrected, is:

    a. $48,200

    b. $48,700

    c. $50,500

    d. $51,800

TRUE/FALSE

Instructions: Indicate whether each of the following statements is true or false by placing a check mark in the appropriate column.

                                                     True   **False**

1. Most businesses use the accrual basis of accounting. ....   _____   _____

2. When the reduction in prepaid expenses is not properly recorded, this causes the asset accounts and expense accounts to be overstated. ....   _____   _____

3. Accumulated depreciation accounts may be referred to as contra asset accounts. ....   _____   _____

4. If the adjusting entry to record accrued wages at the end of the year is omitted, net income, owner's equity, and total assets will be overstated. ....   _____   _____

5. If the debit portion of an adjusting entry debits an expense, the credit portion must credit either a contra asset or a liability account. ....   _____   _____

6. The adjusting entry to record depreciation of fixed assets consists of a debit to a depreciation expense account and a credit to an accumulated depreciation account. ....   _____   _____

7. When services are not paid for until after they have been performed, the accrued expense is recorded in the accounts by an adjusting entry at the end of the accounting period. ....   _____   _____

8. A deferral is an expense that has not been paid or a revenue that has not been received. ....   _____   _____

9. Accrued expenses may be described on the balance sheet as accrued liabilities. ....   _____   _____

10. The amount of accrued revenue is recorded by debiting a liability account and crediting a revenue account. ....   _____   _____

EXERCISE 3-1

Don Taylor closes his books at the end of each year (December 31). On May 1 of the current year, Don insured the business assets for three years at a premium of $5,400.

Instructions:

(1) Using the T accounts below, enter the adjusting entry that should be made by Taylor as of December 31 to record the amount of insurance expired as of that date. The May 1 premium payment is recorded in the T accounts.

Cash	Prepaid Insurance	Insurance Expense
May 1 5,400	May 1 5,400	

(2) Taylor's balance sheet as of December 31 should show the asset value of the unexpired insurance as .... $ _____

(3) Taylor's income statement for the year ended December 31 should show insurance expense of .... $ _____

EXERCISE 3-2

Jan Olin closes her books at the end of each month. Olin has only one employee, who is paid at the rate of $50 per day. The employee is paid every Friday at the end of the day. Each workweek is composed of five days, starting on Monday. Assume that the Fridays of this month (October) fall on the 7th, 14th, 21st, and 28th.

Instructions:

(1) Using the T accounts below, enter the four weekly wage payments for October. Then enter the adjusting entry that should be made by Olin as of October 31 to record the salary owed the employee but unpaid as of that date.

Cash	Salary Expense	Salaries Payable

(2) Olin's income statement for October should show total salary expense of .... $ _____

(3) Olin's balance sheet as of October 31 should show a liability for salaries payable of .... $ _____

EXERCISE 3-3

Keller Co.'s unearned rent account has a balance of $6,000 as of December 31 of the current year. This amount represents the rental of an apartment for a period of one year. The lease began on December 1 of the current year.

Instructions: Using the T accounts below, record the adjusting entry as of December 31 to recognize the rent income for the appropriate portion of the year. Then journalize the entry.

Unearned Rent	Rent Revenue
Dec. 1 6,000	

JOURNAL   PAGE

	DATE	DESCRIPTION	POST. REF.	DEBIT	CREDIT	
1						1
2						2
3						3
4						4
5						5

EXERCISE 3-4

Garret Co. has accrued but uncollected interest of $320 as of December 31 on a note receivable.

Instructions: Using the T accounts below, record the adjusting entry for accrued interest income as of December 31. Then journalize the entry.

Interest Receivable	Interest Revenue

JOURNAL   PAGE

	DATE	DESCRIPTION	POST. REF.	DEBIT	CREDIT	
1						1
2						2
3						3
4						4
5						5

PROBLEM 3-1

An unadjusted trial balance for Bob's Service Company as of July 31, 20-- is shown below.

Bob's Service Company
Unadjusted Trial Balance
July 31, 20--

Cash	9,218	
Accounts Receivable	7,277	
Supplies	2,750	
Prepaid Rent	8,712	
Tools & Equipment	21,829	
Accumulated Depreciation		1,535
Accounts Payable		7,117
Bob Jones, Capital		37,417
Bob Jones, Drawing	3,234	
Service Fees		28,699
Salary Expense	15,929	
Miscellaneous Expense	5,819	
	74,768	74,768

The data needed to determine end-of-month adjustments are as follows:

(a) Salaries accrued but not paid at the end of the month amount to $2,000.

(b) The $8,712 debit in the prepaid rent account is the payment of one year's rent on July 1.

(c) The supplies on hand as of July 31 cost $1,000.

(d) Depreciation of the tools and equipment for July is estimated at $400.

(e) Fees for service rendered in July but collected in August amount to $2,100.

Instructions:

(1) Journalize the adjusting entries. Add additional accounts as needed.

(2) Determine the balances of the accounts affected by the adjusting entries and prepare an adjusted trial balance.

(1)   **JOURNAL**   PAGE _____

	DATE		DESCRIPTION	POST. REF.	DEBIT	CREDIT	
1							1
2							2
3							3
4							4
5							5
6							6
7							7
8							8
9							9
10							10
11							11
12							12
13							13
14							14
15							15
16							16
17							17
18							18
19							19
20							20
21							21
22							22
23							23
24							24
25							25
26							26
27							27
28							28
29							29
30							30
31							31
32							32
33							33
34							34
35							35
36							36

(2)

4

Completing the Accounting Cycle

QUIZ AND TEST HINTS

The following hints may be helpful to you in preparing for a quiz or a test over the material covered in Chapter 4.

1. Terminology is important in this chapter. Do the Matching Exercise on page 159 in the text.

2. The preparation of the work sheet is an important part of this chapter. Although most instructors will not require you to prepare a work sheet from scratch, a test question might include a partially completed work sheet that you would be asked to complete.

3. Be thoroughly familiar with the financial statements presented in Exhibit 5 in the text. Know the financial statement captions and how the statements tie together. In a test situation, you may be provided with partially completed financial statements that you would be asked to complete.

4. You should be able to prepare the formal adjusting entries and closing entries in general journal form. You may have to prepare these entries from a completed work sheet.

5. The accounting cycle is an essential part of accounting. Expect multiple-choice or other types of short answer questions related to the accounting cycle.

6. Your instructor may or may not have discussed the material in the end-of-chapter appendix on reversing entries. If your instructor covered the appendix, you should know what adjusting entries normally require reversing entries, and be able to prepare reversing entries.

FILL IN THE BLANK—Part A

Instructions: Answer the following questions or complete the statements by writing the appropriate words or amounts in the answer blanks.

1. A(n) _____ _____ is a working paper that accountants may use to summarize adjusting entries and the account balances for the financial statements.

2. A(n) _____ _____ is a customer's written promise to pay an amount and possibly interest at an agreed rate.

3. Liabilities that will be due within a short time (usually one year or less) and that are to be paid out of current assets are called _____ _____.

4. In completing the work sheet, the adjusted amount for office equipment is extended to the _____ _____ Debit column.

5. In completing the work sheet, the adjusted amount for the owner's drawing account is extended to the _____ _____ Debit column.

6. After all of the account balances have been extended to the Income Statement columns of the work sheet, the totals of the Debit and Credit columns are $89,900 and $99,500, respectively. The difference of $9,600 is the _____ _____ for the period.

7. After all of the account balances have been extended to the Balance Sheet columns of the work sheet, the totals of the Debit and Credit columns are $94,300 and $110,500, respectively. The difference of $16,200 is the _____ _____ for the period.

8. Revenue and expense account balances are transferred to the _____ _____ account at the end of a period.

9. The drawing account is closed at the end of the period by crediting it for its balance and debiting the _____ _____ account.

10. The fees earned account is closed at the end of the period by debiting it for its balance and crediting the _____ _____ account.

11. The income summary account (net income) is closed at the end of the period by debiting it for its balance and crediting the _____ _____ account.

12. The trial balance prepared after the closing entries have been posted is called the _____-_____ trial balance.

13. A fiscal year that ends when business activities have reached the lowest point in the annual operating cycle is called the _____ _____ _____.

14. The _____ _____ begins with analyzing and journalizing transactions and ends with the post-closing trial balance.

15. The excess of the current assets over current liabilities is called the _____ _____ of a business.

FILL IN THE BLANK—Part B

Instructions: Answer the following questions or complete the statements by writing the appropriate words or amounts in the answer blanks.

1. Cash and other assets that are expected to be converted to cash or sold or used up within one year or less through the normal operations of the business are classified on the balance sheet as _____ _____.

2. The _____, _____, and _____, section of the balance sheet includes equipment, machinery, buildings, and land.

3. Liabilities that will not be due for usually more than one year are classified on the balance sheet as _____-_____ _____.

4. In completing the work sheet, the adjusted amount for depreciation expense is extended to the _____ _____ Debit column.

5. In completing the work sheet, the adjusted amount for the fees earned account is extended to the _____ _____ Credit column.

6. After all of the account balances have been extended to the Income Statement columns of the work sheet, the totals of the Debit and Credit columns are $120,000 and $115,000, respectively. The difference of $5,000 is the _____ _____ for the period.

7. After all of the account balances have been extended to the Balance Sheet columns of the work sheet, the totals of the Debit and Credit columns are $280,000 and $240,000, respectively. The difference of $40,000 is the _____ _____ for the period.

8. The _____ _____ transfer the balances of the revenue, expense, and drawing accounts to the owner's capital account.

9. Revenue and expense account balances are transferred to the _____ _____ account at the end of a period.

10. The drawing account is closed at the end of the period by crediting it and debiting the _____ _____ account.

11. The office salaries account is closed at the end of the period by crediting it and debiting the _____ _____ account.

12. The income summary account (net loss) is closed at the end of the period by crediting it and debiting the _____ _____ account.

13. The _____ _____ is the annual accounting period adopted by a business.

14. _____ refers to the ability of a business to pays its debts.

15. The _____ ratio is computed by dividing current assets by current liabilities.

MULTIPLE CHOICE

Instructions: Circle the best answer for each of the following questions.

1. Notes receivable are written claims against:
   a. creditors
   b. owner's equity
   c. customers
   d. assets

2. A work sheet is completed by:
   a. extending the adjusted trial balance amounts to the Income Statement and Balance Sheet columns
   b. totaling the Adjustment columns
   c. extending the work sheet adjustments to the Adjusted Trial Balance columns
   d. all the above

3. If the Income Statement Credit column is greater than the Income Statement Debit column:
   a. a net income exists
   b. a net loss exists
   c. an asset account is debited
   d. a liability account is credited

4. After all of the account balances have been extended to the Balance Sheet columns of the work sheet, the totals of the Debit and Credit columns are $377,750 and $387,750, respectively. What is the amount of net income or net loss for the period?
   a. $10,000 net income
   b. $10,000 net loss
   c. $377,750 net income
   d. $387,750 net income

5. After all of the account balances have been extended to the Income Statement columns of the work sheet, the totals of the Debit and Credit columns are $62,300 and $67,600, respectively. What is the amount of the net income or net loss for the period?
   a. $5,300 net income
   b. $5,300 net loss
   c. $62,300 net income
   d. $67,600 net loss

6. Which of the following accounts should be closed to Income Summary at the end of the fiscal year?

    a. Lisa Murray, Drawing

    b. Accumulated Depreciation—Equipment

    c. Sales

    d. Accounts Payable

7. Which of the following accounts will be closed at the end of the fiscal year by debiting Lisa Murray, Capital?

    a. Salaries Expense

    b. Sales

    c. Lisa Murray, Drawing

    d. Accounts Receivable

8. Which of the following accounts will ordinarily appear in the post-closing trial balance?

    a. Salaries Expense

    b. Lisa Murray, Drawing

    c. Sales

    d. Lisa Murray, Capital

9. The maximum length of an accounting period is normally:

    a. 6 months

    b. 1 year

    c. 2 years

    d. 3 years

10. The complete sequence of accounting procedures for a fiscal period is frequently called the:

    a. work sheet process

    b. opening and closing cycle

    c. accounting cycle

    d. fiscal cycle

TRUE/FALSE

Instructions: Indicate whether each of the following statements is true or false by placing a check mark in the appropriate column.

		True	**False**
1.	The balance of Accumulated Depreciation—Equipment is extended to the Income Statement columns of the work sheet.	_____	_____
2.	The difference between the Debit and Credit columns of the Income Statement section of the work sheet is normally larger than the difference between the Debit and Credit columns of the Balance Sheet section.....................	_____	_____
3.	The first item normally presented in the statement of owner's equity is the balance of the owner's capital account at the beginning of the period.	_____	_____
4.	The balance that is transferred from the income summary account to the capital account is the net income or net loss for the period..	_____	_____
5.	The balances of the accounts reported in the balance sheet are carried from year to year and are called temporary accounts.	_____	_____
6.	An account titled Income Summary is normally used for transferring the revenue and expense account balances to the owner's capital account at the end of the period.	_____	_____
7.	If the Income Statement Debit column is greater than the Income Statement Credit column, the difference is net income.	_____	_____
8.	A type of working paper frequently used by accountants prior to the preparation of financial statements is called a post-closing trial balance.	_____	_____
9.	At the end of the period, the balances are removed from the temporary accounts and the net effect is recorded in the permanent account by means of closing entries.	_____	_____
10.	The annual accounting period adopted by a business is known as its fiscal year..	_____	_____

EXERCISE 4-1

The account titles and Adjustments columns of the work sheet for Sally's Small Engine Repair are listed below.

Sally's Small Engine Repair
Work Sheet
For Month Ended August 31, 20--

	Adjustments			
	Debit		Credit	
Cash				
Accounts Receivable	(e)	3,200		
Supplies			(c)	700
Prepaid Rent			(b)	560
Tools/Equipment				
Accumulated Depreciation			(d)	1,000
Accounts Payable				
Sally Sand, Capital				
Sally Sand, Drawing				
Repair Fees			(e)	3,200
Salary Expense	(a)	1,500		
Miscellaneous Expense				
Salaries Payable			(a)	1,500
Rent Expense	(b)	560		
Supplies Expense	(c)	700		
Depreciation Expense	(d)	1,000		

Instructions: Prepare journal entries for the adjustments indicated for Sally's Small Engine Repair.

JOURNAL   PAGE

	DATE		DESCRIPTION	POST. REF.	DEBIT	CREDIT	
1							1
2							2
3							3
4							4
5							5
6							6
7							7
8							8
9							9
10							10
11							11
12							12
13							13
14							14

EXERCISE 4-2

Instructions: The journal, the income summary account, the service fees account, the salary expense account, and the supplies expense account of Tony Brown as of March 31, the first month of the current fiscal year, follow. In the journal, prepare the entries to close Brown's revenue and expense accounts into the income summary account. Then post to the ledger.

JOURNAL   PAGE 7

	DATE	DESCRIPTION	POST. REF.	DEBIT	CREDIT	
1						1
2						2
3						3
4						4
5						5
6						6
7						7
8						8
9						9
10						10
11						11
12						12

ACCOUNT   *Income Summary*   ACCOUNT NO.   45

DATE	ITEM	POST. REF.	DEBIT	CREDIT	BALANCE DEBIT	BALANCE CREDIT

ACCOUNT   *Service Fees*   ACCOUNT NO.   50

DATE		ITEM	POST. REF.	DEBIT	CREDIT	BALANCE DEBIT	BALANCE CREDIT
20-- Mar.	15		5		4 8 5 0		4 8 5 0
	31		6		14 3 7 5		19 2 2 5

ACCOUNT   *Salary Expense*   ACCOUNT NO.   58

DATE		ITEM	POST. REF.	DEBIT	CREDIT	BALANCE	
						DEBIT	CREDIT
20-- Mar.	31		5	8 5 5 0		8 5 5 0	

ACCOUNT   *Supplies Expense*   ACCOUNT NO.   67

DATE		ITEM	POST. REF.	DEBIT	CREDIT	BALANCE	
						DEBIT	CREDIT
20-- Mar.	15		5	2 4 3 0		2 4 3 0	
	25		6	1 7 2 0		4 1 5 0	
	31		6	1 2 8 0		5 4 3 0	

PROBLEM 4-1

The partially completed ten-column work sheet of Castle Shop for the fiscal year ended April 30, 20--, appears on the following page. The following adjustment data have been entered in the Adjustments columns of the work sheet:

(a) Supplies on hand as of April 30, 20--, $1,800.

(b) Rent prepaid for 12 months on April 1, $9,504.

(c) Depreciation on tools and equipment during the year, $1,000.

(d) Wages accrued but not paid as of April 30, 20--, $2,000.

(e) Accrued fees earned but not recorded as of April 30, 20--, $3,000.

(f) Unearned fees as of April 30, 20--, $1,500.

Instructions:

(1) Complete the ten-column work sheet.

(2) Prepare an income statement, statement of owner's equity, and a balance sheet.

Castle

Work

For the Year

#	ACCOUNT TITLE	TRIAL BALANCE DEBIT	TRIAL BALANCE CREDIT	ADJUSTMENTS DEBIT	ADJUSTMENTS CREDIT	#
1	Cash	1 00 56				1
2	Accounts Receivable	7 93 8		(e) 3 00 0		2
3	Supplies	3 00 0			(a) 1 20 0	3
4	Prepaid Rent	9 50 4			(b) 7 92	4
5	Tools & Equipment	2 3 81 4				5
6	Accumulated Depreciation		1 67 4		(c) 1 00 0	6
7	Accounts Payable		7 76 4			7
8	Unearned Fees		2 00 0	(f) 5 00		8
9	Castle, Capital		3 8 81 8			9
10	Castle, Drawing	3 52 8				10
11	Service Fees		3 1 30 8		(e) 3 00 0	11
12					(f) 5 00	12
13	Wages Expense	1 7 37 6		(d) 2 00 0		13
14	Miscellaneous Expense	6 34 8				14
15		8 1 56 4	8 1 56 4			15
16						16
17	Wages Payable				(d) 2 00 0	17
18	Rent Expense			(b) 7 92		18
19	Supplies Expense			(a) 1 20 0		19
20	Depreciation Expense			(c) 1 00 0		20
21				8 49 2	8 49 2	21
22						22
23						23
24						24
25						25
26						26
27						27
28						28
29						29
30						30
31						31
32						32
33						33
34						34

Shop _____

Sheet _____

Ended April 30, 20--

	ADJUSTED TRIAL BALANCE		INCOME STATEMENT		BALANCE SHEET		
	DEBIT	CREDIT	DEBIT	CREDIT	DEBIT	CREDIT	
1							1
2							2
3							3
4							4
5							5
6							6
7							7
8							8
9							9
10							10
11							11
12							12
13							13
14							14
15							15
16							16
17							17
18							18
19							19
20							20
21							21
22							22
23							23
24							24
25							25
26							26
27							27
28							28
29							29
30							30
31							31
32							32
33							33
34							34

PROBLEM 4-2

Instructions:

(1) On the basis of the data in the Adjustments columns of the work sheet in Problem 4-1, journalize the adjusting entries.

(2) On the basis of the data in the Income Statement and Balance Sheet columns of the work sheet in Problem 4-1, journalize the closing entries.

JOURNAL   PAGE

	DATE	DESCRIPTION	POST. REF.	DEBIT	CREDIT	
1						1
2						2
3						3
4						4
5						5
6						6
7						7
8						8
9						9
10						10
11						11
12						12
13						13
14						14
15						15
16						16
17						17
18						18
19						19
20						20
21						21
22						22
23						23
24						24
25						25
26						26
27						27
28						28
29						29

JOURNAL

PAGE _____

	DATE		DESCRIPTION	POST. REF.	DEBIT	CREDIT	
1							1
2							2
3							3
4							4
5							5
6							6
7							7
8							8
9							9
10							10
11							11
12							12
13							13
14							14
15							15
16							16
17							17
18							18
19							19
20							20
21							21
22							22
23							23
24							24
25							25
26							26
27							27
28							28
29							29
30							30
31							31
32							32
33							33
34							34
35							35
36							36

5

Accounting Systems and Internal Controls

QUIZ AND TEST HINTS

The following hints may be helpful to you in preparing for a quiz or a test over the material covered in Chapter 5.

1. You should be familiar with the terminology related to accounting systems and internal controls. Pay close attention to the terms related to a business' internal control structure. Do the Matching Exercise on pages 204–205 before any quiz or test.

2. Chapter 5 focuses on the recording of transactions using subsidiary ledgers and special journals. Carefully review the content and format of the various special journals illustrated throughout the chapter.

3. Your instructor may provide a list of transactions and ask you to identify the journal in which each transaction would be recorded. Remember, if a transaction does not fit into any of the special journals, it would be recorded in the general journal. In addition, any time the accounts receivable or accounts payable accounts are debited or credited, their related subsidiary ledgers must also be posted. The diagram on page 189 is helpful in indicating the types of transactions recorded in each special journal. In addition, the Illustrative Problem is typical of the problems that commonly appear on quizzes and tests.

FILL IN THE BLANK—Part A

Instructions: Answer the following questions or complete the statements by writing the appropriate words or amounts in the answer blanks.

1. All cash payments are recorded in the _____ _____ journal.

2. _____ _____ is the intentional act of deceiving an employer for personal gain.

3. Computer equipment used for data input/output and internal data management and processing is called _____.

4. A journal that is designed to be used for recording a single type of transaction is called a _____ journal.

5. The policies and procedures used to safeguard assets, ensure accurate business information, and ensure compliance with laws and regulations are called _____ _____.

6. The purchase of supplies on account would be recorded in the _____ journal.

7. The adjusting entry for depreciation expense would be recorded in the _____ journal.

8. The payment of a note payable at its due date would be recorded in the _____ _____ journal.

9. The closing entries at the end of the period would be recorded in the _____ journal.

10. The total of the revenue journal is posted at the end of the month to the fees earned and _____ _____ accounts.

11. The total of the credit column of the cash payments journal is posted at the end of the month to the _____ account.

12. Computer software that performs a specific task, such as word processing or spreadsheet, is called _____ software.

13. All sales of services on account are recorded in the _____ journal.

14. The computer software that provides the basic instructions to the computer and serves as the interface between the user and the computer is called the _____ system.

15. The primary ledger, when used in conjunction with subsidiary ledgers, that contains all of the balance sheet and income statement accounts is called the _____ ledger.

FILL IN THE BLANK—Part B

Instructions: Answer the following questions or complete the statements by writing the appropriate words or amounts in the answer blanks.

1. All cash receipts are recorded in the _____ _____ journal.

2. The subsidiary ledger containing the individual accounts with customers is called the _____ _____ subsidiary ledger.

3. The methods and procedures used by a business to collect, classify, summarize, and report financial data for use by management and external users is called the _____ system.

4. The subsidiary ledger containing the individual accounts with creditors is called the _____ _____ subsidiary ledger.

5. The purchase of supplies for cash would be recorded in the _____ _____ journal.

6. The adjusting entry for accrued fees earned would be recorded in the _____ journal.

7. The issuance of an invoice to a customer for services rendered on account would be recorded in the _____ journal.

8. The receipt of cash in payment of an account from a customer would be recorded in the _____ _____ journal.

9. The total of the revenue journal is posted at the end of the month to the accounts receivable and _____ _____ accounts.

10. The total of the credit column of the purchases journal is posted at the end of the month to the _____ _____ account.

11. The control environment, risk assessment, control procedures, monitoring, and information and communication are all _____ of internal control.

12. The _____ account in the general ledger summarizes the balances of the accounts in a subsidiary ledger.

13. All items purchased on account are recorded in the _____ journal.

14. Entries that do not "fit" in any of the special journals are recorded in a two-column journal called the _____ journal.

15. A ledger containing individual accounts with a common characteristic is called a _____ ledger.

MULTIPLE CHOICE

Instructions: Circle the best answer for each of the following questions.

1. The job of installing or changing an accounting system is made up of three phases: (1) analysis, (2) design, and (3):
   a. installation
   b. verification
   c. management
   d. implementation

2. Which of the following is not an element of the internal control framework?
   a. risk assessment
   b. control environment
   c. management
   d. monitoring

3. The individual amounts in the "Accounts Payable Cr." column of the purchases journal are posted to the appropriate account in the:
   a. general ledger
   b. general journal
   c. accounts payable subsidiary ledger
   d. accounts payable journal

4. Which of the following transactions should be recorded in the revenue journal?
   a. the purchase of supplies on account
   b. the receipt of cash for services rendered
   c. the billing of fees earned on account
   d. the payment of an account payable

5. The controlling account in the general ledger that summarizes the individual accounts with creditors in a subsidiary ledger is titled:
   a. Accounts Payable
   b. Purchases
   c. Accounts Receivable
   d. Sales Returns and Allowances

6. Internal control policies and procedures provide reasonable assurance that:
   a. the company will not be sued
   b. a net income will be earned
   c. management is competent
   d. business information is accurate

7. The controlling account for the customers ledger is:
   a. Cash
   b. Accounts Receivable
   c. Accounts Payable
   d. Fees Earned

8. When are the amounts entered in the "Accounts Receivable Cr." column of the revenue journal posted?
   a. at regular intervals
   b. at the end of each month
   c. whenever the accounts receivable control account is posted
   d. whenever adjusting entries are prepared and posted

9. Which of the following is not considered a control procedure?
   a. rotating duties among employees
   b. separating responsibilities for custody of assets and accounting for assets
   c. management's operating style
   d. proofs and security measures

10. Which of the following is not a special journal?
    a. revenue journal
    b. general journal
    c. cash receipts journal
    d. purchases journal

TRUE/FALSE

Instructions: Indicate whether each of the following statements is true or false by placing a check mark in the appropriate column.

	True	False
1. The goal of systems design is to identify information needs and how the system should provide the information.	____	____
2. Responsibility for maintaining the accounting records should be separated from the responsibility for custody of the firm's assets...	____	____
3. Transactions involving the payment of cash for any purpose usually are recorded in a purchases journal.	____	____
4. When there are a large number of individual accounts with a common characteristic, it is common to place them in a separate ledger called a detail ledger.	____	____

	True	False

5. For each transaction recorded in the purchases journal, the credit is entered in the "Accounts Payable Cr." column. ____ ____

6. Acquisitions on account that are not provided for in special debit columns are recorded in the purchases journal in the final set of columns called "Misc.".. ____ ____

7. Debits to creditors' accounts for invoices paid are recorded in the "Accounts Payable Dr." column of the cash payments journal. .... ____ ____

8. At the end of each month, the total of the amount column of the revenue journal is posted as a debit to Cash and a credit to Fees Earned. .... ____ ____

9. Each amount in the "Other Accounts Cr." column of the cash receipts journal must be posted individually to an appropriate general ledger account.................................... ____ ____

10. Accounting systems must be continually reviewed for possible revisions in order to keep pace with the changing information needs of businesses. .... ____ ____

11. Many special journals are modified in practice to adapt them to meet the specific needs of a business. .... ____ ____

12. The high cost of computer hardware and software makes computerized accounting systems unaffordable to small- and medium-size businesses. .... ____ ____

13. After all posting has been completed for the month, if the sum of balances in the accounts receivable subsidiary ledger does not agree with the balance of the accounts receivable account in the general ledger, the errors must be located and corrected. .... ____ ____

14. The primary ledger that contains all of the balance sheet and income statement accounts is called the general ledger.. ____ ____

15. If a business uses computers to process accounting data, the concepts and methods for a manual system are not relevant. .... ____ ____

EXERCISE 5-1

Wilco Co. is a computer consulting business. Wilco Co. maintains a cash receipts journal, cash payments journal, revenue journal, purchases journal, and general journal. Selected transactions of Wilco Co. for the month of February are listed below.

Instructions: Indicate the journal in which each of the transactions would be recorded.

Transaction	Journal
Feb. 1. Purchased supplies on account from Winkler's Wholesale.	_____
6. Wilco Co. rendered services to Phil's Grocery Store for cash.	_____
8. Received credit from Winkler's Wholesale for supplies returned.	_____
11. Issued check no. 1099 for payment of supplies purchased on February 1, less return on February 8, to Winkler's Wholesale.	_____
18. Billed Sally's Shop-N-Save for services rendered on account.....	_____
28. Received full payment on account from Tony's Grocery Store...	_____

EXERCISE 5-2

The following transactions were completed by Mezza Co. during October of the current year.

Oct. **3.** Billed Blanders Co. for services rendered on account, Invoice No. 2883, $8,250.

  4. Billed Montana Co. for services rendered on account, Invoice No. 2884, $5,000.

  8. Issued to Blanders Co. a credit for $1,000 due to a misunderstanding of services performed.

  13. Received cash from Blanders Co. in payment of Invoice No. 2883.

  14. Received cash from Montana Co. in payment of Invoice No. 2884.

  25. Received cash for office supplies returned to the manufacturer, $300.

  31. Services rendered for cash in October, $39,600.

Instructions: Record the above transactions in the revenue journal, cash receipts journal, or general journal given below.

REVENUE JOURNAL

DATE	INVOICE NO.	ACCOUNT DEBITED	POST. REF.	ACCTS. REC. DR. FEES EARNED CR.

CASH RECEIPTS JOURNAL

DATE	ACCOUNT CREDITED	POST. REF.	OTHER ACCOUNTS CR.	ACCOUNTS REC. CR.	CASH DR.

JOURNAL

PAGE

	DATE		DESCRIPTION	POST. REF.	DEBIT	CREDIT	
1							1
2							2
3							3
4							4
5							5
6							6
7							7
8							8
9							9
10							10

EXERCISE 5-3

The following transactions related to purchases and cash payments were completed by Kent Company during March of the current year.

March **2.** Purchased store supplies on account from Eastside Co., $1,250.

8. Purchased store supplies on account from Bench Co., $600.

9. Received credit from Eastside Co., $300 for supplies returned.

16. Issued Check No. 230 to Bench Co. in payment of the balance due.

20. Issued Check No. 231 for a cash purchase of office supplies, $250.

27. Issued Check No. 232 to Eastside Co. in payment of the balance due.

28. Purchased the following on account from James & Co.: store supplies, $800; office supplies, $100.

Instructions: Record the above transactions in the purchases journal, cash payments journal, or the general journal given on the next page.

PURCHASES JOURNAL

DATE		ACCOUNT CREDITED	POST. REF.	ACCOUNTS PAYABLE CR.	STORE SUPPLIES DR.	OFFICE SUPPLIES DR.	OTHER ACCOUNTS DR.

CASH PAYMENTS JOURNAL

DATE		CK. NO.	ACCOUNT DEBITED	POST. REF.	OTHER ACCOUNTS DR.	ACCOUNTS PAY. DR.	CASH CR.

JOURNAL   PAGE

	DATE		DESCRIPTION	POST. REF.	DEBIT	CREDIT	
1							1
2							2
3							3
4							4
5							5
6							6
7							7
8							8
9							9
10							10
11							11

PROBLEM 5-1

Kleco Co., an architectural services firm, completed the following transactions with customers on account during September of the current year.

Sept. 8. Invoice No. 210 to Robert Poon, $1,220.

12. Invoice No. 225 to Jeff Lucas, $750.

24. Invoice No. 260 to Pamela Stark, $860.

30. Invoice No. 290 to Steve Kocan, $2,500.

Instructions:

(1) Record the above transactions in the revenue journal below.

(2) Post the individual items from the revenue journal to the T accounts for customers. Indicate that each item has been posted by placing a check mark (✔) in the Post. Ref. column of the revenue journal.

(3) Post the total of the revenue journal to the T accounts for Accounts Receivable and Fees Earned. Indicate that the posting is completed by inserting the appropriate account numbers in the journal under the amount posted.

REVENUE JOURNAL

DATE	INVOICE NO.	ACCOUNT DEBITED	POST. REF.	ACCTS. REC. DR. FEES EARNED CR.

GENERAL LEDGER   **ACCOUNTS RECEIVABLE LEDGER**

Accounts Receivable 113   Steve Kocan   Jeff Lucas

Fees Earned   411   Robert Poon   Pamela Stark

(4) Determine that the sum of the balances of the individual accounts in the accounts receivable subsidiary ledger agrees with the balance of the accounts receivable controlling account in the general ledger by completing the following summary form.

Steve Kocan	$_____
Jeff Lucas	_____
Robert Poon	_____
Pamela Stark	_____
Total accounts receivable	$_____

PROBLEM 5-2

Willbury's, a retail store, completed the following transactions with creditors on account during April of the current year.

April 14. Purchased store supplies on account from Mills Co., $300.

16. Purchased office supplies on account from Quick Co., $175.

22. Purchased store equipment on account from Mills Co., $5,250.

30. Purchased store supplies on account from Mills Co., $280.

Instructions:

(1) Record the above transactions in the purchases journal below.

(2) Post the individual items from the purchases journal to the T accounts in the general and accounts payable subsidiary ledgers. Indicate that each item has been posted by placing a check mark (✔) or an account number in the appropriate Post. Ref. column of the purchases journal.

(3) Post the totals of the purchases journal to the general ledger T accounts. Insert the appropriate account numbers in the journal under the amount posted.

PURCHASES JOURNAL

DATE	ACCOUNT CREDITED	POST. REF.	ACCOUNTS PAYABLE CR.	STORE SUPPLIES DR.	OFFICE SUPPLIES DR.	OTHER ACCOUNTS DR.		
						ACCOUNT	POST. REF.	AMOUNT

GENERAL LEDGER   **ACCTS. PAYABLE LEDGER**

Store Supplies 115	Office Supplies 116	Mills Co.

Store Equipment 121	Accounts Payable 211	Quick Co.

(4) Determine that the sum of the balances of the individual accounts in the accounts payable subsidiary ledger agrees with the balance of the accounts payable controlling account in the general ledger by completing the following summary form:

Mills Co. .... $ _____

Quick Co. .... _____

Total accounts payable .... $ _____

PROBLEM 5-3

The "Totals" line and one other line of the purchases journal of Hamilton Co. for the month of October are shown below. Also shown are selected T accounts taken from Hamilton's general ledger.

Instructions:

(1) Verify the equality of the debits and the credits in Hamilton's purchases journal for October by completing the following schedule:

Debit Totals		Credit Totals	
Store Supplies	_____	Accounts Payable ..	_____
Office Supplies	_____		
Other Accounts ...	_____		
Total	_____	Total	_____

(2) Post all amounts that require posting to the T accounts provided. Show the appropriate posting references in the purchases journal.

PURCHASES JOURNAL

DATE		ACCOUNT CREDITED	POST. REF.	ACCOUNTS PAYABLE CR.	STORE SUPPLIES DR.	OFFICE SUPPLIES DR.	OTHER ACCOUNTS DR.		
							ACCOUNT	POST. REF.	AMOUNT
	29	Hartkemeyer Co.	✔	7,620			Store Equip.		7,620
	31			15,890	3,650	1,250			10,990

GENERAL LEDGER

Store Supplies   115

Office Supplies   116

Store Equipment   121

Accounts Payable   211

6

Accounting for Merchandising Businesses

QUIZ AND TEST HINTS

The following hints may be helpful to you in preparing for a quiz or a test over the material covered in Chapter 6.

1. This chapter introduces merchandising business terminology that you should know. Do the Matching Exercise on page 258.

2. You should be able to prepare general journal entries for the types of transactions illustrated in the chapter. Be sure you can compute purchases discounts and sales discounts. Review the chapter illustrations. The Illustrative Problem in the Chapter Review is an excellent review of the types of entries you might have to prepare.

3. The accounting for transportation costs can be confusing, but you will probably be required to prepare one or more journal entries, or answer one or more multiple-choice questions, involving such costs. Review the chapter discussion and illustration related to such costs.

4. The illustration of the journal entries for both the buyer and seller of merchandise on pages 238–239 of the chapter provides an excellent review. Often, instructors will require students to prepare journal entries based upon the same data for both the buyer and the seller.

5. Review the chart of accounts for a merchandising business as a basis for distinguishing the types of accounts used by merchandising businesses.

6. A major portion of this chapter describes the preparation of financial statements for a merchandising business. Particular emphasis is placed on preparing the income statement. Practice preparing the financial statements for NetSolutions. Your instructor may provide partially completed financial statements, and you will be required to complete the statements.

7. You should be able to prepare the adjusting and closing entries for a merchandising business. These entries are similar to those you prepared in earlier chapters.

8. If your instructor lectures on accounting systems for merchandisers using Appendix 1 to the chapter, you may expect some questions related to special journals for merchandising businesses. Oftentimes instructors will provide a list of merchandise transactions and ask which special journal each should be recorded in. Also, you should know which general ledger

accounts are affected when the column totals of the special journals are posted at the end of the accounting period.

9. If your instructor lectures on preparing a merchandising work sheet from the Appendix 2 to the chapter, you may expect some questions related to the work sheet. Oftentimes instructors provide a partially completed work sheet and require students to complete it. You may find it a helpful exercise to cover up portions of Exhibit 18, and see if you know how to complete the covered sections. Except for the merchandising related accounts, a merchandising business work sheet is similar to others you have prepared.

10. If your instructor lectures on the periodic inventory system using the appendix at the end of the text, you may have to prepare journal entries, a work sheet, and financial statements using this system.

FILL IN THE BLANK—Part A

Instructions: Answer the following questions or complete the statements by writing the appropriate words or amounts in the answer blanks.

1. The cost that is reported as an expense when merchandise is sold is called

   _____ _____ _____ _____.

2. Revenue is normally reported on the income statement of a service enterprise as fees earned. In contrast, revenue for a merchandising business is normally reported as _____.

3. Gross profit minus _____ _____ yields net income for a merchandising business.

4. _____ _____ is merchandise on hand (not sold) at the end of an accounting period.

5. The _____ inventory system does not show the amount available for sale or sold during the period.

6. A(n) _____ is the bill that the seller sends to the buyer.

7. A buyer refers to returned merchandise or an adjustment for defective merchandise as a(n) _____ _____ _____

   _____.

8. A seller refers to discounts offered to the buyer for early payment as

   _____ _____.

9. A seller informs the buyer of the amount that they propose to credit to the buyer's account receivable by issuing a _____ memorandum.

10. If the buyer pays the transportation costs from the shipping point to the final destination, the freight terms are referred to as _____

    _____ _____.

11. A sales invoice for $5,000, terms 1/10, n/30, FOB shipping point, is paid within the discount period. Transportation costs of $75 are paid and added to the invoice. The amount of the discount is _____.

12. A return of $300 has been recorded against a purchase invoice of $3,300, terms 2/10, n/30. The invoice is paid within the discount period. The amount of the discount is _____.

13. Merchandise with a list price of $1,000 is sold with a trade discount of 30%, terms 2/10, n/30. The amount to be recorded in the sales account is

    _____.

14. The _____-_____ form of income statement contains several sections, subsections, and subtotals.

15. Expenses incurred in the administration or general operations of the business are reported on the income statement as _____ expenses.

16. The excess of operating expenses over gross profit is _____

    _____ _____.

17. Expenses that cannot be traced directly to operations are reported on the income statement as _____ expenses.

18. The amount by which the merchandise for sale, as indicated by the balance of the merchandise inventory account, is larger than the total amount of merchandise counted during the physical inventory is referred to as _____ _____.

19. Balances of selected accounts at the end of the year, before adjustments, are as follows: Sales, $900,000; Sales Returns and Allowances, $50,000; Sales Discounts, $10,000; Cost of Merchandise Sold, $600,000; Selling Expenses, $80,000; Administrative Expenses, $25,500; Interest Revenue, $5,000; Interest Expense, $2,000. The gross profit is _____.

20. The _____ form of balance sheet reports assets, liabilities, and owner's equity in a downward sequence.

FILL IN THE BLANK—Part B

Instructions: Answer the following questions or complete the statements by writing the appropriate words or amounts in the answer blanks.

1. Sales minus cost of merchandise sold is called _____ _____.

2. Gross profit minus _____ _____ yields net income.

3. In the _____ inventory system each purchase and sale of merchandise is recorded in an inventory account when the transactions occur.

4. A _____ _____ is a detailed listing of the merchandise for sale at the end of the accounting period.

5. A buyer refers to discounts taken for early payment of an invoice as _____ _____.

6. A buyer informs the seller of the amount the buyer proposes to debit to the seller's account payable by issuing a _____ memorandum.

7. A seller refers to returned merchandise or an adjustment for defective merchandise as a(n) _____ _____ _____ _____.

8. Discounts from the list prices in published catalogs or special discounts offered to certain classes of buyers are called _____ _____.

9. If the seller pays the transportation costs from the shipping point to the final destination, the freight terms are referred to as _____ _____.

10. A sales invoice for $8,000, terms 2/10, n/30, FOB shipping point, is paid within the discount period. Transportation costs of $125 are paid and added to the invoice. The amount of the discount is _____.

11. A sales invoice for $15,000, terms 1/10, n/30, FOB shipping point, is paid within the discount period. Transportation costs of $250 are paid and added to the invoice. The total amount paid by the buyer is _____.

12. A return of $500 has been recorded against a purchase invoice of $3,800, terms 1/10, n/30. The invoice is paid within the discount period. The amount of the discount is _____.

13. A buyer purchased merchandise for $10,000, terms 1/10, n/30, FOB destination. The seller pays transportation costs of $500. If the buyer pays the invoice within the discount period, the amount paid by the buyer is

    _____.

14. Merchandise with a list price of $12,000 is sold with a trade discount of 45%, terms 2/10, n/30. The amount to be recorded in the sales account is

    _____.

15. Expenses that are incurred directly in the selling of merchandise are reported on the income statement as _____ expenses.

16. The excess of gross profit over total operating expenses is _____

    _____ _____.

17. Revenue from sources other than the primary operating activity of a business is reported on the income statement as _____ _____.

18. The _____-_____ form of income statement deducts the total of all expenses from the total of all revenues.

19. Balances of selected accounts at the end of the year, before adjustments, are as follows: Sales, $750,000; Sales Returns and Allowances, $25,000; Sales Discounts, $10,000; Cost of Merchandise Sold, $500,000; Selling Expenses, $80,000; Administrative Expenses, $20,000; Interest Revenue, $5,000; Interest Expense, $2,000. The gross profit is _____.

20. The _____ form of balance sheet reports assets on the left-hand side and the liabilities and owner's equity on the right-hand side.

MULTIPLE CHOICE

Instructions: Circle the best answer for each of the following questions.

1. The basic differences between the financial statements of a merchandising business and a service business include reporting cost of merchandise sold on the income statement and the:

    a. owner's equity section of the balance sheet

    b. other income section of the income statement

    c. inclusion of merchandise inventory on the balance sheet as a current asset

    d. inclusion of an owner's equity statement

2. A buyer receives an invoice for $60 dated June 10. If the terms are 2/10, n/30, and the buyer pays the invoice within the discount period, what amount will the seller receive?

    a. $60

    b. $58.80

    c. $48

    d. $1.20

3. When a seller of merchandise allows a customer a reduction from the original price for defective goods, the seller usually issues to the customer a(n):

    a. debit memorandum

    b. credit memorandum

    c. sales invoice

    d. inventory slip

4. When the seller prepays the transportation costs and the terms of sale are FOB shipping point, the seller records the payment of the transportation costs by debiting:

    a. Accounts Receivable

    b. Sales

    c. Transportation In

    d. Accounts Payable

5. If the seller collects sales tax at the time of sale, the seller credits the tax to:

    a. Sales

    b. Accounts Receivable

    c. Sales Tax Payable

    d. Sales Tax Receivable

6. The account that appears in the chart of accounts for a merchandising business but not for a service business is:

    a. Accounts Receivable

    b. Advertising Expense

    c. Sales Returns and Allowances

    d. Accumulated Depreciation

7. The excess of net revenue from sales over the cost of merchandise sold is called:

    a. gross profit

    b. operating profit

    c. net profit from operations

    d. merchandising income

8. Income from operations is computed by subtracting from gross profit the:

    a. selling expenses

    b. general expenses

    c. total administrative expenses

    d. total operating expenses

9. After all adjusting entries are posted, the balances of all asset, liability, revenue, and expense accounts correspond exactly to the amounts in the:

    a. work sheet trial balance

    b. general journal

    c. post-closing trial balance

    d. financial statements

10. In a multiple-step income statement of a merchandising business, which of the following would appear as "other income"?

    a. sales

    b. interest revenue

    c. sales discounts

    d. sales returns and allowances

TRUE/FALSE

Instructions: Indicate whether each of the following statements is true or false by placing a check mark in the appropriate column.

	True	False
1. The two main systems for accounting for merchandise held for sale are called periodic and perpetual....................	____	____
2. In a perpetual inventory system, purchases of merchandise are recorded in the purchases account.	____	____
3. In a periodic inventory system, no attempt is made to record the cost of merchandise sold at the date of the sale.	____	____
4. A discount offered the purchaser of goods as a means of encouraging payment before the end of the credit period is known as a bank discount.	____	____
5. Credit terms of "2/10, n/30" mean that the buyer may deduct 2% of the amount of the invoice if payment is made within 10 days of the invoice date........................	____	____
6. If the seller is to absorb the cost of delivering the goods, the terms are stated FOB (free on board) shipping point. ...	____	____
7. The liability for the sales tax is incurred at the time the seller receives payment from the buyer.............................	____	____
8. The purchases returns and allowances are credited to Merchandise Inventory.	____	____
9. The chart of accounts for a merchandising business will differ from that of a service business.............................	____	____
10. The work sheet procedures for a merchandising business are significantly different from those of a service business.	____	____
11. The physical inventory taken at the end of the period is normally larger than the amount of the balance of the merchandise inventory account.	____	____
12. Any merchandise inventory shrinkage is normally debited to the merchandise inventory account.............................	____	____
13. Expenses incurred directly and entirely in connection with the sale of merchandise are called administrative expenses.	____	____
14. Revenue from sources such as income from interest, rent, dividends, and gains resulting from the sale of fixed assets is classified as income from operations.............................	____	____
15. The single-step form of income statement has the advantage of being simple, and it emphasizes total revenues and total expenses as the factors that determine net income.	____	____

		True	**False**
16.	Gross profit is not calculated in the single-step form of income statement.	_____	_____
17.	The excess of gross profit over total operating expenses is called income from operations.	_____	_____
18.	The traditional balance sheet arrangement of assets on the left-hand side with the liabilities and owner's equity on the right-hand side is called the report form.	_____	_____
19.	After the adjusting and closing entries have been recorded and posted, the general ledger accounts that appear on the balance sheet have no balances.	_____	_____
20.	The closing entries are recorded in the journal immediately following the adjusting entries.	_____	_____

EXERCISE 6-1

Instructions: Prepare entries for each of the following related transactions of Foley Co. in the journal given below.

(1) Purchased $5,000 of merchandise from Phillips Co. on account, terms 2/10, n/30.

(2) Paid Phillips Co. on account for purchases, less discount.

(3) Purchased $3,500 of merchandise from Farris Co. on account, terms FOB shipping point, n/30, with prepaid shipping costs of $80 added to the invoice.

(4) Returned merchandise from Farris Co., $900.

(5) Paid Farris Co. on account for purchases, less return.

JOURNAL

PAGE

	DATE	DESCRIPTION	POST. REF.	DEBIT	CREDIT	
1						1
2						2
3						3
4						4
5						5
6						6
7						7
8						8
9						9
10						10
11						11
12						12
13						13
14						14
15						15
16						16
17						17
18						18
19						19
20						20
21						21
22						22
23						23
24						24
25						25

EXERCISE 6-2

Instructions: Prepare entries for each of the following related transactions of Wilson Co. in the journal given below.

(1) Sold merchandise on nonbank credit cards and reported accounts to the card company, $3,150. The cost of the merchandise sold was $2,000.

(2) Sold merchandise for cash, $2,850. The cost of the merchandise sold was $1,380.

(3) Received cash from card company for nonbank credit card sales, less $100 service fee.

(4) Sold merchandise on account to Rask Co., $4,500, terms 2/10, n/30, FOB shipping point. Prepaid transportation costs of $150 at the customer's request. The cost of the merchandise sold was $3,100.

(5) Received merchandise returned by Rask Co., $400. The cost of the merchandise returned was $275.

(6) Received cash on account from Rask Co. for sale and transportation costs, less returns and discount.

JOURNAL   PAGE

	DATE	DESCRIPTION	POST. REF.	DEBIT	CREDIT	
1						1
2						2
3						3
4						4
5						5
6						6
7						7
8						8
9						9
10						10
11						11
12						12
13						13
14						14
15						15
16						16
17						17
18						18
19						19
20						20
21						21

JOURNAL

	DATE		DESCRIPTION	POST. REF.	DEBIT	CREDIT	
1							1
2							2
3							3
4							4
5							5
6							6
7							7
8							8
9							9
10							10
11							11
12							12
13							13
14							14
15							15
16							16
17							17
18							18
19							19
20							20

EXERCISE 6-3

Baker Co. had the following purchases and sales transactions during the month of January.

Jan. **3.** Purchased $25,000 of merchandise on account from Zeff Co., terms 2/10, n/30.

5. Returned merchandise purchased on account from Zeff Co. on January 3, $5,000.

12. Sold merchandise on account to Smith Co., $50,000, terms 1/10, n/30. The cost of the merchandise sold was $35,000.

13. Paid Zeff Co. for purchase on January 3, on account, less return and discount.

15. Received merchandise return on account from Smith Co., $8,000. The cost of the merchandise returned was $5,600.

22. Received payment in full on account from Smith Co., less return and discount.

Instructions: Prepare journal entries for the preceding transactions.

JOURNAL

	DATE		DESCRIPTION	POST. REF.	DEBIT	CREDIT	
1							1
2							2
3							3
4							4
5							5
6							6
7							7
8							8
9							9
10							10
11							11
12							12
13							13
14							14
15							15
16							16
17							17
18							18
19							19
20							20
21							21
22							22
23							23
24							24
25							25
26							26
27							27
28							28
29							29
30							30
31							31
32							32
33							33
34							34
35							35
36							36

PROBLEM 6-1

The following transactions were selected from among those completed by the Bowman Company during September of the current year:

Sept. **3.** Purchased merchandise on account from Axel Co., list price $10,000, trade discount 15%, terms FOB destination, 1/10, n/30.

4. Purchased office supplies for cash, $800.

6. Sold merchandise on account to Hart Co., list price $5,000, trade discount 20%, terms 2/10, n/30. The cost of merchandise sold was $3,000.

7. Returned $2,000 of the merchandise purchased on September 3 from Axel Co.

10. Purchased merchandise for cash, $5,000.

12. Sold merchandise on nonbank credit cards and reported accounts to the card company, $5,500. The cost of merchandise sold was $3,200.

13. Paid Axel Co. on account for purchase of September 3, less return of September 7 and discount.

16. Received cash on account from sale of September 6 to Hart Co., less discount.

20. Received cash from card company for nonbank credit sales of September 12, less $300 service fee.

24. Sold merchandise to Wilcox Co., $3,000, terms 1/10, n/30. The cost of merchandise sold was $1,750.

26. Sold merchandise for cash, $2,200. The cost of merchandise sold was $1,400.

30. Received merchandise returned by Wilcox Co. from sale on September 24, $1,000. The cost of the merchandise returned was $600.

Instructions: Journalize the transactions for the Bowman Co., using the journal forms provided below and on the following pages.

JOURNAL   PAGE

	DATE		DESCRIPTION	POST. REF.	DEBIT	CREDIT	
1							1
2							2
3							3
4							4
5							5
6							6
7							7
8							8
9							9
10							10

JOURNAL

	DATE	DESCRIPTION	POST. REF.	DEBIT	CREDIT	
1						1
2						2
3						3
4						4
5						5
6						6
7						7
8						8
9						9
10						10
11						11
12						12
13						13
14						14
15						15
16						16
17						17
18						18
19						19
20						20
21						21
22						22
23						23
24						24
25						25
26						26
27						27
28						28
29						29
30						30
31						31
32						32
33						33
34						34
35						35
36						36

JOURNAL

PAGE

	DATE		DESCRIPTION	POST. REF.	DEBIT	CREDIT	
1							1
2							2
3							3
4							4
5							5
6							6
7							7
8							8
9							9
10							10

PROBLEM 6-2

The following accounts and their normal balances were taken from the general ledger of Miller Co. after the adjusting entries have been posted for the fiscal year ending March 31.

Cash	43,100
Notes Receivable	6,000
Accounts Receivable	107,780
Interest Receivable	520
Merchandise Inventory	115,800
Office Supplies	1,250
Prepaid Insurance	8,740
Delivery Equipment	60,150
Accum. Depr.—Delivery Equipment	22,950
Accounts Payable	75,300
Salaries Payable	2,000
R. W. Miller, Capital	193,650
R. W. Miller, Drawing	30,000
Sales	1,016,700
Sales Returns and Allowances	13,010
Cost of Merchandise Sold	681,060
Sales Salaries Expense	78,250
Advertising Expense	13,090
Delivery Expense	42,100
Depreciation Expense—Delivery Equipment	9,050
Misc. Selling Expense	13,950
Office Salaries Expense	55,800
Office Supplies Expense	9,100
Insurance Expense	16,000
Misc. Admin. Exp.	6,870
Interest Revenue	1,020

Instructions:

(a) Prepare a multiple-step income statement for Miller Co.

(b) Prepare a single-step income statement for Miller Co.

(c) Assume that the inventory shrinkage for Miller Co. for the period ending March 31 was $4,200. Prepare the adjusting entry to record the inventory shrinkage.

(a)

Multiple-Step Income Statement

(b)

Single-Step Income Statement

(c)   **JOURNAL**   PAGE

	DATE	DESCRIPTION	POST. REF.	DEBIT	CREDIT	
1						1
2						2
3						3
4						4
5						5
6						6

PROBLEM 6-3

Using the information in Problem 6-2, prepare a statement of owner's equity for Miller Co.

PROBLEM 6-4

Using the information in Problem 6-2, prepare a balance sheet in report form for Miller Co. as of March 31, 20--.

7

Cash

QUIZ AND TEST HINTS

The following hints may be helpful to you in preparing for a quiz or a test over the material covered in Chapter 7.

1. You may expect some general terminology questions (usually true/false or multiple-choice) related to internal control over cash receipts and cash payments. Do the Matching Exercise on page 297. You should be generally familiar with the basic components of a voucher system.

2. You should be able to prepare journal entries to establish and replenish cash funds, including cash change funds and petty cash. In replenishing such funds, the cash short and over account may need to be debited (short) or credited (over).

3. You should be able to prepare a bank reconciliation of the type illustrated in the chapter. Instructors often include short bank reconciliations of the type shown in the Illustrative Problem of the text and in Problem 7-1 of this Study Guide. Attempt to work the Illustrative Problem and the Study Guide Problem 7-1 without looking at the solution.

4. Be able to identify in which section of the bank reconciliation different types of reconciling items would be included. The form of the reconciliation illustrated on page 290 may be a helpful study aid. Have a friend read off the reconciling items from the chapter illustration of the bank reconciliation on page 290, and identify whether the item would appear in the section of the reconciliation beginning with "Cash balance according to bank statement" or the section beginning with "Cash balance according to depositor's records."

    Note that sometimes instructors may refer to the "Cash balance according to bank statement" as the "Balance per bank" and "Cash balance according to depositor's records" as "Balance per books."

5. Finally, you should read over and be generally familiar with the presentation of cash on the balance sheet.

FILL IN THE BLANK—Part A

Instructions: Answer the following questions or complete the statements by writing the appropriate words or amounts in the answer blanks.

1. Coins, currency (paper money), checks, money orders, and money on deposit that are available for unrestricted withdrawal from banks and other financial institutions are reported in the financial statements as _____.

2. Most companies' invoices are designed so that customers return a portion of the invoice called a _____ _____.

3. A _____ system is a set of procedures for authorizing and recording liabilities and cash payments.

4. Vouchers are ordinarily filed in the unpaid voucher file in order of _____ date.

5. A _____ _____ _____ system uses computers rather than paper (money, checks, etc.) to effect cash transactions.

6. A _____ _____ details the items responsible for the difference between the cash balance reported in the bank statement and the balance of the cash account in the ledger.

7. In a bank reconciliation, a bank debit memorandum for a customer's check returned because of insufficient funds is _____ _____ the cash balance according to the depositor's records.

8. In a bank reconciliation, checks outstanding are _____ _____ the cash balance according to the bank statement.

9. A company erroneously recorded a check issued for $180 as $810. On the bank reconciliation, the difference of $630 would be added to the cash balance according to the _____ _____.

10. Highly liquid investments that are usually reported with cash on the balance sheet are called _____ _____.

FILL IN THE BLANK—Part B

Instructions: Answer the following questions or complete the statements by writing the appropriate words or amounts in the answer blanks.

1. Procedures designed to detect theft or misuse of cash are called _____ controls.

2. At the beginning of a work shift, each cash register clerk is given a cash drawer that contains a predetermined amount of cash. The amount of cash in each drawer is called a _____ fund.

3. If Cash Short and Over has a credit balance at the end of the period, the balance would be reported on the income statement in the section entitled

   _____ _____.

4. A _____ is a special form for recording relevant data about a liability and the details of its payment.

5. A voucher for the purchase of goods is normally supported by the supplier's invoice, a purchase order, and a _____ _____.

6. A _____ _____ fund is used to pay relatively small amounts.

7. In a bank reconciliation, a bank credit memorandum for a note receivable collected by the bank is _____ _____ the cash balance according to the depositor's records.

8. In a bank reconciliation, deposits in transit are _____ _____ the cash balance according to the bank statement.

9. In a bank reconciliation, a bank debit memorandum for service charges is _____ _____ the cash balance according to the depositor's records.

10. The ratio of cash and cash equivalents to current liabilities is called the _____ ratio.

MULTIPLE CHOICE

Instructions: Circle the best answer for each of the following questions.

1. For good internal control over cash receipts, remittance advices should be separated from cash received by mail and sent directly to the:
   a. treasurer
   b. cashier's department
   c. accounting department
   d. voucher clerk

2. An important characteristic of the voucher system is the requirement that:
   a. vouchers be prepared by the treasurer
   b. vouchers be paid immediately after they are prepared
   c. paid vouchers are filed by due date
   d. a voucher be prepared for each major expenditure

3. The bank on which a check is drawn is known as the:
   a. drawer
   b. drawee
   c. payee
   d. creditor

4. In a bank reconciliation, deposits not recorded by the bank are:
   a. added to the balance according to the bank statement
   b. deducted from the balance according to the bank statement
   c. added to the balance according to the depositor's records
   d. deducted from the balance according to the depositor's records

5. The amount of the outstanding checks is included on the bank reconciliation as:
   a. an addition to the balance per bank statement
   b. a deduction from the balance per bank statement
   c. an addition to the balance per depositor's records
   d. a deduction from the balance per depositor's records

6. Receipts from cash sales of $7,500 were recorded incorrectly as $5,700. What entry is required in the depositor's accounts?
   a. debit Cash; credit Accounts Receivable
   b. debit Cash; credit Sales
   c. debit Accounts Receivable; credit Cash
   d. debit Sales; credit Cash

7. Accompanying the bank statement was a credit memorandum for a short-term, non-interest-bearing note collected by the bank. What entry is required in the depositor's accounts?

   a. debit Cash; credit Miscellaneous Income

   b. debit Cash; credit Notes Receivable

   c. debit Accounts Receivable; credit Cash

   d. debit Notes Receivable; credit Cash

8. What entry is required in the depositor's accounts to record outstanding checks?

   a. debit Cash; credit Accounts Payable

   b. debit Accounts Receivable; credit Cash

   c. debit Accounts Payable; credit Cash

   d. No entry is required.

9. Journal entries based on the bank reconciliation are required on the depositor's books for:

   a. additions to the balance according to the depositor's records

   b. deductions from the balance according to the depositor's records

   c. both a and b

   d. both additions to and deductions from the balance according to the bank's records

10. The entry to record the replenishment of the petty cash fund includes a debit to various expense and asset accounts and a credit to:

   a. Cash

   b. Petty Cash

   c. Accounts Receivable

   d. various liability accounts

TRUE/FALSE

Instructions: Indicate whether each of the following statements is true or false by placing a check mark in the appropriate column.

		True	False
1.	There are four parties to a check.	_____	_____
2.	The drawer is the one to whose order the check is drawn.	_____	_____
3.	In a bank reconciliation, checks issued that have not been paid by the bank are added to the balance according to the bank statement.	_____	_____
4.	Bank memorandums not recorded by the depositor require entries in the depositor's accounts.	_____	_____
5.	For a greater degree of internal control, the bank reconciliation should be prepared by an employee who does not engage in or record cash transactions with the bank.	_____	_____
6.	If there is a debit balance in the cash short and over account at the end of the fiscal period, this represents income to be included in "Miscellaneous general income" in the income statement.	_____	_____
7.	It is common practice for businesses to require that every payment of cash be evidenced by a check signed by the owner.	_____	_____
8.	After vouchers are paid, it is customary to file them in numerical sequence in the paid voucher file.	_____	_____
9.	Petty Cash should be debited when the petty cash fund is replenished.	_____	_____
10.	A voucher system is a set of methods and procedures for authorizing and recording liabilities and cash payments.	_____	_____

EXERCISE 7-1

A comparison of the bank statement and the accompanying canceled checks and memorandums with the records of Pearl Co. for the month of September of the current year revealed the following reconciling items:

(1) A check drawn for $25 had been erroneously charged by the bank for $250.

(2) The bank collected $1,920 on a note left for collection. The face of the note was $1,800.

(3) Bank service charges for September totaled $28.

(4) Check No. 231, written to Stanley Optical Warehouse for $2,500, and Check No. 236, written to Stella's Janitorial Service for $100, were outstanding.

(5) A deposit of $5,250 made on September 30 was not recorded on the bank statement.

(6) A canceled check for $1,100, returned with the bank statement, had been recorded erroneously in the check register as $1,000. The check was a payment on account to Charlie's Optical Supply.

Instructions: In the following general journal, prepare any necessary entries that Pearl Co. should make as a result of these reconciling items. The accounts have not been closed.

JOURNAL   PAGE

	DATE	DESCRIPTION	POST. REF.	DEBIT	CREDIT	
1						1
2						2
3						3
4						4
5						5
6						6
7						7
8						8
9						9
10						10
11						11
12						12
13						13
14						14
15						15
16						16
17						17
18						18

EXERCISE 7-2

Instructions: In the general journal provided below, prepare the entries to record the following transactions:

(1) Established a petty cash fund of $400.

(2) Replenished the fund, based on the following summary of petty cash receipts. (The amount of cash in the fund is now $128.34.)

Office supplies, $80.25

Miscellaneous selling expense, $115.33

Miscellaneous administrative expense, $78.05

JOURNAL   PAGE

	DATE	DESCRIPTION	POST. REF.	DEBIT	CREDIT	
1						1
2						2
3						3
4						4
5						5
6						6
7						7
8						8
9						9
10						10
11						11
12						12
13						13
14						14
15						15
16						16
17						17
18						18
19						19
20						20
21						21
22						22
23						23
24						24
25						25
26						26
27						27

PROBLEM 7-1

On September 30 of the current year, Dumont Co.'s checkbook showed a balance of $7,540, and the bank statement showed a balance of $8,510. A comparison of the bank statement and Dumont's records as of September 30 revealed the following:

(a) A deposit of $1,900, mailed to the bank by Dumont on September 29, was not included in the bank statement of September 30.

(b) The following checks were outstanding: Check No. 255 for $325, Check No. 280 for $100, Check No. 295 for $700.

(c) Check No. 289 in payment of a voucher had been written for $140 and had been recorded at that amount by the bank. However, Dumont had recorded it in the check register as $410.

(d) A check for $910 received from a customer was deposited in the bank. The bank recorded it at the correct amount, but Dumont recorded it at $190.

(e) Included with the bank statement was a credit memorandum for $780, representing the proceeds of a $700 note receivable left at the bank for collection. This had not been recorded on Dumont's books.

(f) Included with the bank statement was a debit memorandum for $25 for service charges that had not been recorded on Dumont's books.

Instructions:

(1) Complete the bank reconciliation below.

(2) In the general journal, prepare the entry or entries that Dumont should make as a result of the bank reconciliation.

Dumont Co.
Bank Reconciliation
September 30, 20--

Balance according to bank statement .... $
Add:

Deduct:

Adjusted balance .... $

Balance according to depositor's records .... $
Add:

Deduct:

Adjusted balance .... $

(2)   **JOURNAL**   PAGE

	DATE		DESCRIPTION	POST. REF.	DEBIT	CREDIT	
1							1
2							2
3							3
4							4
5							5
6							6
7							7
8							8
9							9
10							10
11							11
12							12
13							13
14							14
15							15
16							16
17							17
18							18
19							19
20							20
21							21
22							22
23							23
24							24
25							25
26							26
27							27
28							28
29							29
30							30
31							31
32							32
33							33
34							34
35							35
36							36

8

Receivables

QUIZ AND TEST HINTS

The following hints may be helpful to you in preparing for a quiz or a test over the material covered in Chapter 8.

1. You should be able to determine the amount of the adjusting entry for uncollectible receivables (the allowance method) for both estimation methods presented in the chapter (percentage of sales and aging of receivables). Note that the percentage of sales method is the easiest to use since the amount of the entry is the same as the estimate of the uncollectible sales. The aging method requires the entry to be made for an amount that will result in the estimated balance of the allowance account.

2. You should be able to determine the due date, interest, and maturity value of a note receivable.

3. You may be tested on a problem requiring a series of general journal entries that encompass both uncollectible accounts receivable and notes receivable. The materials presented in this Study Guide and the Illustrative Problem in the text provide an excellent review.

4. Finally, study the new terminology introduced in this chapter for possible multiple-choice, matching, or true/false questions. Do the Matching Exercise on page 332.

FILL IN THE BLANK—Part A

Instructions: Answer the following questions or complete the statements by writing the appropriate words or amounts in the answer blanks.

1. All money claims against other entities, including people, business firms, and other organizations are called _____.

2. A(n) _____ _____ is a formal, written instrument of credit that has been received for the amount a customer owes.

3. The _____ method of accounting for uncollectible accounts provides an expense for uncollectible receivables in advance of their write-off.

4. The _____ _____ _____ is a process of analyzing the accounts receivable and classifying them according to various age groupings, with the due date being the base point for determining age.

5. Allowance for Doubtful Accounts has a debit balance of $1,500 at the end of the year, before adjustments. Sales for the year amounted to $740,000, and sales returns and allowances amounted to $25,000. If uncollectible accounts expense is estimated at 1% of net sales, the amount of the appropriate adjusting entry will be ___7150___.

6. Allowance for Doubtful Accounts has a debit balance of $2,500 at the end of the year, before adjustments. Sales for the year amounted to $950,000, and sales returns and allowances amounted to $20,000. If the analysis of the accounts in the customers' ledger indicates doubtful accounts of $30,000, the amount of the appropriate adjusting entry will be ___32500___.

7. The maturity value of a $300,000, 90-day, 12% note receivable is _____.

8. The due date of a 90-day note receivable dated July 12 is ___OCT 10___.

9. A note that the maker fails to pay on the due date is referred to as a _____ note.

10. _____ _____ _____ measures how frequently during the year the accounts receivable are being converted to cash.

FILL IN THE BLANK—Part B

Instructions: Answer the following questions or complete the statements by writing the appropriate words or amounts in the answer blanks.

1. A(n) _____ receivable is created by selling merchandise or services on credit.

2. The operating expense incurred because of the failure to collect receivables is recorded as _____ _____ expense.

3. The _____ _____-_____ method of accounting for uncollectible accounts recognizes an expense only when accounts are judged to be worthless.

4. At the end of the fiscal year, after the accounts are closed, Accounts Receivable has a balance of $350,000 and Allowance for Doubtful Accounts has a credit balance of $40,000. The expected realizable value of the receivables is _____.

5. Allowance for Doubtful Accounts has a credit balance of $800 at the end of the year, before adjustments. If an analysis of receivables indicates doubtful accounts of $11,200, the amount of the appropriate adjusting entry is ___10400___.

6. The amount that is due at the maturity or due date of a note is called the _____ _____.

7. The maturity value of a $150,000, 60-day, 15% note receivable is _____.

8. The due date of a 120-day note receivable dated on August 18 is _____.

9. The _____ _____ _____ _____ _____ _____ is an estimate of the length of time the accounts receivable have been outstanding, expressed in days.

10. A written promise to pay a sum of money on demand or at a definite time is called a(n) _____ note.

MULTIPLE CHOICE

Instructions: Circle the best answer for each of the following questions.

1. When the allowance method is used in accounting for uncollectible accounts, any uncollectible account is written off against the:

   a. allowance account

   b. sales account

   c. accounts receivable account

   d. uncollectible accounts expense account

2. When the direct write-off method is used in accounting for uncollectible accounts, any uncollectible account is written off against the:

   a. allowance account

   b. sales account

   c. accounts receivable account

   d. uncollectible accounts expense account

3. What is the type of account and normal balance of Allowance for Doubtful Accounts?

   a. asset, debit

   b. asset, credit

   c. contra asset, debit

   d. contra asset, credit

4. Assume that the allowance account has a credit balance of $170 at the end of the year, before adjustments. If the estimate of uncollectible accounts based on aging the receivables is $3,010, the amount of the adjusting entry for uncollectible accounts would be:

   a. $170

   b. $2,840

   c. $3,010

   d. $3,180

5. Assume that the allowance account has a debit balance of $250 at the end of the year, before adjustments. If the estimate of uncollectible accounts based on sales for the period is $2,200, the amount of the adjusting entry for uncollectible accounts would be:

   a. $250

   b. $1,950

   c. $2,200

   d. $2,450

6. After the accounts are adjusted and closed at the end of the fiscal year, Accounts Receivable has a balance of $430,000 and Allowance for Doubtful Accounts has a balance of $25,000. What is the expected realizable value of the accounts receivable?

   a. $25,000

   b. $405,000

   c. $430,000

   d. $455,000

7. On a promissory note, the one making the promise to pay is called the:

   a. payee

   b. creditor

   c. maker

   d. noter

8. The amount that is due on a note at the maturity or due date is called the:

   a. terminal value

   b. face value

   c. book value

   d. maturity value

9. The due date of a 90-day note dated July 1 is:

   a. September 28

   b. September 29

   c. September 30

   d. October 1

10. A 60-day, 12% note for $15,000, dated May 1, is received from a customer on account. The maturity value of the note is:

   a. $14,700

   b. $15,000

   c. $15,300 ——

   d. $16,200

TRUE/FALSE

Instructions: Indicate whether each of the following statements is true or false by placing a check mark in the appropriate column.

		True	False
1.	The method of accounting which provides in advance for receivables deemed uncollectible is called the allowance method.	____	____
2.	The process of analyzing the receivable accounts in order to estimate the uncollectibles is sometimes called aging the receivables.	____	____
3.	The direct write-off method of accounting for uncollectible receivables provides for uncollectible accounts in the year of sale.	____	____
4.	Estimation of uncollectible accounts based on the analysis of receivables emphasizes the current net realizable value of the receivables.	____	____
5.	The allowance method of accounting for uncollectible receivables emphasizes the matching of uncollectible expense with the related sales.	____	____
6.	The term *notes* includes all money claims against people, organizations, or other debtors.	____	____
7.	Accounts and notes receivable originating from sales transactions are sometimes called trade receivables.	____	____
8.	For good internal control, an employee who handles the accounting for notes and accounts receivable should not be involved with credit approvals or collections of receivables.	____	____
9.	When a note is received from a customer on account, it is recorded by debiting Notes Receivable and crediting Sales.	____	____
10.	Jacob Co. issues a 90-day, 12% note on May 13; the due date of the note is August 11.	____	____

EXERCISE 8-1

Star Co. uses the allowance method of accounting for uncollectibles. On March 31, 20--, Star deemed that an amount of $3,150 due from Jane Eades was uncollectible and wrote it off. On May 8, 20--, Eades paid the $3,150.

Instructions:

(1) Prepare the entry to write off the account on March 31.

(2) Prepare the entry to reinstate the account on May 8, and to record the cash received.

JOURNAL   PAGE

	DATE		DESCRIPTION	POST. REF.	DEBIT	CREDIT	
1							1
2							2
3							3
4							4
5							5
6							6
7							7
8							8
9							9
10							10
11							11

EXERCISE 8-2

Coco Co. uses the direct write-off method of accounting for uncollectibles. On August 31, 20--, Coco deemed that an amount of $550 due from Don Shore was uncollectible and wrote it off. On October 8, 20--, Shore paid the $550.

Instructions:

(1) Prepare the entry to write off the account on August 31.

(2) Prepare the entry to reinstate the account on October 8, and to record the cash received.

JOURNAL   PAGE

	DATE		DESCRIPTION	POST. REF.	DEBIT	CREDIT	
1							1
2							2
3							3
4							4
5							5
6							6
7							7
8							8
9							9
10							10
11							11

EXERCISE 8-3

Instructions: Using the basic formula for interest and assuming a 360-day year, compute the interest on the following notes.

1. $8,000 at 12% for 30 days .... $ _____

2. $3,500 at 6% for 60 days .... $ _____

3. $2,000 at 12% for 90 days .... $ _____

4. $8,000 at 9% for 30 days .... $ _____

5. $7,500 at 6% for 60 days .... $ _____

6. $12,000 for 90 days at 9% .... $ _____

7. $5,250 for 120 days at 12% .... $ _____

EXERCISE 8-4

The following data regarding the current assets of Walton Company were selected from the accounting records after adjustment at the end of the current fiscal year:

Accounts Receivable	$35,000
Allowance for Doubtful Accounts	1,200
Cash	37,500
Interest Receivable	9,900
Notes Receivable	20,000

Instructions: Prepare the Current Assets section of the balance sheet for Walton Company.

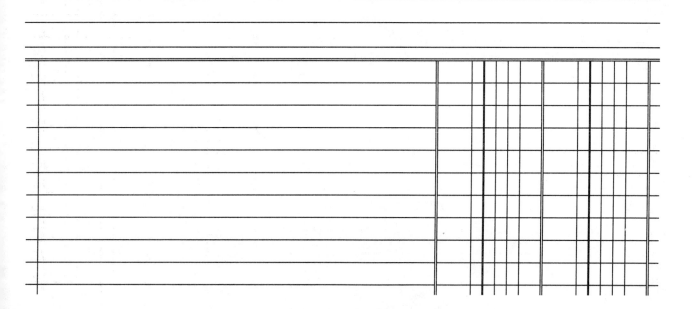

PROBLEM 8-1

Instructions: Prepare the appropriate general journal entries for each of the following situations.

(1) Net sales for the year are $800,000, uncollectible accounts expense is estimated at 3% of net sales, and the allowance account has a $425 credit balance before adjustment. Prepare the adjusting entry at year end for the uncollectibles.

(2) Based on an analysis of accounts in the customers' ledger, estimated uncollectible accounts total $6,280, and the allowance account has a $325 credit balance before adjustment. Prepare the adjusting entry at year end for the uncollectibles.

(3) A $3,500 account receivable from Bentley Co. is written off as uncollectible. The allowance method is used.

(4) A $1,235 account receivable from Apple Co., which was written off three months earlier, is collected in full. The allowance method is used.

JOURNAL   PAGE

	DATE		DESCRIPTION	POST. REF.	DEBIT	CREDIT	
1							1
2							2
3							3
4							4
5							5
6							6
7							7
8							8
9							9
10							10
11							11
12							12
13							13
14							14
15							15
16							16
17							17
18							18
19							19
20							20
21							21
22							22

PROBLEM 8-2

Instructions: Prepare the general journal entries to record the following transactions. (Omit explanations.)

(1) Pequot Co. received a 60-day, 12% note for $8,000 from a customer, Dave Davidson, in settlement of Davidson's account.

(2) Davidson failed to pay the note in (1) at maturity.

(3) Ten days after the maturity of the note in (1), Davidson paid Pequot in full, including interest at 11% for this 10-day period.

(4) Pequot received a 90-day, 10% note for $3,000 from a customer, Sue Smith, in settlement of Smith's account.

(5) The note in (4) was dishonored at maturity.

JOURNAL

PAGE

	DATE		DESCRIPTION	POST. REF.	DEBIT	CREDIT	
1							1
2							2
3							3
4							4
5							5
6							6
7							7
8							8
9							9
10							10
11							11
12							12
13							13
14							14
15							15
16							16
17							17
18							18
19							19
20							20
21							21
22							22
23							23
24							24
25							25

9

Inventories

QUIZ AND TEST HINTS

The following hints may be helpful to you in preparing for a quiz or a test over the material covered in Chapter 9.

1. You should carefully review the new terminology introduced in this chapter. Do the Matching Exercise on page 373.

2. The chapter emphasizes determining the cost of inventory using the first-in, first-out (fifo), last-in, first-out (lifo), and average cost methods. Most instructors ask questions related to these cost flow assumptions using the perpetual and periodic inventory systems. The Illustrative Problem in the Chapter Review is an excellent study aid for this type of question.

3. The retail method and gross profit method of estimating inventory are also popular subjects for quiz and test questions with instructors. Be prepared to work each method.

FILL IN THE BLANK—Part A

Instructions: Answer the following questions or complete the statements by writing the appropriate words or amounts in the answer blanks.

1. A detailed listing of merchandise on hand is called a(n) _____ _____.

2. At the end of the year, the physical inventory is overstated. As a result, the cost of merchandise sold will be _____.

3. At the end of the year, the physical inventory is understated. As a result, the owner's capital reported on the balance sheet will be

    _____.

4. The _____-_____, _____-_____ method of costing inventory is based on the assumption that the most recent merchandise inventory costs should be charged against revenue.

5. On June 1, there was beginning inventory of 5 units at $100 per unit. During June, the following three purchases were made: June 7, 10 units at $110 per unit; June 17, 15 units at $115 per unit; and June 23, 8 units at $116 per unit. If 12 units are on hand on June 30, the total cost of the ending inventory using the last-in, first-out method is _____.

6. During a period of consistently falling prices, the _____ (fifo or lifo) method will result in reporting the greater amount of gross profit.

7. The _____-_____-_____-_____-_____ method reports inventory at the lower of its cost or current market value (replacement cost).

8. During July, merchandise available for sale at cost and retail is $240,000 and $400,000, respectively. If $25,000 of merchandise at retail is on hand on July 31, the estimated cost of the merchandise on hand on July 31 is

    _____.

9. The _____ _____ method estimates inventory cost based on the relationship of gross profit to sales.

10. The _____ _____ ratio measures the relationship between the volume of goods (merchandise) sold and the amount of inventory carried during the period.

FILL IN THE BLANK—Part B

Instructions: Answer the following questions or complete the statements by writing the appropriate words or amounts in the answer blanks.

1. At the end of the year, the physical inventory is overstated. As a result, net income will be _____.

2. At the end of the year, the physical inventory is understated. As a result, gross profit will be _____.

3. The _____-_____, _____-_____ method of costing inventory is based on the assumption that the costs of merchandise sold should be charged against revenue in the order in which the costs were incurred.

4. The _____ _____ method costs inventory based upon the assumption that costs should be charged against revenue in accordance with the weighted average unit costs of the items sold.

5. On June 1, there was beginning inventory of 5 units at $100 per unit. During June, the following three purchases were made: June 7, 10 units at $110 per unit; June 17, 15 units at $115 per unit; and June 23, 8 units at $116 per unit. If 12 units are on hand on June 30, the total cost of the ending inventory using the first-in, first-out method is _____.

6. The estimated selling price of an item of inventory less any direct costs of disposal, such as sales commissions, is called _____ _____ _____.

7. If the cost of an item of inventory is $50, the current replacement cost is $45, and the selling price is $80, the amount included in inventory according to the lower-of-cost-or-market concept is _____.

8. The _____ _____ method estimates inventory cost based on the relationship of the cost of merchandise available for sale to the retail price of the same merchandise.

9. During November, the cost of merchandise available for sale was $750,000. Sales of $900,000 were made during November at an average gross profit of 30% of sales. Using the gross profit method, the estimated cost of the inventory on hand on November 30 is _____.

10. The _____ _____ _____ _____ _____ _____ is a measure of the length of time it takes to acquire, sell, and replace the inventory.

MULTIPLE CHOICE

Instructions: Circle the best answer for each of the following questions.

1. If merchandise inventory at the end of the period is understated:
   a. gross profit will be overstated
   b. owner's equity will be overstated
   c. net income will be understated
   d. cost of merchandise sold will be understated

2. If merchandise inventory at the end of period 1 is overstated and at the end of period 2 is correct:
   a. gross profit in period 2 will be understated
   b. assets at the end of period 2 will be overstated
   c. owner's equity at the end of period 2 will be understated
   d. cost of merchandise sold in period 2 will be understated

3. The following units of a particular item were purchased and sold during the period:

Beginning inventory	10 units at $5
First purchase	15 units at $6
Sale	10 units
Second purchase	10 units at $7
Sale	8 units
Third purchase	15 units at $8
Sale	17 units

   What is the total cost of the 15 units on hand at the end of the period, as determined under the perpetual inventory system by the lifo costing method?
   a. $80
   b. $90
   c. $100
   d. $120

4. Assuming the data given in No. 3, determine the total cost of the 15 units on hand at the end of the period assuming a perpetual inventory system and the fifo costing method.
   a. $80
   b. $90
   c. $100
   d. $120

5. Assuming the data given in No. 3, determine the total cost of the 15 units on hand at the end of the period assuming a periodic inventory system and the lifo costing method.

   a. $80

   b. $90

   c. $100

   d. $120

6. Assuming the data given in No. 3, determine the total cost of the 15 units on hand at the end of the period assuming a periodic inventory system and the fifo costing method.

   a. $80

   b. $90

   c. $99

   d. $120

7. Assuming the data given in No. 3, determine the total cost of the 15 units on hand at the end of the period assuming a periodic inventory system and the average costing method.

   a. $80

   b. $90

   c. $99

   d. $120

8. During a period of rising prices, the inventory costing method that will result in the lowest amount of net income is:

   a. fifo

   b. lifo

   c. average cost

   d. perpetual

9. If the replacement price of an item of inventory is lower than its cost, the use of the lower of cost or market method:

   a. is not permitted unless a perpetual inventory system is maintained

   b. is recommended in order to maximize the reported net income

   c. tends to overstate the gross profit

   d. reduces gross profit for the period in which the decline occurred

10. When lifo is strictly applied to a perpetual inventory system, the unit cost prices assigned to the ending inventory will not necessarily be those associated with the earliest unit costs of the period if:

    a. a physical inventory is taken at the end of the period

    b. physical inventory records are maintained throughout the period in terms of quantities only

    c. at any time during a period the number of units of a commodity sold exceeds the number previously purchased during the same period

    d. moving average inventory cost is maintained

TRUE/FALSE

Instructions: Indicate whether each of the following statements is true or false by placing a check mark in the appropriate column.

	True	False
1. If merchandise inventory at the end of the period is understated, gross profit will be overstated.		X
2. The two principal systems of inventory accounting are periodic and physical.		X
3. When terms of a sale are FOB destination, title usually does not pass to the buyer until the commodities are delivered.		
4. If merchandise inventory at the end of the period is overstated, owner's equity at the end of the period will be understated.		
5. During a period of rising prices, the inventory costing method that will result in the highest amount of net income is lifo.		
6. If the cost of units purchased and the prices at which they were sold remained stable, all three inventory methods would yield the same results.		
7. When the rate of inflation is high, the larger gross profits that result from using the fifo method are frequently called inventory profits.		
8. As used in the phrase "lower of cost or market," *market* means selling price.		
9. When the retail inventory method is used, inventory at retail is converted to cost on the basis of the ratio of cost to replacement cost of the merchandise available for sale.		
10. Merchandise inventory is usually presented on the balance sheet immediately following receivables.		

EXERCISE 9-1

At the fiscal year end of October 31, 2003, the merchandise inventory was understated by $5,000. The error was discovered in 2004.

Instructions: In the spaces provided below, indicate the effect of the error on the sales, cost of merchandise sold, gross profit, net income, merchandise inventory (October 31, 2003), current assets, total assets, liabilities, and owner's equity for the year ending October 31, 2003. For each item, indicate (1) whether it is understated, overstated, or correct; and (2) the dollar amount of the error, if any.

Sales

(1) _____

(2) _____

Cost of Merchandise Sold

(1) _____

(2) _____

Gross Profit

(1) _____

(2) _____

Net Income

(1) _____

(2) _____

Merchandise Inventory (October 31, 2003)

(1) _____

(2) _____

Current Assets

(1) _____

(2) _____

Total Assets

(1) _____

(2) _____

Liabilities

(1) _____

(2) _____

Owner's Equity

(1) _____

(2) _____

EXERCISE 9-2

The following information was taken from the records of Dawkins Co. for the year ended June 30, 2003.

Merchandise inventory, July 1, 2002 .... $130,000
Merchandise inventory, June 30, 2003 125,000
Purchases 600,000
Purchases returns and allowances 45,000
Purchases discounts 10,000
Sales 875,000
Transportation in 7,500

Instructions: Prepare a partial income statement for Dawkins Co. through the reporting of gross profit.

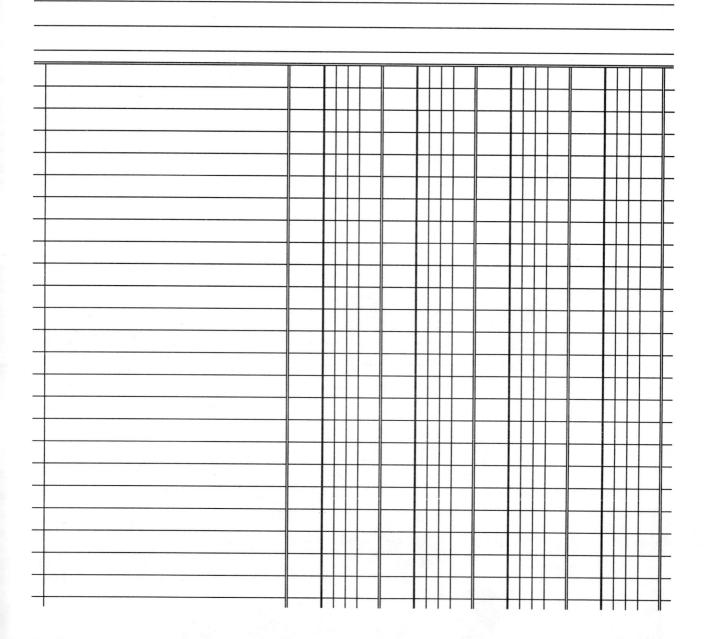

EXERCISE 9-3

Instructions: Complete the following summary, which illustrates the application of the lower-of-cost-or-market rule to individual inventory items of Unks Co.

	Quantity	Unit Cost Price	Unit Market Price	Total Cost	Total Lower of Cost or Market
Commodity A	750	$5.00	$4.80	$ _____	$ _____
Commodity B	460	6.00	7.00	_____	_____
Commodity C	200	7.25	6.00	_____	_____
Commodity D	300	4.80	4.30	_____	_____
Total				$ _____	$ _____

PROBLEM 9-1

Hawkins Co. is a small wholesaler of hiking shoes. The accounting records show the following purchases and sales of the Mountain model during the first year of business.

A physical count of the Mountain model at the end of the year reveals that 12 are still on hand.

Purchases					Sales	
Date	Units	Price	Total Cost		Date	Units
Jan. 10	10	$48	$ 480		Feb. 10	8
Feb. 15	100	54	5,400		Apr. 1	95
July 3	65	55	3,575		Aug. 10	65
Nov. 1	35	58	2,030		Nov. 15	30
Total	210		$11,485			198

Instructions:

(1) Determine the cost of the Mountain model inventory as of December 31 by means of the first-in, first-out (fifo) method with a perpetual inventory system.

INVENTORY (Fifo Perpetual)

Date Purchased	Units	Price	Total Cost

(2) Determine the cost of the Mountain Model inventory as of December 31 by means of the last-in, first-out (lifo) method with a perpetual inventory system.

INVENTORY (Lifo Perpetual)

Date Purchased	Units	Price	Total Cost

(3) Determine the cost of the Mountain model inventory as of December 31 by means of the first-in, first-out (fifo) method with a periodic inventory system.

INVENTORY (Fifo Periodic)

Date Purchased	Units	Price	Total Cost

(4) Determine the cost of the Mountain model inventory as of December 31 by means of the last-in, first-out (lifo) method with a periodic inventory system.

INVENTORY (Lifo Periodic)

Date Purchased	Units	Price	Total Cost

(5) Determine the cost of the Mountain model inventory as of December 31 by means of the average cost method with a periodic system. (Round unit cost to two decimal places.)

INVENTORY (Average Cost)

Average unit cost = $_____ = $_____

_____ units in the inventory @ $_____ = $_____

PROBLEM 9-2

Bartle Co. began operating on January 1 of the current year. During the year, Bartle sold 28,000 units at an average price of $80 each, and made the following purchases:

Date of Purchase	Units	Unit Price	Total Cost
January 1	5,400	$50	$ 270,000
March 1	4,100	54	221,400
June 1	4,800	56	268,800
September 1	8,400	61	512,400
November 1	5,400	69	372,600
December 1	1,900	73	138,700
	30,000		$1,783,900

Instructions: Using the periodic inventory system, determine the ending inventory, the cost of merchandise sold, and the gross profit for Bartle, using each of the following methods of inventory costing: **(1)** fifo, **(2)** lifo, and **(3)** average cost. (Round unit cost to two decimal places.)

	(1) Fifo	**(2)** Lifo	**(3)** Average Cost
Sales	$	$	$
Purchases	$ 1,783,900	$ 1,783,900	$ 1,783,900
Less ending inventory	$	$	$
Cost of merchandise sold	$	$	$
Gross profit	$	$	$

PROBLEM 9-3

Knish Co. operates a department store and takes a physical inventory at the end of each calendar year. However, Knish likes to have a balance sheet and an income statement available at the end of each month in order to study financial position and operating trends. Knish estimates inventory at the end of each month for accounting statement preparation purposes. The following information is available as of August 31 of the current year:

	Cost	Retail
Merchandise inventory, August 1	$118,500	$170,000
Purchases in August	307,125	481,400
Purchases returns and allowances—August ...	8,000	8,900
Sales in August		493,200
Sales returns and allowances—August		14,200

Instructions:

(1) Determine the estimated cost of the inventory on August 31, using the retail method.

	Cost	Retail
Merchandise inventory, August 1	$	$
Purchases in August (net)		
Merchandise available for sale	$	$

Ratio of cost to retail:

$$\frac{\$\underline{\hspace{2cm}}}{\$} = \underline{\hspace{1cm}} \%$$

	Retail
Sales in August (net)	
Merchandise inventory, August 31, at retail	$
Merchandise inventory, August 31, at estimated cost ($_____ × _____%)	$

(2) Determine the estimated cost of inventory on August 31, using the gross profit method. On the basis of past experience, Knish estimates a rate of gross profit of 30% of net sales.

Merchandise inventory, August 1	$
Purchases in August (net)	
Merchandise available for sale	$
Sales in August (net)	$
Less estimated gross profit ($_____ × _____%)	
Estimated cost of merchandise sold	$
Estimated merchandise inventory, August 31	$

10

Fixed Assets and Intangible Assets

QUIZ AND TEST HINTS

The following hints may be helpful to you in preparing for a quiz or a test over the material covered in Chapter 10.

1. The chapter emphasizes the computation of depreciation. You should be able to compute depreciation using each of the three methods: straight-line, units-of-production, and declining-balance. If your instructor lectures on the sum-of-the-years-digits method of depreciation in the appendix to the chapter, you should also be prepared to compute depreciation under this method.

2. A common question on quizzes and tests involves the recording of fixed asset disposals. You should be able to prepare general journal entries for disposals, including the exchange of similar assets. Exhibit 6 may be useful for reviewing the journal entries of exchanges of similar assets.

3. The chapter introduces a significant amount of new terminology. These terms lend themselves to numerous multiple-choice and matching questions. Do the Matching Exercise on pages 415—416.

4. You should expect some questions related to intangible assets. The computation of amortization is relatively simple, and it is similar to the units-of-production depreciation method. This section of the chapter lends itself to multiple-choice questions.

FILL IN THE BLANK—Part A

Instructions: Answer the following questions or complete the statements by writing the appropriate words or amounts in the answer blanks.

1. Long-term or relatively permanent tangible assets that are used in the normal business operation are called _____ assets.

2. Surveying fees incurred in connection with securing title of land for use by a business is debited to the _____ account.

3. The cost of a special foundation incurred in connection with the acquisition of a secondhand machine would be debited to the _____ account.

4. The estimated value of a fixed asset at the end of its useful life is called _____ value.

5. The _____-_____-_____ method is a method of depreciation that provides for depreciation expense based on the expected productive capacity of a fixed asset.

6. The cost of a fixed asset minus accumulated depreciation on the asset is called the _____ value.

7. A useful life of 4 years is equivalent to a straight-line depreciation rate of _____.

8. Equipment acquired on the first day of the current fiscal year for $50,000 has an estimated life of 4 years or 25,000 hours and a residual value of $5,000. Depreciation for the current year using the straight-line method is _____.

9. Equipment acquired on the first day of the current fiscal year for $50,000 has an estimated life of 4 years or 25,000 hours and a residual value of $5,000. Depreciation for the current year using the declining-balance method (using twice the straight-line rate) is _____.

10. Equipment acquired on the first day of the current fiscal year for $50,000 has an estimated life of 4 years or 25,000 hours and a residual value of $5,000. The equipment was used for 7,000 hours during the current year. Depreciation for the current year using the units-of-production method is _____.

11. The costs of acquiring fixed assets, adding to a fixed asset, improving a fixed asset, or extending a fixed asset's useful life are called _____ expenditures.

12. An expenditure that improves a fixed asset's operating efficiency or capacity for its remaining useful life is called a(n) _____.

13. The amount a seller allows a buyer for a fixed asset that is traded in for a similar asset is called a(n) _____-_____ _____.

14. Old equipment with a book value of $25,000 is traded in on similar equipment priced at $70,000. A trade-in allowance of $30,000 is allowed on the old equipment, and the balance is paid in cash. The new equipment should be recorded at a cost of _____.

15. _____ leases treat the leased assets as purchased assets for the accounts.

16. The process of transferring the cost of natural resources to an expense account is called _____.

17. _____ is the periodic transfer of a cost of an intangible asset to expense.

18. _____ are exclusive rights to produce and sell goods with one or more unique features.

19. The cost of a patent is amortized by debiting Amortization Expense—Patents and crediting _____.

20. A name, term, or symbol used to identify a business and its products is called a _____.

FILL IN THE BLANK—Part B

Instructions: Answer the following questions or complete the statements by writing the appropriate words or amounts in the answer blanks.

1. The cost of razing an unwanted building on land purchased for use by a business is debited to the _____ account.

2. The systematic, periodic transfer of the cost of a fixed asset to expense during its expected useful life is called _____.

3. The _____-_____ method is a method of depreciation that provides for equal periodic depreciation expense over the estimated life of a fixed asset.

4. The _____-_____ method is a method of depreciation that provides declining periodic depreciation expense over the estimated life of a fixed asset.

5. A useful life of 5 years is equivalent to a straight-line depreciation rate of _____.

6. Equipment acquired on the first day of the current fiscal year for $80,000 has an estimated life of 5 years or 25,000 hours and a residual value of $10,000. Depreciation for the current year using the straight-line method is _____14000_____.

7. Equipment acquired on the first day of the current fiscal year for $80,000 has an estimated life of 5 years or 25,000 hours and a residual value of $10,000. Depreciation for the current year using the declining-balance method (using twice the straight-line rate) is _____.

8. Equipment acquired on the first day of the current fiscal year for $80,000 has an estimated life of 5 years or 25,000 hours and a residual value of $10,000. The equipment was used for 6,000 hours during the current year. Depreciation for the current year using the units-of-production method is ___*16800*___.

9. Depreciation methods that provide for a higher depreciation amount in the first year of the asset's use, followed by a gradually declining amount of depreciation, are referred to as _____ depreciation methods.

10. Costs that benefit only the current period or costs incurred for normal maintenance and repairs of fixed assets are called _____ expenditures.

11. An expenditure that increases the useful life of an asset beyond its original estimate is called a(n) _____ _____.

12. _____ is the amount a buyer owes a seller when a fixed asset is traded in on a similar asset.

13. Old equipment with a book value of $25,000 is traded in on similar equipment priced at $70,000. A trade-in allowance of $18,000 is allowed on the old equipment, and the balance is paid in cash. The new equipment should be recorded at a cost of _____.

14. _____ leases do not meet the criteria for capital leases and thus are accounted for as operating expenses.

15. Long-term assets that are useful in the operations of a business, are not held for sale, and are without physical qualities are called _____ assets.

16. _____ is an intangible asset of a business that is created from such favorable factors as location, product quality, reputation, and managerial skill.

17. A(n) _____ is an exclusive right to publish and sell a literary, artistic, or musical composition.

18. Depletion expense related to a mineral ore deposit is recorded by debiting Depletion Expense and crediting _____ _____.

19. Research and development costs are normally accounted for as _____ _____ _____ in the period in which they are incurred.

20. The ratio of _____ _____ _____ _____-_____ _____ provides a measure of the margin of safety to creditors.

MULTIPLE CHOICE

Instructions: Circle the best answer for each of the following questions.

1. If unwanted buildings are located on land acquired for a plant site, the cost of their removal, less any salvage recovered, should be charged to the:
   a. expense accounts
   b. building account
   c. land account
   d. accumulated depreciation account

2. The depreciation method used most often in the financial statements is the:
   a. straight-line method
   b. declining-balance method
   c. units-of-production method
   d. MACRS method

3. The depreciation method that would provide the highest reported net income in the early years of an asset's life would be:
   a. straight-line
   b. declining-balance
   c. 150% straight-line
   d. accelerated

4. Equipment with an estimated useful life of 5 years and an estimated residual value of $1,000 is acquired at a cost of $15,000. Using the declining-balance method (at twice the straight-line rate), what is the amount of depreciation for the first year of use of the equipment?
   a. $2,600
   b. $3,000
   c. $5,600
   d. $6,000

5. Equipment that cost $20,000 was originally estimated to have a useful life of 5 years and a residual value of $2,000. The equipment has been depreciated for 2 years using straight-line depreciation. During the third year it is estimated that the remaining useful life is 2 years (instead of 3) and that the residual value is $1,000 (instead of $2,000). The depreciation expense on the equipment in year 3 using the straight-line method would be:
   a. $5,500
   b. $5,900
   c. $6,000
   d. $7,500

6. Assume that a drill press is rebuilt during its sixth year of use so that its useful life is extended 5 years beyond the original estimate of 10 years. In this case, the cost of rebuilding the drill press should be charged to the appropriate:

    a. expense account

    b. accumulated depreciation account

    c. asset account

    d. liability account

7. Old equipment which cost $11,000 and has accumulated depreciation of $6,300 is given, along with $9,000 in cash, for the same type of new equipment with a price of $15,600. At what amount should the new equipment be recorded?

    a. $15,600

    b. $15,300

    c. $13,700

    d. $9,000

8. Assume the same facts as in No. 7, except that the old equipment and $11,500 in cash is given for the new equipment. At what amount should the new equipment be recorded for financial accounting purposes?

    a. $16,200

    b. $15,600

    c. $11,500

    d. $10,900

9. In a lease contract, the party who legally owns the asset is the:

    a. contractor

    b. operator

    c. lessee

    d. lessor

10. Which of the following items would not be considered an intangible asset?

    a. mineral ore deposits

    b. patent

    c. copyright

    d. goodwill

TRUE/FALSE

Instructions: Indicate whether each of the following statements is true or false by placing a check mark in the appropriate column.

		True	False
1.	The declining-balance method provides for a higher depreciation charge in the first year of use of the asset, followed by a gradually declining periodic charge...............	____	____
2.	The method of depreciation which yields a depreciation charge that varies with the amount of asset usage is known as the units-of-production method.	____	____
3.	In using the declining-balance method, the asset should not be depreciated below the net book value......................	____	____
4.	Accelerated depreciation methods are most appropriate for situations in which the decline in productivity or earning power of the asset is proportionately greater in the early years of its use than in later years.....................................	____	____
5.	MACRS depreciation methods permit the use of asset lives that are often much shorter than the actual useful life.	____	____
6.	When an old fixed asset is traded in for a new fixed asset having a similar use, proper accounting treatment prohibits recognition of a gain.	____	____
7.	A lease that transfers ownership of the leased asset to the lessee at the end of the lease term should be classified as an operating lease...	____	____
8.	Long-lived assets that are without physical characteristics but useful in the operations of a business are classified as fixed assets...	____	____
9.	Fully depreciated assets should be retained in the accounting records until disposal has been authorized and they are removed from service...	____	____
10.	Intangible assets are usually reported on the balance sheet in the current asset section.......................................	____	____

EXERCISE 10-1

A fixed asset acquired on January 2 at a cost of $420,000 has an estimated useful life of 8 years. Assuming that it will have a residual value of $20,000, determine the depreciation for each of the first two years (a) by the straight-line method and (b) by the declining-balance method, using twice the straight-line rate.

(a) Straight-line method   Depreciation

       Year 1 ....   _____

       Year 2 ....   _____

(b) Declining-balance method   Depreciation

       Year 1 ....   _____

       Year 2 ....   _____

EXERCISE 10-2

Bidwell Co. uses the units-of-production method for computing the depreciation on its machines. One machine, which cost $88,000, is estimated to have a useful life of 22,000 hours and no residual value. During the first year of operation, this machine was used a total of 5,200 hours. Record the depreciation of this machine on December 31, the end of the first year. (Omit explanation.)

JOURNAL   PAGE

	DATE	DESCRIPTION	POST. REF.	DEBIT	CREDIT	
1						1
2						2
3						3
4						4
5						5
6						6
7						7
8						8
9						9
10						10
11						11
12						12
13						13

EXERCISE 10-3

On March 8, Tilly's Wholesale decides to sell for $2,000 cash some fixtures for which it paid $4,000 and on which it has taken total depreciation of $2,500 to date of sale. Record this sale. (Omit explanation.)

JOURNAL   PAGE

	DATE		DESCRIPTION	POST. REF.	DEBIT	CREDIT	
1							1
2							2
3							3
4							4
5							5
6							6
7							7
8							8
9							9
10							10

EXERCISE 10-4

Mine-It Co. paid $2,400,000 for some mineral rights in Idaho. The deposit is estimated to contain 800,000 tons of ore of uniform grade. Record the depletion of this deposit on December 31, the end of the first year, assuming that 80,000 tons are mined during the year. (Omit explanation.)

JOURNAL   PAGE

	DATE		DESCRIPTION	POST. REF.	DEBIT	CREDIT	
1							1
2							2
3							3
4							4
5							5
6							6
7							7
8							8
9							9
10							10

EXERCISE 10-5

Stables Co. acquires a patent at the beginning of its calendar (fiscal) year for $100,000. Although the patent will not expire for another ten years, it is expected to be of value for only five years. Record the amortization of this patent at the end of the fiscal year. (Omit explanation.)

JOURNAL   PAGE

	DATE	DESCRIPTION	POST. REF.	DEBIT	CREDIT	
1						1
2						2
3						3
4						4
5						5
6						6
7						7
8						8
9						9
10						10
11						11
12						12
13						13

PROBLEM 10-1

Bishop Company purchased equipment on January 1, 20XA, for $80,000. The equipment is expected to have a useful life of 4 years or 15,000 operating hours and a residual value of $5,000. The equipment was used 3,400 hours in 20XA, 4,000 hours in 20XB, 6,000 hours in 20XC, and 1,600 hours in 20XD.

Instructions: Determine the amount of depreciation expense for the years ended December 31, 20XA, 20XB, 20XC, and 20XD, for each method of depreciation in the table below.

Year	Straight-Line	Declining-Balance	Units-of-Production
20XA			
20XB			
20XC			
20XD			
Total			

PROBLEM 10-2

Getco Co. has a sales representative who must travel a substantial amount. A car for this purpose was acquired January 2 four years ago at a cost of $20,000. It is estimated to have a total useful life of 4 years or 100,000 miles.

Instructions:

(1) Record the annual depreciation on Getco's car at the end of the first and third years of ownership using the straight-line method, assuming no residual value, and using a December 31 year end. (Omit explanation.)

(2) Record the annual depreciation on Getco's car at the end of the first and third years of ownership using the declining-balance method at twice the straight-line rate and a December 31 year end. (Omit explanation.)

(3) Record the annual depreciation on Getco's car at the end of the first and third years of ownership using the units-of-production method, assuming no residual value, and using a December 31 year end. The car was driven 35,000 miles in the first year and 28,000 miles in the third year. (Omit explanation.)

JOURNAL

PAGE

	DATE	DESCRIPTION	POST. REF.	DEBIT	CREDIT	
1						1
2						2
3						3
4						4
5						5
6						6
7						7
8						8
9						9
10						10
11						11
12						12
13						13
14						14
15						15
16						16
17						17
18						18
19						19
20						20
21						21

PROBLEM 10-3

(a) Braso Co. is planning to trade in its present truck for a new model on April 30 of the current year. The existing truck was purchased May 1 three years ago at a cost of $15,000, and accumulated depreciation is $12,000 through April 30 of the current year. The new truck has a list price of $20,700. Ralston Motors agrees to allow Braso $3,500 for the present truck, and Braso agrees to pay the balance of $17,200 in cash.

Instructions: Record the exchange in general journal form according to acceptable methods of accounting for exchanges. (Omit explanation.)

JOURNAL   PAGE

	DATE	DESCRIPTION	POST. REF.	DEBIT	CREDIT	
1						1
2						2
3						3
4						4
5						5
6						6
7						7
8						8
9						9

(b) Assume the same facts as in (a), except that the allowance on the present truck is $1,000 and Braso agrees to pay the balance of $19,700 in cash.

Instructions: Record the exchange according to acceptable methods of accounting for exchanges.

JOURNAL   PAGE

	DATE	DESCRIPTION	POST. REF.	DEBIT	CREDIT	
1						1
2						2
3						3
4						4
5						5
6						6
7						7
8						8
9						9

11

Current Liabilities

QUIZ AND TEST HINTS

The following hints may be helpful to you in preparing for a quiz or a test over the material covered in Chapter 11.

1. A major focus of this chapter is on the computation of payroll. You should be able to compute total earnings, social security and Medicare tax, state and federal unemployment tax, and net pay and prepare the necessary journal entries. Review the chapter illustrations related to these computations.

2. The journal entries for vacation pay, pensions, and warranty expense are fairly easy to do. Spend a few minutes reviewing these entries.

3. Most instructors will ask some questions related to notes payable. You should be able to compute interest and prepare the necessary journal entries, including an adjusting entry for accrued interest. Also, carefully review the discounting of notes.

4. The Illustrative Problem is a good overall review of the types of journal entries you might have to prepare on a test or a quiz. Try to work the problem without looking at the solution. Check your answer. If you made any errors, review those sections of the chapter. If you still don't understand the answer, ask your instructor for help.

5. Do the Matching Exercise on page 456.

FILL IN THE BLANK—Part A

Instructions: Answer the following questions or complete the statements by writing the appropriate words or amounts in the answer blanks.

1. The maturity value of a 90-day, 12%, $30,000 note payable is

   _____.

2. In buying equipment, a business issues a $90,000, 180-day note dated January 17, which the seller discounts at 12%. The cost of the equipment would be recorded at _____.

3. The total earnings of an employee for a payroll period is called _____ pay.

4. _____ _____ is the amount the employer is obligated to pay the employee after payroll deductions.

5. _____ _____ _____
   _____ tax is used to finance federal programs for old-age and disability benefits (social security) and health insurance for the aged (Medicare).

6. A(n) _____ _____ _____ is a detailed record of each employee's earnings.

7. Employer's payroll taxes become liabilities when the related employee payroll is _____.

8. A pension plan that promises employees a fixed annual pension benefit based on years of service and compensation levels is called a(n) _____ _____ plan.

9. Rights to benefits that employees earn during their term of employment but take effect after they retire are called _____ benefits.

10. The _____ ratio measures the ability to pay current liabilities within a short period of time.

FILL IN THE BLANK—Part B

Instructions: Answer the following questions or complete the statements by writing the appropriate words or amounts in the answer blanks.

1. The maturity value of a 120-day, 9%, $75,000 note payable is

   _____.

2. In buying a building, a business issues a $240,000, 120-day note dated August 3, which the seller discounts at 10%. The cost of the building would be recorded at _____.

3. The interest deducted from the maturity value of a note is called the

   _____.

4. The _____ rate is used in computing the interest to be deducted from the maturity value of a note.

5. Gross pay less payroll deductions is _____ pay.

6. A(n) _____ _____ is a multicolumn form used to assemble and summarize payroll data at the end of each payroll period.

7. The employer's matching portion of the Federal Insurance Contribution Act (FICA) tax that represents the contribution to health insurance for senior citizens is credited to _____ _____ Payable.

8. _____ is the total amount paid to employees for a certain period.

9. Benefits provided to employees in addition to wages and salaries are called _____ benefits.

10. A pension plan that requires a fixed amount of money to be invested for the employee's behalf during the employee's working years is called a(n) _____ _____ plan.

MULTIPLE CHOICE

Instructions: Circle the best answer for each of the following questions.

1. The interest charged by the bank, at the rate of 12%, on a 90-day, non-interest-bearing note payable for $75,000 is:
   a. $1,000
   b. $2,250
   c. $3,000
   d. $9,000

2. The cost of a product warranty should be included as an expense:
   a. in the period of the sale of the product
   b. in the period of the collection of the cash from the sale of the product
   c. in the future period when the product is repaired or replaced
   d. in the future period when the cost of repairing the product is paid

3. An employee's rate of pay is $8 per hour, with time and a half for hours worked in excess of 40 during a week. If the employee works 50 hours during a week and has social security tax withheld at a rate of 6.0%, Medicare tax withheld at a rate of 1.5%, and federal income tax withheld at a rate of 15%, the employee's net pay for the week is:
   a. $440
   b. $374
   c. $341
   d. $310

4. An employee receives an hourly rate of $18, with time and a half for all hours worked in excess of 40 during a week. Payroll data for the current week are as follows: hours worked, 45; federal income tax withheld, $350; cumulative earnings for year prior to current week, $49,700; social security tax rate, 6.0%; Medicare tax rate, 1.5%. What is the gross pay for the employee?

   a. $475

   b. $505

   c. $720

   d. $855

5. Prior to the last weekly payroll period of the calendar year, the cumulative earnings of employees A and B are $79,800 and $21,000, respectively. Their earnings for the last completed payroll period of the year are $1,000 each. The amount of earnings subject to social security tax is $80,000, and the tax rate is 6%. All earnings are subject to Medicare tax at 1.5%. Assuming that the payroll will be paid on December 29, what will be the employer's total FICA tax (social security and Medicare) for this payroll period on the two salary amounts of $1,000 each?

   a. $75

   b. $90

   c. $102

   d. $150

6. Payroll taxes levied against employees become liabilities:

   a. when earned by the employee

   b. at the end of an accounting period

   c. the first of the following month

   d. at the time the liability for the employee's wages is paid

7. Which of the following items would not be considered a fringe benefit?

   a. vacations

   b. employee pension plans

   c. health insurance

   d. FICA benefits

8. For proper matching of revenues and expenses, the estimated cost of fringe benefits must be recognized as an expense of the period the:

   a. employee earns the benefit

   b. employee is paid the benefit

   c. fringe benefit contract is signed

   d. fringe benefit contract becomes effective

9. The inputs into a payroll system may be classified as either constants or variables. All of the following are variables except for:

   a. number of hours worked

   b. vacation credits

   c. number of income tax withholding allowances

   d. number of days sick leave with pay

10. An aid in internal control over payrolls that indicates employee attendance is a(n):

   a. payroll register

   b. employee earnings record

   c. "In and Out" card

   d. payroll check

TRUE/FALSE

Instructions: Indicate whether each of the following statements is true or false by placing a check mark in the appropriate column.

		True	False
1.	The total earnings of an employee for a payroll period are called gross pay.	___	___
2.	Only employers are required to contribute to the Federal Insurance Contributions Act program.	___	___
3.	All states require that unemployment compensation taxes be withheld from employees' pay.	___	___
4.	Most employers are also subject to federal and state payroll taxes based on the amount earned by their employees, not the amount paid.	___	___
5.	The amounts withheld from employees' earnings have an effect on the firm's debits to the salary or wage expense accounts.	___	___
6.	All payroll taxes levied against employers become liabilities at the time the related remuneration is paid to employees.	___	___
7.	The recording procedures when special payroll checks are used are different from the procedures when the checks are drawn on the regular bank account.	___	___
8.	Depending on when it is to be paid, vacation liability may be classified in the balance sheet as either a current liability or a long-term liability.	___	___
9.	To properly match revenues and expense, employees' vacation pay should be accrued as a liability as the vacation rights are earned.	___	___

True   False

10. In order for revenues and expenses to be matched properly, a liability to cover the cost of a product warranty must be recorded in the period when the product is repaired. ..... _____   _____

11. Potential liabilities that may arise in the future because of past transactions are called contingent liabilities. .... _____   _____

12. All changes in the constants of the payroll system, such as changes in pay rates, should be properly authorized in writing.. _____   _____

13. The net periodic pension cost of a defined benefit plan is debited to Pension Expense, the amount funded is credited to Cash, and any unfunded amount is credited to Unfunded Pension Revenue.. _____   _____

14. Examples of postretirement benefits from an employer may include dental care, eye care, medical care, life insurance, tuition assistance, or tax services. .... _____   _____

15. The rate used by a bank in discounting a note is called the prime rate.. _____   _____

EXERCISE 11-1

Instructions: In each of the following situations, determine the correct amount.

(1) An employee of a firm operating under the Federal Wage and Hour Law worked 50 hours last week. If the hourly rate of pay is $14, what is the employee's gross earnings for the week?

(2) During the current pay period, an employee earned $2,000. Prior to the current period, the employee earned (in the current year) $79,500. If the social security tax is 6.0% on the first $80,000 of annual earnings and the Medicare tax rate is 1.5% on all earnings, what is the total amount to be withheld from the employee's pay this period?

(3) During the current pay period, an employee earned $3,000. Prior to the current period, the employee earned (in the current year) $137,800. Using the social security and Medicare tax rates and bases in (2), compute the total amount to be withheld from the employee's pay this period.

(4) Using the rates and maximum bases in (2), compute the total amount of social security and Medicare tax withheld from the pay of an employee who has earned $10,000 during the year but has actually received only $9,700, with the remaining $300 to be paid in the next year.

EXERCISE 11-2

Instructions: Prepare the general journal entries to record each of the following items for Wiler Co. for the year ended December 31. (Omit explanations.)

(1) Accrued employee vacation pay at the end of the year is $3,225.

(2) The estimated product warranty liability at the end of the year is 3% of sales of $150,000.

(3) A partially funded pension plan is maintained for employees at an annual cost of $40,000. At the end of the year, $27,500 is paid to the fund trustee and the remaining accrued pension liability is recognized.

JOURNAL

PAGE

	DATE	DESCRIPTION	POST. REF.	DEBIT	CREDIT	
1						1
2						2
3						3
4						4
5						5
6						6
7						7
8						8
9						9
10						10
11						11
12						12
13						13
14						14
15						15
16						16
17						17
18						18
19						19
20						20
21						21
22						22
23						23
24						24
25						25
26						26
27						27

PROBLEM 11-1

The weekly gross payroll of O'Brien Co. on December 7 amounts to $50,000, distributed as follows: sales salaries, $34,000; office salaries, $16,000. The following amounts are to be withheld: social security tax, $3,000; Medicare tax, $750; employees' income tax, $7,500; union dues, $900; and United Way, $450.

Instructions: Omitting explanations, prepare general journal entries to:

(1) Record the payroll.

(2) Record the payment of the payroll.

(3) Record the employer's payroll taxes. Assume that the entire payroll is subject to social security tax at 6.0%, Medicare tax at 1.5%, federal unemployment tax at .8%, and state unemployment tax at 5.4%.

(4) Record the employer's payroll taxes. Assume that $40,000 of payroll is subject to social security tax at 6.0% and $50,000 is subject to Medicare tax at 1.5%. Assume that none of the payroll is subject to federal or state unemployment tax.

JOURNAL   PAGE

	DATE	DESCRIPTION	POST. REF.	DEBIT	CREDIT	
1						1
2						2
3						3
4						4
5						5
6						6
7						7
8						8
9						9
10						10
11						11
12						12
13						13
14						14
15						15
16						16
17						17
18						18
19						19
20						20
21						21
22						22

JOURNAL

PAGE

	DATE	DESCRIPTION	POST. REF.	DEBIT	CREDIT	
1						1
2						2
3						3
4						4
5						5
6						6
7						7
8						8
9						9
10						10
11						11
12						12
13						13
14						14
15						15
16						16
17						17
18						18
19						19
20						20
21						21
22						22
23						23
24						24
25						25
26						26
27						27
28						28
29						29
30						30
31						31
32						32
33						33
34						34
35						35
36						36

PROBLEM 11-2

Instructions: For the employees listed below, compute the individual taxes indicated as well as total taxes by type and by employee. Assume the social security tax rate is 6.0% on the first $80,000 of annual earnings, the Medicare tax rate is 1.5% on all earnings, the state unemployment tax rate is 5.4% on a maximum of $7,000, and the federal unemployment tax rate is .8% on a maximum of $7,000.

| | | | | Employer's Taxes | | | | |
Employee	Annual Earnings	Social Security Tax	Medicare Tax	Social Security Tax	Medicare Tax	State Unemploy- ment	Federal Unemploy- ment	Total
Avery	$ 12,000							
Johnson	5,000							
Jones	59,000							
Smith	70,000							
Wilson	141,000							
Total	$290,000							

PROBLEM 11-3

Instructions: Prepare the general journal entries to record the following transactions. (Omit explanations.)

(1) Audrey Newman issued a 90-day, 12% note for $2,000 to Mayday Co. for a $2,000 overdue account.

(2) Newman paid the note in (1) at maturity.

(3) Paula Wheat borrowed $8,000 from the bank and gave the bank a 90-day, 11% note.

(4) Wheat paid the note in (3) at maturity.

(5) Randy Lucky borrowed $6,000 from the bank, giving a 60-day, non-interest-bearing note that was discounted at 9%.

(6) Lucky paid the note recorded in (5) at maturity.

JOURNAL

PAGE

	DATE	DESCRIPTION	POST. REF.	DEBIT	CREDIT	
1						1
2						2
3						3
4						4
5						5
6						6
7						7
8						8
9						9
10						10
11						11
12						12
13						13
14						14
15						15
16						16
17						17
18						18
19						19
20						20
21						21
22						22
23						23
24						24

Corporations: Organization, Capital Stock Transactions, and Dividends

QUIZ AND TEST HINTS

The following hints may be helpful to you in preparing for a quiz or a test over the material covered in Chapter 12.

1. Many new terms related to the corporate form of organization are introduced in this chapter that may be tested using true/false or multiple-choice questions. Do the Matching Exercise on pages 493–494.

2. You should be able to compute the amount of dividends allocated between nonparticipating cumulative preferred stock and common stock.

3. You should be able to prepare journal entries for the issuance of par and no-par stock, treasury stock transactions, and cash and stock dividends. Expect at least one problem requiring such entries.

4. It is unlikely that you will be required to prepare a journal entry for organization costs. However, you may be asked a multiple-choice question related to organization costs.

FILL IN THE BLANK—Part A

Instructions: Answer the following questions or complete the statements by writing the appropriate words or amounts in the answer blanks.

1. Shares of ownership of a corporation are called _____.

2. The owners' equity in a corporation is reported on the balance sheet under the caption _____ _____.

3. Net income retained in a corporation is reported on the balance sheet as _____ _____.

4. The stockholders' equity section of a balance sheet is composed of preferred $7 stock, $250,000; discount on preferred stock, $25,000; common stock, $750,000; premium on common stock, $100,000; retained earnings, $190,000; treasury stock, $80,000. The total paid-in capital is _____.

5. Stock in the hands of stockholders is called _____ stock.

6. When a corporation has issued only one class of stock, it is called _____ stock.

7. A class of preferred stock whose dividend rights are usually limited to a certain amount is referred to as _____ preferred stock.

8. A company has outstanding stock that is composed of 10,000 shares of $5 cumulative, nonparticipating, $50 par preferred stock and 150,000 shares of $10 par common stock. Preferred dividends were passed last year, and no dividends have been paid thus far in the current year. A total of $280,000 in dividends is to be distributed. The total amount of dividends to be paid on the preferred stock is _____.

9. When the issuance price of a stock exceeds its par value, the stock is said to have been issued at a _____.

10. Land is acquired by issuing 5,000 shares of $20 par common stock with a current market price of $32 per share. The land should be recorded at a cost of _____.

11. If a corporation issues stock and then reacquires the stock, the stock reacquired is referred to as _____ stock.

12. A company purchases 500 shares of its $50 par common stock for $32,500 cash. The effect (increase, decrease, or none) of this purchase on the company's retained earnings is _____ (indicate amount and effect).

13. A _____ is a cash distribution of earnings by a corporation to its shareholders.

14. A balance sheet indicated 20,000 shares of common stock authorized, 8,000 shares issued, and 1,500 shares of treasury stock. If a cash dividend of $5 per share is declared on the common stock, the total amount of the dividend is _____.

15. The effect of a stock dividend on the stockholders' equity of a corporation's balance sheet is to increase paid-in capital and decrease _____ _____.

FILL IN THE BLANK—Part B

Instructions: Answer the following questions or complete the statements by writing the appropriate words or amounts in the answer blanks.

1. The owners of a corporation are the _____.

2. Capital contributed to a corporation by the stockholders and others is reported on the balance sheet as _____-_____ capital.

3. A debit balance in the retained earnings account is called a(n) _____.

4. A value, similar to par value, approved by the board of directors of a corporation for no-par stock is called _____ value.

5. A class of stock with preferential rights over common stock is called _____ stock.

6. _____ preferred stock has a right to receive regular dividends that have been passed (not declared) before any common stock dividends are paid.

7. A company has outstanding stock that is composed of 25,000 shares of $3 cumulative, nonparticipating, $100 par preferred stock and 150,000 shares of $10 par common stock. Preferred dividends were passed last year, and no dividends have been paid thus far in the current year. A total of $140,000 in dividends is to be distributed. The total amount of dividends to be paid on the preferred stock is _____.

8. When the par value of a stock exceeds its issuance price, the stock is said to have been issued at a _____.

9. A company purchases 500 shares of its $50 par common stock for $32,500 cash. The effect (increase, decrease, or none) of this purchase on the company's paid-in capital is _____ (indicate amount and effect).

10. The stockholders' equity section of a balance sheet is composed of preferred $7 stock, $250,000; discount on preferred stock, $25,000; common stock, $750,000; premium on common stock, $100,000; retained earnings, $100,000 deficit; treasury stock, $80,000. The total stockholder's equity is _____.

11. A _____ _____ is the reduction in the par or stated value of common stock and the issuance of a proportionate number of additional shares.

12. A corporation announced a 5-for-1 stock split of its $100 par value stock, which is currently trading for $180. The estimated market value of the stock after the split is _____.

13. A _____ _____ is a distribution of shares of stock to its stockholders.

14. The _____ value is the monetary amount printed on a stock certificate.

15. The _____ _____ is a ratio computed by dividing the annual dividends paid per share of common stock by the market price per share at a specific date, and it indicates the rate of return to stockholders in terms of cash dividend distributions.

MULTIPLE CHOICE

Instructions: Circle the best answer for each of the following questions.

1. Which of the following is not a characteristic of the corporate form of organization?

    a. ownership represented by shares of stock

    b. separate legal existence

    c. unlimited liability of stockholders

    d. earnings subject to the federal income tax

2. The amount printed on a stock certificate is known as:

    a. stated value

    b. premium

    c. discount

    d. par value

3. Assume that a corporation has outstanding 5,000 shares of $6 cumulative preferred stock of $100 par and dividends have been passed for the preceding four years. What is the amount of preferred dividends that must be declared in the current year before a dividend can be declared on common stock?

    a. $90,000

    b. $120,000

    c. $150,000

    d. $180,000

4. When a corporation purchases its own stock, what account is debited for the cost of the stock?

    a. Common Stock Subscribed

    b. Treasury Stock

    c. Preferred Stock

    d. Common Stock Receivable

5. The excess of the proceeds from selling treasury stock over its cost should be credited to:

    a. Retained Earnings

    b. Premium on Capital Stock

    c. Gain from Sale of Treasury Stock

    d. Paid-In Capital from Sale of Treasury Stock

6. The claims of the (?) must first be satisfied upon liquidation of a corporation.

    a. preferred stockholders

    b. cumulative preferred stockholders

    c. common stockholders

    d. creditors

7. A company with 20,000 authorized shares of $20 par common stock issued 12,000 shares at $50. Subsequently, the company declared a 5% stock dividend on a date when the market price was $60 per share. What is the amount transferred from the retained earnings account to paid-in capital accounts as a result of the stock dividend?

    a. $36,000

    b. $30,000

    c. $12,000

    d. $6,000

8. The charter of a corporation provides for the issuance of 100,000 shares of common stock. Assume that 60,000 shares were originally issued and 5,000 were subsequently reacquired. What is the number of shares outstanding?

    a. 5,000

    b. 55,000

    c. 60,000

    d. 100,000

9. The entry to record the issuance of common stock at a price above par would include a credit to:

   a. Donated Capital

   b. Retained Earnings

   c. Treasury Stock

   d. Paid-In Capital in Excess of Par—Common Stock

10. A corporation purchases 10,000 shares of its own $20 par common stock for $35 per share, recording it at cost. What will be the effect on total stockholders' equity?

    a. increase, $200,000

    b. increase, $350,000

    c. decrease, $200,000

    d. decrease, $350,000

TRUE/FALSE

Instructions: Indicate whether each of the following statements is true or false by placing a check mark in the appropriate column.

	True	False
1. A partnership is similar to a proprietorship except that it has more than one owner.	____	____
2. A corporation may acquire, own, and dispose of property in its corporate name.	____	____
3. The two main sources of stockholders' equity are paid-in capital and long-term debt.	____	____
4. The common stockholders have a greater chance of receiving regular dividends than do preferred stockholders.	____	____
5. The board of directors has the sole authority to distribute earnings to the stockholders in the form of dividends.	____	____
6. The specified minimum stockholders' contribution that a corporation is required by law to retain for protection of its creditors is called legal capital.	____	____
7. Preferred stock for which dividend rights are limited to a certain amount is said to be noncumulative.	____	____
8. When par stock is issued for more than par, the excess of the contract price over par is termed a premium.	____	____
9. Sales of treasury stock result in a net decrease in paid-in capital.	____	____

True   False

10. Expenditures incurred in organizing a corporation, such as legal fees, taxes, fees paid to the state, and promotional costs, are charged to an intangible asset account entitled Goodwill.. _____   _____

11. A commonly used method for accounting for the purchase and resale of treasury stock is the derivative method.......... _____   _____

12. A major objective of a stock split is to increase stock-holders' equity. .... _____   _____

13. Paid-in capital and retained earnings are two major sub-divisions of stockholders' equity... _____   _____

14. A liability for a dividend is normally recorded in the accounting records on the date of record........................... _____   _____

15. An accounting entry is required to record a stock dividend.   _____   _____

EXERCISE 12-1

Prepare the entries in general journal form to record each of the following unrelated transactions. (Omit explanations.)

(1) Cannuck Corp. issued 20,000 shares of no-par common stock for cash at $35 per share.

JOURNAL   PAGE

	DATE	DESCRIPTION	POST. REF.	DEBIT	CREDIT	
1						1
2						2
3						3
4						4
5						5

(2) Dunlo Corp. issued 20,000 shares of $25 par common stock for cash at $25 per share.

JOURNAL   PAGE

	DATE	DESCRIPTION	POST. REF.	DEBIT	CREDIT	
1						1
2						2
3						3
4						4
5						5

(3) Erickson Corp. issued 20,000 shares of $50 par common stock for cash at $60 per share.

JOURNAL

PAGE

	DATE		DESCRIPTION	POST. REF.	DEBIT	CREDIT	
1							1
2							2
3							3
4							4
5							5
6							6
7							7

(4) Felix Corp. issued 10,000 shares of $10 par common stock in exchange for new manufacturing equipment with a fair market value of $145,000.

JOURNAL

PAGE

	DATE		DESCRIPTION	POST. REF.	DEBIT	CREDIT	
1							1
2							2
3							3
4							4
5							5
6							6
7							7

(5) Huddley Corp. issued 10,000 shares of $25 par preferred stock for cash at $30 per share.

JOURNAL

PAGE

	DATE		DESCRIPTION	POST. REF.	DEBIT	CREDIT	
1							1
2							2
3							3
4							4
5							5
6							6
7							7

EXERCISE 12-2

Prepare the entries in general journal form to record each of the following treasury stock transactions of Pinell Corp. using the cost basis method. (Omit explanations.)

(1) On October 1, Pinell purchased 2,000 shares of treasury stock at $75.

(2) On October 31, Pinell sold 800 shares of the treasury stock it purchased on October 1 at $82.

(3) On November 20, Pinell sold 100 shares of the treasury stock it purchased on October 1 at $70.

JOURNAL   PAGE

	DATE	DESCRIPTION	POST. REF.	DEBIT	CREDIT	
1						1
2						2
3						3
4						4
5						5
6						6
7						7
8						8
9						9
10						10
11						11
12						12
13						13
14						14
15						15
16						16
17						17
18						18
19						19
20						20
21						21
22						22
23						23
24						24
25						25
26						26
27						27
28						28

EXERCISE 12-3

Journalize the following transactions of Copper Corp. (Omit explanations.)

(1) On February 20, Copper declared a $60,000 cash dividend.

(2) On March 22, Copper paid the cash dividend declared on February 20.

(3) On December 15, Copper declared a 5% stock dividend on 160,000 shares of $20 par value common stock with a market value of $25 per share.

(4) On January 14, Copper issued the stock certificates for the stock dividend declared on December 15.

(5) On February 20, Copper declared a 2 for 1 stock split, exchanging 380,000 shares of $10 par common stock for 190,000 shares of $20 par common stock.

JOURNAL

PAGE

	DATE	DESCRIPTION	POST. REF.	DEBIT	CREDIT	
1						1
2						2
3						3
4						4
5						5
6						6
7						7
8						8
9						9
10						10
11						11
12						12
13						13
14						14
15						15
16						16
17						17
18						18
19						19
20						20
21						21
22						22
23						23
24						24
25						25
26						26

PROBLEM 12-1

Pattering Corp. has 4,000 shares of $10 par common stock outstanding and 1,000 shares of $100 par 8% preferred stock outstanding. Pattering expects to pay annual dividends of $7,000, $9,000, $28,000, and $48,000 respectively for the next four years.

Instructions: By completing the following forms, indicate how the dividends should be distributed in each case if the preferred stock is given the rights or the restrictions indicated.

(1) The preferred stock is cumulative and nonparticipating.

Year	Total Dividends	Preferred Dividends		Common Dividends	
		Total	Per Share	Total	Per Share
1	$ 7,000				
2	9,000				
3	28,000				
4	48,000				

(2) The preferred stock is noncumulative and nonparticipating.

Year	Total Dividends	Preferred Dividends		Common Dividends	
		Total	Per Share	Total	Per Share
1	$ 7,000				
2	9,000				
3	28,000				
4	48,000				

PROBLEM 12-2

The stockholders' equity of Southland Corp. consists of 100,000 shares of $25 par stock, additional paid-in capital of $1,500,000, and retained earnings of $6,440,000. Theodore Rafael owns 1,000 of the outstanding shares.

Instructions:

(1) In Column A below, fill in the blanks with the appropriate figures based on the data given.

(2) In Column B, fill in the blanks with the appropriate figures based on the data given, but after a $1.50 per share cash dividend has been declared and paid.

(3) In Column C, fill in the blanks with the appropriate figures based on the data given, but after a 5% stock dividend has been declared and distributed. The market value of Southland Corp.'s stock is $30. (Ignore the instructions in (2) when making these calculations.)

	A	B	C
	Before Any Dividend	After Cash Dividend	After Stock Dividend
a. Total number of shares outstanding......................................			
b. Total par value of shares outstanding......................................			
c. Total additional paid-in capital			
d. Total retained earnings			
e. Total stockholders' equity.................			
f. Amount required to pay a $1.50 per share cash dividend next year. (Assume no further changes in the capital structure.)...................			
g. Percentage of total stock owned by Rafael			
h. Total number of shares owned by Rafael..			
i. Total par value of Rafael's shares ...			
j. Total equity of Rafael's shares.........			

13

Corporations: Income and Taxes, Stockholders' Equity, and Investments in Stocks

QUIZ AND TEST HINTS

The following hints may be helpful to you in preparing for a quiz or a test over the material covered in Chapter 13.

1. Many new terms are introduced in this chapter. Oftentimes terms are tested using true/false or multiple-choice questions. Do the Matching Exercise on pages 531–532.

2. The discussion of the reporting of unusual items in the financial statements is an important part of this chapter. You should be able to describe each of the types of unusual items and how they are reported in the financial statements. Be especially careful in studying how discontinued operations, extraordinary items, and changes in accounting principles are reported on the income statement, including the reporting of earnings per common share. The Illustrative Problem in the text is a good review of the reporting of unusual items. You might also look for several multiple-choice questions related to this topic.

3. You should be able to prepare a simple stockholders' equity section of a balance sheet and a simple retained earnings statement.

4. Various types of journal entries are illustrated throughout this chapter. You should be able to prepare journal entries for the income taxes and investments in stocks.

FILL IN THE BLANK—Part A

Instructions: Answer the following questions or complete the statements by writing the appropriate words or amounts in the answer blanks.

1. The _____ income is used as a base for determining the amount of taxes owed.

2. Income before income tax reported on the income statement for the first year of operations is $300,000. Because of timing differences in accounting and tax methods, the taxable income for the same year is $250,000. If the income tax rate is 50%, the amount of income tax expense reported on the income statement should be _____.

3. When a company disposes of operations of a major line of business for a company (such as a division, a department, or a certain class of customer), the gain or loss is reported on the income statement as a gain or loss from _____ operations.

4. Events and transactions that (1) are significantly different (unusual) from the typical or the normal operating activities of a business and (2) occur infrequently are reported in the income statement as _____ _____.

5. A company which recently decided to stop producing and selling its products in foreign markets would report the resulting loss on its income statement as a(n) _____ _____ _____ _____.

6. Net income per share of common stock outstanding during a period is called _____ _____ _____.

7. Errors in a prior period's net income that arise from mathematical mistakes or from mistakes in applying accounting principles are called _____-_____ _____.

8. All changes in stockholders' equity during a period except those resulting from investments by stockholders and dividends should be reported as part of _____ income.

9. Securities that management intends to actively trade for profit are referred to as _____ securities.

10. The balance sheet caption _____ _____ is used to report investments in income-yielding securities that can be quickly sold and converted to cash as needed.

11. The _____ method is used in accounting for an investment in common stock, by which the investment account is adjusted for the investor's share of periodic net income and property dividends of the investee.

12. A _____ is the creation of a new corporation by the transfer of assets and liabilities of two or more existing corporations that are then dissolved.

13. The corporation that is controlled by a parent company is referred to as the _____ company.

14. The _____-_____-_____ method is used in accounting for a business combination in which one corporation exchanges its voting common stock for a controlling share of the voting common stock of another corporation.

15. The portion of a subsidiary corporation's stock owned by outsiders is called

_____ _____.

FILL IN THE BLANK—Part B

Instructions: Answer the following questions or complete the statements by writing the appropriate words or amounts in the answer blanks.

1. Differences between taxable income and income before income tax that reverse or turn around in later years are called _____ differences.

2. Income before income tax reported on the income statement for the first year of operations is $300,000. Because of timing differences in accounting and tax methods, the taxable income for the same year is $250,000. If the income tax rate is 50%, the amount of deferred income tax payable is

_____.

3. A company that has never experienced a loss from a hurricane would report an uninsured hurricane loss on its income statement as a(n)

_____ _____.

4. The amount of retained earnings that is restricted and therefore is unavailable for use as dividends is called a(n) _____.

5. A statement of _____ _____ summarizes significant changes in stockholders' equity that have occurred during a period.

6. Preferred or common stock are referred to as _____ securities.

7. Securities that management expects to sell in the future, but which are not actively traded for profit, are referred to as _____-_____-_____ securities.

8. The difference between the fair market values of the securities and their cost is a(n) _____ gain or loss.

9. The _____ method is used in accounting for an investment in common stock, by which the investor recognizes as income its share of cash dividends of the investee.

10. A _____ is the joining of two corporations in which the acquiring company acquires all the assets and liabilities of another corporation that is then dissolved.

11. The balance sheet caption _____ is used to report long-term investments in stocks not intended as a source of cash in the normal operations of the business.

12. The corporation owning all or a majority of the voting stock of another corporation is referred to as the _____ company.

13. The _____ method is used in accounting for a business combination in which a corporation acquires the controlling share of the voting common stock of another corporation by paying cash, exchanging other assets, issuing debt, or some combination of these methods.

14. The combining of parent and subsidiary financial statements for reporting purposes results in _____ financial statements.

15. The _____-_____ ratio is computed by dividing a corporation's stock market price per share at a specific date by the company's annual earnings per share.

MULTIPLE CHOICE

Instructions: Circle the best answer for each of the following questions.

1. During its first year of operations, a corporation elected to use the straight-line method of depreciation for financial reporting purposes and the sum-of-the-years-digits method for reporting taxable income. If the income tax is 40% and the amount of depreciation expense is $200,000 under the straight-line method and $300,000 under the sum-of-the-years-digits method, what is the amount of income tax deferred to future years?

    a. $40,000

    b. $80,000

    c. $100,000

    d. $120,000

2. All of the following are examples of items that create temporary differences except:

    a. A method of recognizing revenue when the sale is made is used for financial statements, and a method of recognizing revenue at the time the cash is collected is used for tax reporting.

    b. Warranty expense is recognized in the year of sale for financial statements and when paid for tax reporting.

    c. An accelerated depreciation method is used for tax reporting, and the straight-line method is used for financial statements.

    d. Interest income on municipal bonds is recognized for financial statements and not for tax reporting.

3. Which of the following would appear as an extraordinary item on the income statement?

    a. correction of an error in the prior year's financial statements

    b. gain resulting from the sale of fixed assets

    c. loss on sale of temporary investments

    d. loss on condemnation of land

4. Earnings per share is required to be presented on the face of the income statement for:

    a. extraordinary items

    b. discontinued operations

    c. income from continuing operations and net income

    d. all of the above

5. All changes in stockholders' equity during a period except those resulting from investments by stockholders and dividends is the definition of:

    a. income from continuing operations

    b. comprehensive income

    c. net income

    d. retained earnings

6. The receipt of cash dividends on a long-term investment in common stock is accounted for as a debit to Cash and a credit to Dividend Revenue. Which of the following methods is being used to account for the investment?

    a. equity method

    b. market method

    c. cost method

    d. revenue method

7. The receipt of cash dividends on a long-term investment in common stock is accounted for as a debit to Cash and a credit to Investment in Spacek Inc. Which of the following methods is being used to account for the investment?

    a. equity method

    b. market method

    c. cost method

    d. revenue method

8. During the year in which Parent Company owned 75% of the outstanding common stock of Subsidiary Company, Subsidiary reported net income of $200,000 and dividends declared and paid of $50,000. What is the amount of net increase in the Investment in Subsidiary account for the year?

    a. $37,500

    b. $112,500

    c. $200,000

    d. $250,000

9. An investor purchased 800 shares of common stock, $50 par, for $96,000. Subsequently, 200 shares were sold for $115 per share. What is the amount of gain or loss on the sale?

   a. $1,000 loss

   b. $1,000 gain

   c. $4,000 loss

   d. $4,000 gain

10. In what section of the parent company's balance sheet would the balance of the account Investment in Subsidiary appear?

   a. current assets

   b. temporary investments

   c. investments

   d. stockholders' equity

TRUE/FALSE

Instructions: Indicate whether each of the following statements is true or false by placing a check mark in the appropriate column.

	True	False
1. Income that is exempt from federal taxes, such as interest income on municipal bonds, is an example of a temporary tax difference.	___	___
2. The amount reported as a gain or loss from discontinued operations on the income statement should be reported net of related income tax.	___	___
3. Income tax should be allocated to the fiscal year in which the related income is reported and earned.	___	___
4. To be classified as an extraordinary item, an item must be unusual in nature and infrequent in occurrence.	___	___
5. Over the life of a business, temporary differences reduce the total amount of tax paid.	___	___
6. An appropriation is a restriction of retained earnings that becomes part of paid-in capital of the corporation.	___	___
7. All changes in stockholders' equity during a period except those resulting from investments by stockholders and dividends should be reported as part of comprehensive income.	___	___
8. A change from an unacceptable accounting principle to an acceptable accounting principle is reported as a prior-period adjustment.	___	___

True   False

9. Under the cost method of accounting for investments in stocks, the investor records its share of cash dividends as a decrease in the investment account and an increase in the cash account. ....   _____   _____

10. A corporation that is controlled by another corporation is known as a subsidiary. ....   _____   _____

11. The two methods of accounting for investments in stock are the cost method and the equity method........................   _____   _____

12. When two or more corporations transfer their assets and liabilities to a corporation that has been created for the purpose of the takeover, the combination is called a merger..   _____   _____

13. When two or more corporations become affiliated by means of exchange of the voting stock of one corporation (the parent) for substantially all of the voting common stock of another corporation (the subsidiary), the transaction is termed a purchase. ....   _____   _____

14. Subsequent to acquisition of a subsidiary, a parent company's investment account should be increased periodically for its share of the subsidiary's income........................   _____   _____

15. A note representing a loan by a parent corporation to its subsidiary would appear as a note receivable in the parent's balance sheet and a note payable in the subsidiary's balance sheet...   _____   _____

EXERCISE 13-1

(1) Jabbs Corp. reported $550,000 income before tax on its income statement for the year. Because of temporary differences in accounting and tax methods, taxable income for the year is $320,000. Assuming an income tax rate of 40%, prepare the journal entry to record the income tax expense, liability, and deferred liability of Jabbs Corp.

JOURNAL   PAGE

	DATE		DESCRIPTION	POST. REF.	DEBIT	CREDIT	
1							1
2							2
3							3
4							4
5							5
6							6
7							7
8							8
9							9
10							10

(2) In the following year, Jabbs Corp. reported $500,000 income before income tax. Because of temporary differences in accounting and tax methods, taxable income for this year is $600,000. Assuming an income tax rate of 40%, prepare the journal entry to record the income tax expense, liability, and reduction of the deferred liability of Jabbs Corp.

JOURNAL   PAGE

	DATE		DESCRIPTION	POST. REF.	DEBIT	CREDIT	
1							1
2							2
3							3
4							4
5							5
6							6
7							7
8							8
9							9
10							10

EXERCISE 13-2

Mills Corp. estimates its income tax expense for the year to be $250,000. At the end of the year, Mills Corp. determines that its actual income tax for the year is $280,000.

(1) Prepare the entry to record one of the four estimated income tax payments.

JOURNAL

PAGE _____

	DATE	DESCRIPTION	POST. REF.	DEBIT	CREDIT	
1						1
2						2
3						3
4						4
5						5
6						6
7						7
8						8
9						9
10						10
11						11
12						12

(2) Prepare the entry to record the additional income tax liability for the year.

JOURNAL

PAGE _____

	DATE	DESCRIPTION	POST. REF.	DEBIT	CREDIT	
1						1
2						2
3						3
4						4
5						5
6						6
7						7
8						8
9						9
10						10
11						11
12						12

PROBLEM 13-1

The following accounts and their balances appear in the ledger of Charleston Corporation on December 31, the end of the current fiscal year.

Common Stock, $25 par	$2,500,000
Paid-In Capital in Excess of Par—Common Stock.......................	500,000
Paid-In Capital in Excess of Par—Preferred Stock	375,000
Paid-In Capital in Excess of Par—Treasury Stock.......................	4,000
Preferred $10 Stock, $100 par..	750,000
Retained Earnings..	1,000,000
Treasury Stock—Common	50,000

Instructions: Prepare the stockholders' equity section of the balance sheet as of December 31, the end of the current year. Ten thousand shares of preferred and 150,000 shares of common stock are authorized. One thousand shares of common stock are held as treasury stock.

PROBLEM 13-2

(1) Record the following transactions for Richards Inc.

(a) As a long-term investment, Richards Inc. acquires 40,000 shares of Norris Inc. common stock at a cost of $600,000. Richards Inc. uses the equity method of accounting for this investment because it represents 25% of the voting stock of Norris Inc.

(b) On May 18, a cash dividend of $.75 per share is paid by Norris Inc.

(c) Norris Inc. reports net income of $900,000 for the year.

JOURNAL

PAGE

	DATE	DESCRIPTION	POST. REF.	DEBIT	CREDIT	
1						1
2						2
3						3
4						4
5						5
6						6
7						7
8						8
9						9

(2) Record the following transactions for Smith Inc.

(a) As a long-term investment, Smith Inc. acquires 10,000 shares of Kline Inc. common stock at a cost of $150,000. Smith uses the cost method of accounting for this investment, because it represents 5% of the voting stock of Kline Inc.

(b) On September 3, a cash dividend of $.50 per share is paid by Kline Inc.

(c) Kline Inc. reports a net income of $350,000 for the year.

JOURNAL

PAGE

	DATE	DESCRIPTION	POST. REF.	DEBIT	CREDIT	
1						1
2						2
3						3
4						4
5						5
6						6
7						7
8						8

PROBLEM 13-3

Summary data for Wess Corp. for the current fiscal year ended March 31 are as follows:

Cost of merchandise sold..	$1,800,000
Cumulative effect on prior years of changing to a different depreciation method..	80,000
Loss on disposal of a segment of the business	70,000
Income taxes:	
Applicable to a change in depreciation method	18,000
Reduction applicable to loss on disposal of segment	20,000
Applicable to ordinary income	176,000
Reduction applicable to loss from earthquake	48,000
Loss from earthquake	240,000
Operating expenses	100,000
Sales	2,500,000

Instructions: Prepare an income statement for Wess Corp., including a section for earnings per share in the form illustrated in this chapter. There were 50,000 shares of common stock outstanding throughout the year, and the effect of the change in depreciation method was to increase income.

14

Bonds Payable and Investment in Bonds

QUIZ AND TEST HINTS

The following hints may be helpful to you in preparing for a quiz or a test over the material covered in Chapter 14.

1. Study the new terminology introduced in this chapter for possible use in fill-in-the-blank, multiple-choice, or true/false questions. As a review of the key terms, do the Matching Exercise on pages 572–573.

2. It is unlikely that you will see a problem related to the Financing Corporations section of the chapter. Instead, you should focus primarily on being able to prepare the various journal entries illustrated throughout the chapter. The Illustrative Problem is a good study aid for reviewing the various journal entries.

3. If your instructor discussed the computation of present value of bonds payable, you should expect one or more questions on this topic.

4. Be ready to prepare entries for the issuance of bonds at face value, at a discount, and at a premium; for discount and premium amortization; and for bond redemption.

5. Be able to prepare journal entries for bond investments. You will more likely see a question requiring journal entries for the issuance of bonds payable, but occasionally instructors will include short problems on bond investments. You can assess the likelihood of such a problem by the amount of time your instructor spent lecturing on bond investments and whether you were assigned a homework problem on bond investments.

FILL IN THE BLANK—Part A

Instructions: Answer the following questions or complete the statements by writing the appropriate words or amounts in the answer blanks.

1. A corporation issuing bonds enters into a contract with the bondholders. This contract is known as a(n) _____ _____.

2. A corporation reserves the right to redeem _____ bonds before they mature.

3. Bonds issued on the general credit of the issuing corporation are called _____ _____.

4. The _____ rate determines the periodic interest paid on a bond.

5. When the market rate of interest on bonds is lower than the contract rate, the bonds will sell at a(n) _____.

6. Assuming an interest rate of 10%, $110 to be received a year from today is called the _____ _____ of $100 today.

7. The present value of $1,000 to be paid one year later, using an interest rate of 10% is _____.

8. If the market rate of interest is 11%, the present value of $10,000 to be received in each of the next 2 years is _____ (round to the nearest dollar).

9–10. The two methods for amortizing a bond discount are the _____-_____ method and the _____ _____ _____ method.

11. The amount set aside for the payment of bonds at maturity is called a(n) _____ _____.

12. The balance of the bonds payable account (face amount of the bonds) less any unamortized discount or plus any unamortized premium is called the _____ _____.

13. If the balances of Bonds Payable and Discount on Bonds Payable are $400,000 and $12,000, respectively, the carrying amount of the bonds is _____.

14. If $2,000,000 of bonds are sold at 101½, the amount of cash received is _____.

15. Bonds with a face amount of $100,000 were purchased through a broker at 103 plus accrued interest of $2,000 and brokerage commissions of $650. The amount to be debited to the investment account is _____.

16–17. A corporation purchased bonds at a premium several years ago. When this year ends, the company makes an entry to record the amortization of the premium.

16. The account to be debited is _____ _____.

17. The account to be credited is _____ ___ _____.

18. Jones Company has redeemed bonds at 102. The bonds have a face value of $600,000 and an unamortized premium of $10,000. Jones Company will record a gain (or loss) on redemption of _____ (indicate amount and gain or loss).

19. Smith Company intends to hold 10-year bonds until they mature. This asset is called a _____-____-_____ _____.

20. River Company had interest expenses of $2,500,000 and income before tax of $29,000,000. The number of times interest charges are earned is _____.

FILL IN THE BLANK—Part B

Instructions: Answer the following questions or complete the statements by writing the appropriate words or amounts in the answer blanks.

1. All of Sand Company's bonds mature at the same time. These are known as _____ bonds.

2. Bonds that may be exchanged for other securities are called _____ bonds.

3. When the contract rate of interest on bonds is lower than the market rate of interest, the bonds sell at a(n) _____.

4. The present value of the face amount of a $1,000, 5-year bond, using an interest rate of 7% is _____.

5. Oliver Company issues 10-year bonds with a face value of $100,000 and annual interest of 12%. The present value of the bonds' interest payments is _____ (round to the nearest dollar).

6. A series of equal cash payments at fixed intervals is called a(n) _____.

7. A firm redeemed bonds at 95. The bonds have a face value of $500,000 and an unamortized discount of $15,000. The firm will record a gain (or loss) on redemption of _____ (indicate amount and gain or loss).

8–11. Under which caption (current assets, investments, fixed assets, current liabilities, long-term liabilities, stockholders' equity) would each of the following appear on the balance sheet?

8. Investment in X Co. Bonds (management intends to hold to maturity in 5 years) would appear in the _____ section of the balance sheet.

9. Premium on Bonds Payable would appear in the _____ _____ section of the balance sheet.

10. Bonds Payable due in ten years would appear in the _____ _____ section of the balance sheet.

11. Bond sinking fund investments would appear in the _____ section of the balance sheet.

12. Bonds with a face value of $75,000 were purchased through a broker at 98 plus accrued interest of $1,000 and brokerage commissions of $350. The amount to be debited to the investment account is _____.

13. If Bonds Payable has a balance of $5,000,000 and Premium on Bonds Payable has a balance of $45,000, the carrying amount of the bonds is _____.

14–16. On April 1, Avery Company issued $4,000,000, 5-year, 12% bonds for $4,280,000. If the bonds pay interest semiannually and if the effective rate of interest is 10%, determine the following:

14. The interest paid on September 30 is _____.

15. The amount of premium amortized on September 30, using the straight-line method is _____.

16. The accrued interest payable on December 31 is _____.

17. In No. 14, the total amount of annual interest expense _____ (increases, decreases, or remains the same) over the life of the bonds as the premium on bonds payable is amortized.

18. A ratio that indicates the likelihood a company will be able to continue paying interest to its debtholders if the company's earnings decrease is called the _____ _____ _____ _____ _____ _____.

19. Canary Company had interest expenses of $8,250,000 and income before tax of $60,500,000. The number of times interest charges are earned is _____.

20. The estimated worth today of an amount of cash to be received (or paid) in the future is called the _____ _____.

MULTIPLE CHOICE

Instructions: Circle the best answer for each of the following questions.

1. A bond that gives the bondholder a right to exchange the bond for other securities under certain conditions is called a:

   a. convertible bond

   b. sinking fund bond

   c. term bond

   d. debenture bond

2. What is the present value of $2,000 to be paid in one year if the current interest rate is 6%?

   a. $1,880

   b. $1,887

   c. $2,000

   d. $2,120

3. The entry to record the amortization of a discount on bonds payable is:

   a. debit Bonds Payable; credit Interest Expense

   b. debit Interest Expense; credit Discount on Bonds Payable

   c. debit Discount on Bonds Payable; credit Interest Expense

   d. debit Discount on Bonds Payable; credit Bonds Payable

4. Under the straight-line method of bond discount amortization, as a bond payable approaches maturity, the total yearly amount of interest expense will:

   a. increase

   b. decrease

   c. remain the same

   d. increase or decrease, depending on the size of the original discount

5. On May 1, a $1,000 bond was purchased as a long-term investment at 104, and $8 was paid as the brokerage commission. If the bond bears interest at 6%, which is paid semiannually on January 1 and July 1, what is the total cost to be debited to the investment account?

   a. $1,000

   b. $1,040

   c. $1,048

   d. $1,068

6. What method of amortizing bond discount or premium is required by generally accepted accounting principles?

   a. declining balance method

   b. future value method

   c. principal method

   d. interest method

7. Bonds that do not provide for any interest payments are called:

   a. interest-free bonds

   b. held-to-maturity securities

   c. sinking-fund bonds

   d. zero-coupon bonds

8. The principal of each bond is also called the:

   a. present value

   b. future value

   c. face value

   d. contract value

9. A special fund accumulated over the life of a bond issue and kept separate from other assets in order to provide for payment of bonds at maturity is called a(n):

   a. sinking fund

   b. investment fund

   c. retirement fund

   d. redemption fund

10. Held-to-maturity securities are classified on the balance sheet as:

   a. current assets

   b. investments

   c. long-term liabilities

   d. sinking-fund assets

TRUE/FALSE

Instructions: Indicate whether each of the following statements is true or false by placing a check mark in the appropriate column.

		True	False
1.	The interest rate specified on the bond indenture is called the contract rate or effective rate.	____	____
2.	If the market rate is lower than the contract rate, the bonds will sell at a discount.	____	____
3.	When zero-coupon bonds are issued, the discount is amortized as interest expense over the life of the bonds.	____	____
4.	The straight-line method of allocating bond discount provides for a constant amount of interest expense each period.	____	____
5.	Bonds that may be exchanged for other securities under certain conditions are called callable bonds.	____	____
6.	When cash is transferred to the sinking fund, it is recorded in an account called Sinking Fund Investments.	____	____
7.	A corporation's earnings per share can be affected by whether it finances its operations with common stock, preferred stock, or bonds.	____	____
8.	If the price paid to redeem bonds is below the bond carrying value, the difference is recorded as a gain.	____	____
9.	The balance in a discount on bonds payable account is reported in the balance sheet as a deduction from the related bonds payable.	____	____
10.	The present value of a future amount becomes less as the interest rate used to compute the present value increases.	____	____

EXERCISE 14-1

(1) Star Corp. issued $500,000 of 10-year, 12% bonds on June 1 of the current year with interest payable on June 1 and December 1. Journalize the entries to record the following selected transactions for the current year:

June 1. Issued the bonds for cash at face amount.

Dec. 1. Paid the interest on the bonds.

JOURNAL   PAGE

	DATE	DESCRIPTION	POST. REF.	DEBIT	CREDIT	
1						1
2						2
3						3
4						4
5						5
6						6
7						7
8						8

(2) On April 1, Turner Inc. issued $1,000,000 of 10-year, 11% bonds, with interest payable semiannually on April 1 and October 1 at an effective interest rate of 12%, receiving cash of $942,645. Journalize the entries to record the following selected transactions for the current year:

Apr. 1. Sold the bonds.

Oct. 1. Made first interest payment and amortized discount for six months using the straight-line method.

JOURNAL   PAGE

	DATE	DESCRIPTION	POST. REF.	DEBIT	CREDIT	
1						1
2						2
3						3
4						4
5						5
6						6
7						7
8						8
9						9
10						10
11						11

(3) On March 1, Sullivan Inc. issued $700,000 of 10-year, 11% bonds at an effective interest rate of 10%. Interest is payable semiannually on March 1 and September 1. Journalize the entries to record the following selected transactions for the current year. (Hint: To complete this portion of the exercise, you must compute the present value of the bonds at the issue date.)

Mar. 1. Sold the bonds.

Sept. 1. Made first interest payment and amortized premium for six months using the straight-line method.

JOURNAL PAGE

	DATE	DESCRIPTION	POST. REF.	DEBIT	CREDIT	
1						1
2						2
3						3
4						4
5						5
6						6
7						7
8						8
9						9
10						10
11						11
12						12

EXERCISE 14-2

Grimes Co. issued $5,000,000 of 10-year bonds at face value on January 1 of the current year.

Instructions:

(1) Assume the bonds are called at 101. Prepare the entry to record the redemption of the bonds.

JOURNAL PAGE

	DATE	DESCRIPTION	POST. REF.	DEBIT	CREDIT	
1						1
2						2
3						3
4						4
5						5

(2) Assume the bonds are purchased on the open market at 98. Prepare the entry to record the redemption of the bonds.

JOURNAL   PAGE

	DATE	DESCRIPTION	POST. REF.	DEBIT	CREDIT	
1						1
2						2
3						3
4						4
5						5

EXERCISE 14-3

Record the following transactions. (Omit explanations.)

(1) On October 1, 20XA, purchased for cash, as a long-term investment, $400,000 of Elgin Inc. 10% bonds at 99 plus accrued interest of $10,000.

(2) On December 31, 20XA received first semiannual interest.

(3) On December 31, 20XA amortized $120 discount on the bond investment.

(4) On December 1, 20XC, sold the bonds at 102 plus accrued interest of $16,667. The carrying amount of the bonds was $397,040 at the time of sale.

JOURNAL   PAGE

	DATE	DESCRIPTION	POST. REF.	DEBIT	CREDIT	
1						1
2						2
3						3
4						4
5						5
6						6
7						7
8						8
9						9
10						10
11						11
12						12
13						13
14						14
15						15
16						16

PROBLEM 14-1

Jackson Inc. issued $2,000,000 of 10-year, 11% bonds with interest payable semiannually.

Instructions:

(1) Compute (a) the cash proceeds and (b) the amount of premium or discount from the sale of the bonds if the effective interest rate is 11%.

(2) Compute (a) the cash proceeds and (b) the amount of premium or discount from the sale of the bonds if the effective interest rate is 12%.

(3) Compute (a) the cash proceeds and (b) the amount of premium or discount from the sale of the bonds if the effective interest rate is 10%.

PROBLEM 14-2

On December 31 of the current fiscal year, Palus Inc. issued $500,000 of 10-year, 11% bonds. The bonds were dated December 31 of the same year. Interest on the bonds is payable on June 30 and December 31 of each year.

Instructions:

Record the following transactions. (Omit explanations and round to the nearest dollar.)

(1) The bonds were sold for $531,161 on December 31 of the current year. The market rate of interest on this date was 10%.

(2) Interest was paid on June 30, and the related amount of bond premium was amortized, based on the straight-line method.

(3) Interest was paid on December 31, and the related amount of bond premium was amortized, based on the straight-line method.

(4) On December 31 (bonds are one year old), one-half of the bonds were redeemed at 103.

JOURNAL   PAGE

	DATE	DESCRIPTION	POST. REF.	DEBIT	CREDIT	
1						1
2						2
3						3
4						4
5						5
6						6
7						7
8						8
9						9
10						10
11						11
12						12
13						13
14						14
15						15
16						16
17						17
18						18
19						19
20						20
21						21
22						22

PROBLEM 14-3

On January 1 of the current fiscal year, Block Co. issued $1,000,000 of 10-year, 10% bonds. The bonds were dated January 1 of the same year. Interest on the bonds is payable on June 30 and December 31 of each year.

Instructions:

Record the following transactions. (Omit explanations and round to the nearest dollar.)

(1) The bonds were sold for $885,295 on January 1 of the current year. The market rate of interest on that date was 12%.

(2) Interest was paid on June 30, and the related amount of bond discount was amortized, based on the straight-line method.

(3) Interest was paid on December 31, and the related amount of bond discount was amortized, based on the straight-line method.

(4) On December 31 (bonds are one year old), one-half of the bonds were redeemed at 98.

JOURNAL

PAGE

	DATE	DESCRIPTION	POST. REF.	DEBIT	CREDIT	
1						1
2						2
3						3
4						4
5						5
6						6
7						7
8						8
9						9
10						10
11						11
12						12
13						13
14						14
15						15
16						16
17						17
18						18
19						19
20						20
21						21
22						22

15

Statement of Cash Flows

QUIZ AND TEST HINTS

The following hints may be helpful to you in preparing for a quiz or a test over the material covered in Chapter 15.

1. Study the new terminology introduced in this chapter for possible use in fill-in-the-blank, multiple-choice, or true/false questions. As a review of the key terms, do the Matching Exercise on pages 618–619.

2. You should be able to classify different types of cash flows as operating, investing, or financing activities. Test questions on this material often appear in a true/false or multiple-choice format.

3. Instructors may emphasize the indirect method, the direct method, or both methods of preparing the statement of cash flows. Adjust your studying to the method or methods that your instructor emphasized during class lectures and in homework assignments. You should be able to prepare a statement of cash flows using one or both methods. Often, instructors will include a partially completed statement of cash flows on an examination and require students to complete it. The Illustrative Problem is a good study aid for both the indirect and direct methods.

4. The work sheets for preparing the statement of cash flows appear in the Appendix to the chapter. Study the Appendix if your instructor has expressed a preference for use of the work sheet in preparing the statement of cash flows.

FILL IN THE BLANK—Part A

Instructions: Answer the following questions or complete the statements by writing the appropriate words or amounts in the answer blanks.

1. The financial statement that reports a firm's major cash inflows and outflows for a period is the _____ _____ _____ _____.

2. The two alternative methods of reporting operating activities in the statement of cash flows are the _____ and _____ methods.

3–7. Indicate the section of the statement of cash flows in which each of the following would appear (answer operating activities, investing activities, or financing activities):

3. Depreciation expense on equipment would appear under _____ activities.

4. Sale of long-term investments would appear under _____ activities.

5. Sale of equipment would appear under _____ activities.

6. Issuance of bonds would appear under _____ activities.

7. Sale of patents would appear under _____ activities.

8–10. This year, Young Company issued 500,000 shares of common stock, inventory increased by $20,000, and a new asset was purchased for $1,000,000. For each of these events, indicate whether net cash flows increased or decreased:

8. Common stock issued. Net cash flows _____.

9. Inventory increased. Net cash flows _____.

10. New asset purchased. Net cash flows _____.

11. Cash dividends of $35,000 were declared during the year. Cash dividends payable were $8,000 and $8,750 at the beginning and end of the year, respectively. The amount of cash flows for payment of dividends during the year is _____.

12. The net income from operations was $75,000, and the only revenue or expense item not affecting cash was depreciation expense of $27,000. The amount of net cash flows from operating activities that would appear on the statement of cash flows is _____.

13. A corporation purchased and retired 3,000 shares of its $50 par common stock, originally issued at par, for $65. Cash flows amounted to _____.

14. If a fixed asset having a book value of $54,000 is sold (for cash) at a gain of $6,000, the total amount reported as a cash flow is _____.

15. The $47,000 net income for the year included a loss of $2,500 on the sale of land. Exclusive of the effect of other adjustments, the amount of net cash flows from operating activities is _____.

16. A corporation issued $1,000,000 of bonds payable at 104. Cash flow from this transaction was _____.

17. If 15,000 shares of $20 par common stock were issued at 22, the amount to be reported in the cash flows from financing activities section of the statement of cash flows would be _____.

18. Cash flows resulting from the redemption of debt securities are classified in the statement of cash flows as related to _____ activities.

19. Jones Company had cash flow from operations of $75,000. This year, dividends paid amounted to $6,000, and the company purchased $9,000 in spare parts for machines used on the factory floor. Jones Company's free cash flow is _____.

20. A cash flow term for which an amount should not be reported in the financial statements because it could mislead readers is _____ _____ _____ _____.

FILL IN THE BLANK—Part B

Instructions: Answer the following questions or complete the statements by writing the appropriate words or amounts in the answer blanks.

1. The _____ method of analyzing operating cash flows begins with net income and adjusts it for revenues and expenses that do not involve the receipt or payment of cash.

2. The statement of cash flows groups cash flow activities as financing, investing, or _____.

3. When the _____ method of reporting cash flows is used, a supplemental schedule reconciling net income and net cash flow from operating activities must also be prepared.

4–8. Indicate the section of the statement of cash flows in which each of the following would appear (answer operating activities, investing activities, or financing activities):

4. Retirement of long-term debt would appear under _____ activities.

5. Sale of common stock would appear under _____ activities.

6. Net income would appear under _____ activities.

7. Payment of cash dividends would appear under _____ activities.

8. Purchase of equipment would appear under _____ activities.

9. _____ investing and financing activities that will affect future cash flows are reported in a separate schedule to the statement of cash flows.

10–11. Indicate whether each of the following items would be added to or deducted from net income on the schedule reconciling net income with cash flows from operating activities:

10. Increase in inventories would be _____ _____ net income.

11. Increase in accounts payable would be _____ _____ net income.

12. If a loss of $15,000 is incurred in selling (for cash) store equipment having a book value of $345,000, the total amount reported as a cash flow is _____.

13. A corporation issued $750,000 of 20-year bonds at 99½. Cash flows were _____.

14. A corporation purchased 25,000 shares of its $100 par common stock, originally issued at par, as treasury stock for $125. Cash flows were _____.

15. Cash dividends of $50,000 were declared during the year. Cash dividends payable were $8,500 and $12,500 at the beginning and end of the year, respectively. The amount of cash flows for the payment of dividends during the year is _____.

16. The net loss from operations was $15,000, and the only revenue or expense item not affecting cash was depreciation expense of $35,000. The amount to be reported as net cash flow from operating activities on the statement of cash flows is _____.

17. In preparing a statement of cash flows under the indirect method, it is efficient to analyze the _____ _____ account first.

18. The $55,000 net income for the year included a gain of $4,000 on the sale of equipment. Exclusive of the effect of other adjustments, the amount of net cash flows from operating activities is _____.

19. Cash flow for interest expense is included on the statement of cash flows as an _____ activity.

20. A measure of cash available for corporate purposes, after productive assets are maintained and the business owners are paid dividends, is called _____ _____ _____.

MULTIPLE CHOICE

Instructions: Circle the best answer for each of the following questions.

1. Which of the following is not one of the major sections of the statement of cash flows?

   a. cash flows from financing activities

   b. cash flows from selling activities

   c. cash flows from operating activities

   d. cash flows from investing activities

2. Noncash investing and financing activities which may have a significant effect on future cash flows are reported:

   a. in the statement of cash flows

   b. in a separate schedule to accompany the statement of cash flows

   c. in the retained earnings statement

   d. in a footnote accompanying the balance sheet

3. Under the indirect method, which of the following items must be deducted from reported net income to determine net cash flow from operating activities?

   a. depreciation of fixed assets

   b. decreases in current assets

   c. decreases in current liabilities

   d. loss on sale of equipment

4. During the past year, Lockhart Inc. declared $40,000 in cash dividends. If the beginning and ending balance of the dividends payable account was $12,000 and $10,000, respectively, what amount of cash paid for dividends will appear in the cash flow from financing activities section of the statement of cash flows?

   a. $30,000

   b. $38,000

   c. $40,000

   d. $42,000

5. Under the direct method, which of the following items must be added to operating expenses reported on the income statement to determine cash payments for operating expenses?

   a. increase in accrued expenses

   b. decrease in prepaid expenses

   c. increase in income taxes payable

   d. increase in prepaid expenses

6. An example of a cash flow from a financing activity is:

   a. receipt of cash from sale of land

   b. receipt of cash from collection of accounts receivable

   c. payment of cash for acquisition of treasury stock

   d. payment of cash for new machinery

7. Which of the following items appears first on the statement of cash flows prepared using the direct method?

   a. retained earnings

   b. cash received from customers

   c. net income

   d. depreciation

8. Which of the following would not be considered a noncash investing and financing activity in preparing a statement of cash flows?

   a. withdrawal of cash by the owner of a business

   b. issuance of common stock to retire long-term debt

   c. acquisition of a manufacturing plant by issuing bonds

   d. issuance of common stock in exchange for convertible preferred stock

9. To convert the cost of merchandise sold as reported on the income statement to cash payments for merchandise, the cost of merchandise sold is increased for the:

   a. increase in inventories

   b. increase in accounts payable

   c. decrease in inventories

   d. decrease in accounts receivable

10. Cash payments for income taxes are included on the statement of cash flows as:

    a. financing activities

    b. investing activities

    c. operating activities

    d. nonoperating activities

11. A loss on the sale of land is reflected on the statement of cash flows by:

    a. adding the loss to the book value of the land to determine the cash flow from investing activities.

    b. deducting the loss from net income to determine the cash flow from operating activities.

    c. deducting the loss from the book value of the land to determine the cash flow from investing activities.

    d. both b and c

TRUE/FALSE

Instructions: Indicate whether each of the following statements is true or false by placing a check mark in the appropriate column.

		True	False
1.	The statement of cash flows is required as part of the basic set of financial statements.	_____	_____
2.	Cash outflows from the payment of cash dividends is a type of financing activity.	_____	_____
3.	Cash receipts from the sale of fixed assets would be classified as a cash flow from investing activities.......................	_____	_____
4.	Under the direct method, depreciation is the first noncash account balance analyzed...	_____	_____
5.	Under the indirect method, increases in current liabilities are deducted from net income reported on the income statement in determining cash flows from operating activities...	_____	_____
6.	Noncash investing and financing activities that may have a significant effect on future cash flows should be included in a separate schedule to the statement of cash flows.	_____	_____
7.	The correct amount to include in cash flows from financing activities is cash dividends paid, not cash dividends declared..	_____	_____
8.	The analysis of retained earnings provides the starting point for determining cash flows from operating activities under the indirect method only...	_____	_____
9.	The direct method provides a more accurate figure of cash flows from operating activities than does the indirect method...	_____	_____
10.	Under the direct method, the increase in the trade receivables account is deducted from sales to determine the cash received from customers.	_____	_____

EXERCISE 15-1

Instructions: Listed in the first column below are selected transactions and account balance changes of Mason Inc. for the current year. Indicate by placing a check mark in the appropriate column(s) how each of the items would be reported in the statement of cash flows.

Item	Operating Activities	Investing Activities	Financing Activities	Schedule of Noncash Investing and Financing Activities
	Cash Flows From			
1. Decrease in prepaid expenses...........				
2. Retirement of bonds........................				
3. Proceeds from sale of investments....				
4. Increase in inventories				
5. Issuance of common stock................				
6. Purchase of equipment				
7. Cash dividends paid...........................				
8. Acquisition of building in exchange for bonds				
9. Amortization of patents				
10. Amortization of discount on bonds payable..				

EXERCISE 15-2

The net income reported on the income statement of Hunter Inc. for the current year was $150,000. Depreciation recorded on equipment and building amounted to $45,000 for the year. Balances of the current asset and current liability accounts at the beginning and end of the year are as follows:

	End of Year	Beginning of Year
Cash	$ 42,875	$ 36,250
Trade receivables (net)	147,500	137,500
Inventories	109,375	93,750
Prepaid expenses	9,250	11,875
Accounts payable (merchandise creditors)	57,000	40,000
Salaries payable	7,625	10,625

Instructions: Prepare the cash flows from operating activities section of the statement of cash flows using the indirect method.

EXERCISE 15-3

The income statement of Hunter Inc. for the current year is as follows:

Sales		$530,000
Cost of merchandise sold		130,000
Gross profit		$400,000
Operating expenses:		
Depreciation expense	$ 45,000	
Other operating expenses	160,000	
Total operating expenses		205,000
Income before income tax		$195,000
Income tax		45,000
Net income		$150,000

Instructions: Using the income statement presented above and the account balances provided in Exercise 15-2, prepare the cash flows from operating activities section of the statement of cash flows using the direct method.

PROBLEM 15-1

The comparative balance sheet of Stellar Inc. at December 31, 2004, appears below.

Stellar Inc.
Comparative Balance Sheet
December 31, 2004 and 2003

	2004	2003	Increase Decrease*
Assets			
Cash	$ 84,000	$ 66,000	$ 18,000
Trade receivables (net)	156,000	144,000	12,000
Inventories	300,000	306,000	6,000*
Prepaid expenses	12,000	14,400	2,400*
Land	80,000	96,000	16,000*
Building	360,000	360,000	0
Accumulated depreciation—building	(120,000)	(91,200)	(28,800)
Equipment	180,000	102,000	78,000
Accumulated depreciation—equipment	(72,000)	(70,800)	(1,200)
Total assets	$980,000	$926,400	$ 53,600
Liabilities			
Accounts payable	$216,000	$208,800	$ 7,200
Dividends payable	24,000	21,600	2,400
Bonds payable	240,000	300,000	60,000*
Total liabilities	$480,000	$530,400	$ 50,400*
Stockholders' Equity			
Common stock	$140,000	$120,000	$ 20,000
Retained earnings	360,000	276,000	84,000
Total stockholders' equity	$500,000	$396,000	$104,000
Total liabilities and stockholders' equity	$980,000	$926,400	$ 53,600

The following additional data were taken from the records of Stellar Inc.:

a. Equipment costing $96,000 was purchased, and fully depreciated equipment costing $18,000 was discarded.

b. Net income, including gain on sale of land, was $114,000. Depreciation expense on equipment was $19,200; on building, $28,800.

c. Bonds payable of $60,000 were retired at face value.

d. A cash dividend of $30,000 was declared.

e. Land costing $36,000 was sold for $54,000, resulting in an $18,000 gain on the sale.

f. Land was acquired by issuing common stock, $20,000.

Instructions: Complete the following statement of cash flows using the indirect method of reporting cash flows from operating activities.

Stellar Inc.
Statement of Cash Flows
For Year Ended December 31, 2004

Cash flows from operating activities:

Net income, per income statement .... $_____

Add: Depreciation .... $_____

Decrease in inventories ....   _____

Decrease in prepaid expenses ....   _____

Increase in accounts payable ....   _____   _____

$_____

Deduct: Increase in trade receivables .... $_____

Gain on sale of land ....   _____   _____

Net cash flow from operating activities .... $_____

Cash flows from investing activities:

Cash received from land sold .... $_____

Less cash paid for purchase of equipment ....   _____

Net cash flow used for investing activities .....   _____

Cash flows from financing activities:

Cash used to retire bonds payable .... $_____

Cash paid for dividends ....   _____

Net cash flow used for financing activities .....   _____

Increase in cash .... $_____

Cash, January 1, 2004 ....   _____

Cash, December 31, 2004 .... $_____

Schedule of Noncash Investing and Financing Activities:

Acquisition of land by issuance of common stock .... $_____

PROBLEM 15-2

The income statement of Stellar Inc. is provided below. Stellar's comparative balance sheet data were provided in Problem 15-1.

Instructions: Complete the statement of cash flows for Stellar Inc. using the direct method of reporting cash flows from operating activities.

Stellar Inc.
Income Statement
For Year Ended December 31, 2004

Sales		$575,000
Cost of merchandise sold		225,000
Gross profit		$350,000
Operating expenses:		
Depreciation expense	$ 48,000	
Other operating expenses	172,000	
Total operating expenses		220,000
Income from operations		$130,000
Other income:		
Gain on sale of land		18,000
Income before income tax		$148,000
Income tax		34,000
Net income		$114,000

Stellar Inc.
Statement of Cash Flows
For Year Ended December 31, 2004

Cash flows from operating activities:

Cash received from customers .... $\underline{\hspace{2cm}}$

Deduct: Cash payments for merchandise ...... $\underline{\hspace{2cm}}$

Cash payments for operating
expenses .... $\underline{\hspace{2cm}}$

Cash payments for income tax .... $\underline{\hspace{2cm}}$ $\underline{\hspace{2cm}}$

Net cash flow from operating activities .... $\underline{\hspace{2cm}}$

Cash flows from investing activities:

Cash received from land sold .... $\underline{\hspace{2cm}}$

Less cash paid for purchase of equipment .... $\underline{\hspace{2cm}}$

Net cash flow used for investing activities ..... $\underline{\hspace{2cm}}$

Cash flows from financing activities:

Cash used to retire bonds payable .... $\underline{\hspace{2cm}}$

Cash paid for dividends .... $\underline{\hspace{2cm}}$

Net cash flow used for financing activities ..... $\underline{\hspace{2cm}}$

Increase in cash .... $\underline{\hspace{2cm}}$

Cash, January 1, 2004 .... $\underline{\hspace{2cm}}$

Cash, December 31, 2004 .... $\underline{\hspace{2cm}}$

Schedule of Noncash Investing and Financing Activities:

Acquisition of land by issuance of common stock .... $\underline{\hspace{2cm}}$

Schedule Reconciling Net Income with Cash Flows from Operating Activities:

Net income, per income statement .... $\underline{\hspace{2cm}}$

Add: Depreciation .... $\underline{\hspace{2cm}}$

Decrease in inventories .... $\underline{\hspace{2cm}}$

Decrease in prepaid expenses .... $\underline{\hspace{2cm}}$

Increase in accounts payable .... $\underline{\hspace{2cm}}$

$\underline{\hspace{2cm}}$

Deduct: Increase in trade receivables .... $\underline{\hspace{2cm}}$

Gain on sale of land .... $\underline{\hspace{2cm}}$

Net cash flow provided by operating activities .... $\underline{\hspace{2cm}}$

16

Financial Statement Analysis

QUIZ AND TEST HINTS

The following hints may be helpful to you in preparing for a quiz or a test over the material covered in Chapter 16.

1. When studying this chapter, you should focus primarily on the various analytical measures described and illustrated. These measures are also summarized on pages 658–659 of the chapter. Pay special attention to each measure's computation, its use, and its classification as either a solvency or profitability measure. A good study aid for the computation of the measures is the Illustrative Problem at the end of the chapter.

2. Instructors often use true/false and multiple-choice questions to test this chapter. Such questions may require the computation of ratios or test your understanding of various terms introduced in the chapter. As a review of the key terms, do the Matching Exercise on pages 665–666.

FILL IN THE BLANK—Part A

Instructions: Answer the following questions or complete the statements by writing the appropriate words or amounts in the answer blanks.

1. Percentage analysis used to show the relationship of the component parts to the total in a single statement is called _____ _____.

2. _____ _____ focuses primarily on the relationship between operating results as reported in the income statement and resources available to the business as reported in the balance sheet.

3. The use of ratios showing the ability of an enterprise to pay its current liabilities is known as _____ _____ _____.

4. _____ is the ability of a business to meet its financial obligations as they come due.

5. _____-_____ statements are prepared in order to compare percentages of the current period with past periods, to compare individual businesses, or to compare one business with industry percentages published by trade associations or financial information services.

6. The ratio of current assets to current liabilities is called the _____ ratio.

7. The ratio of _____ _____ _____ _____ is a profitability measure that shows how effectively a firm utilizes its assets.

8. The ratio of the sum of cash, receivables, and marketable securities to current liabilities is called the _____-_____ ratio.

9. _____ _____ _____ _____ _____ _____ is the ratio of net income available to common shareholders to the number of common shares outstanding.

10. The excess of the current assets of a business over its current liabilities is called _____ _____.

11. _____ _____ _____ is computed by dividing net sales on account by the average net accounts receivable.

12. _____ _____ is computed by dividing the cost of goods sold by the average inventory.

13. The ratio of _____ _____ _____ _____ is a solvency measure that indicates the margin of safety for creditors.

14. The number of times _____ _____ _____ _____ is a measure of the risk that dividends to preferred stockholders may not be paid.

15. If significant amounts of nonoperating income and expense are reported on the income statement, it may be desirable to compute the ratio of _____ _____ _____ to total assets as a profitability measure.

16. The rate earned on _____ _____ focuses only on the rate of profits earned on the amount invested by common stockholders.

17. Earnings per share and _____ per share on common stock are commonly used by investors in assessing alternative stock investments.

18. All publicly held corporations are required to have a(n) _____ _____ of their financial statements.

19. The ratio of _____ _____ _____ _____-_____ _____ is a solvency measure that indicates the margin of safety of the noteholders or bondholders.

20. In a vertical analysis of the income statement, each item is stated as a percent of _____ _____.

FILL IN THE BLANK—Part B

Instructions: Answer the following questions or complete the statements by writing the appropriate words or amounts in the answer blanks.

1. The percentage analysis of increases and decreases in corresponding items in comparative financial statements is called _____ _____.

2. The _____ _____ is a profitability measure that shows the rate of return to common stockholders in terms of cash dividend distributions.

3. The _____ _____ report describes the results of an independent examination of the financial statements.

4. The _____ _____ _____ _____ _____ _____ is computed by dividing the net accounts receivable at the end of the year by the average daily sales on account.

5. The _____ _____ _____ _____ _____ _____ is computed by dividing the inventory at the end of the year by the average daily cost of goods sold.

6. The number of times _____ _____ _____ is a measure of the risk that interest payments will not be made if earnings decrease.

7. The _____ _____ _____ _____ _____ measures the profitability of total assets, without considering how the assets are financed.

8. The _____ _____ _____ _____ _____ is computed by dividing net income by average total stockholders' equity.

9. The difference between the rate earned by a business on the equity of its stockholders and the rate earned on total assets is called _____.

10. The _____-_____ ratio is computed by dividing the market price per share of common stock at a specific date by the annual earnings per share.

11. The _____ _____ section of a corporate annual report normally includes a statement that the financial statements are management's responsibility and that they have been prepared according to generally accepted accounting principles.

12. _____ _____ are cash and other current assets that can be quickly converted to cash.

13. In a _____-_____ statement, all items are expressed as percentages.

14. _____ _____ focuses on the ability of a business to pay or otherwise satisfy its current and noncurrent liabilities.

15. The current ratio is sometimes called the working capital ratio or the _____ ratio.

16. Two measures that are useful for evaluating the management of inventory are the inventory turnover and the _____ _____ _____ _____ _____ _____.

17. A profitability measure often quoted in the financial press and normally reported in the income statement in corporate annual reports is _____ _____ _____.

18. All items in _____-_____ statements are expressed only in relative terms.

19. Quick assets normally include cash, marketable securities, and _____.

20. Management's assessment of the company's internal accounting control system normally is provided in the _____ _____ section of the corporate annual report.

MULTIPLE CHOICE

Instructions: Circle the best answer for each of the following questions.

1. Statements in which all items are expressed only in relative terms (percentages of a common base) are:
   a. relative statements
   b. horizontal statements
   c. vertical statements
   d. common-size statements

2. Which one of the following measures is a solvency measure?
   a. rate earned on total assets
   b. price-earnings ratio
   c. accounts receivable turnover
   d. ratio of net sales to assets

3. Based on the following data for the current year, what is the inventory turnover?

Net sales..	$6,500,000
Cost of goods sold..	$4,000,000
Inventory, beginning of year..........................	$250,000
Inventory, end of year....................................	$345,000
Accounts receivable, beginning of year	$175,000
Accounts receivable, end of year..................	$297,000

   a. 26.7
   b. 16
   c. 13.4
   d. 11.6

4. Based on the following data for the current year, what is the accounts receivable turnover?

Net sales on account.....................................	$6,500,000
Cost of goods sold..	$4,000,000
Inventory, beginning of year..........................	$250,000
Inventory, end of year....................................	$345,000
Accounts receivable, beginning of year	$175,000
Accounts receivable, end of year..................	$297,000

   a. 37.1
   b. 27.5
   c. 21.8
   d. 17

5. Which of the following sections of corporate annual reports normally includes a statement concerning future prospects and risks?

   a. financial highlights section

   b. president's letter

   c. independent auditors' report

   d. management discussion and analysis

6. A measure used in evaluating the efficiency in collecting receivables is:

   a. working capital ratio

   b. acid-test ratio

   c. receivables/inventory ratio

   d. number of days' sales in receivables

7. Based on the following data for the current year, compute the number of times interest charges are earned:

Income before income tax	$510,000
Interest expense	$30,000
Total assets	$4,080,000

   a. 8

   b. 17

   c. 18

   d. 136

8. Based on the following data for the current year, what is the quick ratio?

Cash...	$27,000
Marketable securities................	$23,000
Receivables	$90,000
Inventory	$105,000
Current liabilities	$70,000

   a. 2.0

   b. 3.5

   c. 0.7

   d. 1.5

9. In vertical analysis of the balance sheet, each asset item is stated as a percent of total:

   a. current assets

   b. assets

   c. current liabilities

   d. liabilities

10. Based on the following data for the current year, what is the earnings per share on common stock?

Net income	$460,000
Preferred dividends	$50,000
Interest expense	$24,000
Shares of common stock outstanding	50,000

    a. $9.20

    b. $8.68

    c. $8.20

    d. $7.72

11. Companies with high P/E ratios are usually associated with:

    a. a high dividend yield

    b. high profit growth

    c. low long-term debt to total assets

    d. strong current position

12. Based on the following data, what is the rate earned on total assets?

Net income	$240,000
Preferred dividends	$60,000
Interest expense	$120,000
Interest income	$40,000
Average total assets	$1,000,000

    a. 18%

    b. 28%

    c. 30%

    d. 36%

TRUE/FALSE

Instructions: Indicate whether each of the following statements is true or false by placing a check mark in the appropriate column.

	True	False
1. In horizontal analysis of the income statement, each item is stated as a percentage of total sales.	____	____
2. Solvency is the ability of a business to meet its financial obligations as they come due.	____	____
3. The ratio of net sales to assets provides a solvency measure that shows the margin of safety of the debtholders.	____	____
4. The acid-test ratio or quick ratio is the ratio of the sum of cash, receivables, and marketable securities to current liabilities.	____	____
5. Net sales on account divided by the year-end net accounts receivable gives the accounts receivable turnover.	____	____
6. Net income minus the amount required for preferred dividends divided by the average common stockholders' equity gives the rate earned on common stockholders' equity.	____	____
7. The rate earned on total assets is calculated by subtracting interest expense from net income and dividing this sum by the average total assets.	____	____
8. The tendency on the rate earned on stockholders' equity to vary disproportionately from the rate earned on total assets is referred to as financial leverage.	____	____
9. A profitability measure that shows the rate of return to common stockholders in terms of cash dividends is known as the dividend yield on common stock.	____	____
10. The excess of the current assets of an enterprise over its current liabilities and stockholders' equity is called working capital.	____	____

EXERCISE 16-1

Instructions: Using the condensed income statement information presented below, perform a vertical analysis for Delta Corp. for the years ending December 31, 2003 and 2002, stating each item as a percent of revenues.

	2003	Percent	2002	Percent
Revenues	$450,000		$389,000	
Costs and expenses:				
Cost of sales	$200,000		$176,000	
Selling and administrative expenses	100,000		73,000	
Interest expense	250		396	
Total costs and expenses	$300,250		$249,396	
Earnings before income taxes	$149,750		$139,604	
Income taxes	35,321		33,765	
Net earnings	$114,429		$105,839	

EXERCISE 16-2

Instructions: Using the condensed balance sheet data presented below, perform a horizontal analysis for Carson Inc. on December 31, 2003. Indicate the amount and percent increase (decrease) in the columns provided.

			Increase (Decrease)	
	2003	2002	Amount	Percent
Current assets	$250,000	$219,500		
Fixed assets	435,000	401,600		
Intangible assets	42,000	46,500		
Current liabilities	88,000	80,000		
Long-term liabilities	225,000	250,000		
Common stock	214,000	167,600		
Retained earnings	200,000	170,000		

PROBLEM 16-1

Instructions: Using the information below and on the following page, perform a horizontal analysis for Nordic Inc. by filling in the Amount and Percent columns that are provided. (Round all percents to one decimal place.)

Nordic Inc.
Comparative Income Statement
For the Years Ended December 31, 2003 and 2002

			Increase (Decrease)	
	2003	2002	Amount	Percent
Sales	$690,500	$585,000		
Sales returns and allowances	25,500	23,000		
Net sales	$665,000	$562,000		
Cost of goods sold	420,000	330,000		
Gross profit	$245,000	$232,000		
Seiling expenses	$ 43,000	$ 47,700		
Administrative expenses	31,000	31,000		
Total operating expenses	$ 74,000	$ 78,700		
Operating income	$171,000	$153,300		
Other income	13,000	16,400		
	$184,000	$169,700		
Other expense	58,000	53,500		
Income before income taxes	$126,000	$116,200		
Income taxes	34,000	32,400		
Net income	$ 92,000	$ 83,800		

Nordic Inc.
Comparative Balance Sheet
December 31, 2003 and 2002

Assets	2003	2002	Increase (Decrease) Amount	Percent
Cash	$ 76,000	$ 69,000		
Marketable securities	98,900	130,000		
Accounts receivable (net)	199,000	195,000		
Inventory	450,000	375,000		
Prepaid expenses	28,000	26,300		
Long-term investments	35,000	35,000		
Fixed assets (net)	871,000	835,000		
Intangible assets	18,000	22,800		
Total assets	$1,775,900	$1,688,100		
Liabilities				
Current liabilities	$ 129,000	$ 107,000		
Long-term liabilities	420,000	440,000		
Total liabilities	$ 549,000	$ 547,000		
Stockholders' Equity				
Preferred 3% stock, $100 par	$ 102,000	$ 93,000		
Common stock, $50 par	549,900	530,100		
Retained earnings	575,000	518,000		
Total stockholders' equity	$1,226,900	$1,141,100		
Total liabilities and stockholders' equity	$1,775,900	$1,688,100		

PROBLEM 16-2

Instructions: Using the information below and on the following page, perform a vertical analysis for Voyageur Inc. by filling in the Percent columns on the statements provided. (Round all percents to one decimal place.)

Voyageur Inc.
Comparative Balance Sheet
December 31, 2003 and 2002

	2003		2002	
Assets	Amount	Percent	Amount	Percent
Cash	$ 500,000		$ 425,000	
Marketable securities	200,000		185,000	
Accounts receivable (net)	680,000		575,000	
Inventory	860,000		740,000	
Prepaid expenses	104,000		95,000	
Long-term investments	450,000		410,000	
Fixed assets	6,556,000		5,420,000	
Total assets	$9,350,000	100%	$7,850,000	100%
Liabilities				
Current liabilities	$1,090,000		$1,050,000	
Long-term liabilities	2,150,000		2,050,000	
Total liabilities	$3,240,000		$3,100,000	
Stockholders' Equity				
Preferred 5% stock, $100 par	$ 350,000		$ 350,000	
Common stock, $10 par	2,550,000		2,550,000	
Retained earnings	3,210,000		1,850,000	
Total stockholders' equity	$6,110,000		$4,750,000	
Total liabilities and stockholders' equity	$9,350,000	100%	$7,850,000	100%

Voyageur Inc.
Income Statement
For the Year Ended December 31, 2003

	Amount	Percent
Sales	$12,800,000	
Sales returns and allowances	300,000	
Net sales	$12,500,000	100%
Cost of goods sold	7,550,000	
Gross profit	$ 4,950,000	
Selling expenses	$ 1,550,000	
Administrative expenses	825,000	
Total operating expenses	$ 2,375,000	
Operating income	$ 2,575,000	
Other income	125,000	
	$ 2,700,000	
Other expense (interest)	150,000	
Income before income taxes	$ 2,550,000	
Income taxes	937,000	
Net income	$ 1,613,000	

PROBLEM 16-3

Voyageur Inc. declared $250,000 of common stock dividends during 2003. The price of Voyageur's common stock on December 31, 2003 is $29.75.

Instructions: Using the data for Voyageur Inc. from Problem 16-2, determine the following amounts and ratios for 2003. (Round all ratios to one decimal point.)

		Calculation	Final Result
a.	Working capital		
b.	Current ratio		
c.	Acid-test ratio		
d.	Accounts receivable turnover		
e.	Number of days' sales in receivables		
f.	Inventory turnover		
g.	Number of days' sales in inventory		
h.	Ratio of fixed assets to long-term liabilities		
i.	Ratio of liabilities to stockholders' equity		

	Calculation	Final Result
j. Number of times interest charges earned		
k. Number of times preferred dividends earned		
l. Ratio of net sales to assets		
m. Rate earned on total assets		
n. Rate earned on stockholders' equity		
o. Rate earned on common stockholders' equity		
p. Earnings per share on common stock		
q. Price-earnings ratio		
r. Dividends per share of common stock		
s. Dividend yield		

Solutions

CHAPTER 1

Fill In the Blank—Part A

1. business
2. corporation
3. business stakeholder
4. accounting
5. ethics
6. managerial
7. unit of measure
8. assets
9. owner's equity
10. accounting equation
11. $70,000
12. account payable
13. $130,000
14. $80,000
15. revenue
16. $15,000 net income
17. statement of owner's equity
18. $38,000 net income
19. account
20. $94,000 increase

Fill In the Blank—Part B

1. manufacturing
2. merchandising
3. proprietorship
4. managers
5. financial
6. Financial Accounting Standards Board (FASB)
7. business entity
8. liabilities
9. business transaction
10. prepaid expenses
11. account receivable
12. $80,000
13. $65,500
14. expenses
15. income statement
16. ($5,000) net loss
17. balance sheet
18. $13,500 increase
19. statement of cash flows
20. $29,000 net income

Multiple Choice

1. a. Incorrect. General accounting is not a category of employment by accountants.
   b. Incorrect. Accountants and their staffs who provide services on a fee basis are said to be employed in public accounting.
   c. Incorrect. Independent accounting is not a category of employment by accountants.
   d. *Correct*. Accountants employed by a particular business firm or not-for-profit organization, perhaps as chief accountant, controller, or financial vice-president, are said to be engaged in private accounting.

2. a. Incorrect. Service businesses provide services rather than products to customers.
   b. *Correct*. Manufacturing businesses change basic inputs into products that are sold to individual customers.
   c. Incorrect. Merchandising businesses do not make the products, but instead they purchase them from other businesses and sell them to customers.
   d. Incorrect. A proprietorship is a form of business organization rather than a type of business.

3. a. Incorrect. The cost concept is the basis for entering the exchange price, or cost, into the accounting records.
   b. Incorrect. The objectivity concept requires that the accounting records and reports be based upon objective evidence.
   c. Incorrect. The business entity concept limits the economic data in the accounting system to data related directly to the activities of the business or entity.
   d. *Correct*. The unit of measure concept requires that economic data be recorded in dollars.

4. a. Incorrect. The business entity concept limits the economic data in the accounting system to data related directly to the activities of the business or entity.
   b. *Correct*. The cost concept is the basis for recording the amounts, or cost, into the accounting records.
   c. Incorrect. The matching principle emphasizes matching the expenses with the revenue generated during a period by those expenses.
   d. Incorrect. Proprietorship is not a principle, but instead it is a form of business organization.

5. a. Incorrect.
   b. Incorrect.
   c. Incorrect.
   d. *Correct*. The accounting equation (Assets = Liabilities + Owner's Equity) may also be expressed as Assets − Liabilities = Owner's Equity.

6. a. Incorrect.
   b. Incorrect.
   c. Incorrect.
   d. **Correct**. If total liabilities increased by $20,000 during a period of time and owner's equity increased by $5,000 during the same period, total assets must increase by $25,000. That is, if the right side of the accounting equation increases by $25,000 (Liabilities + Owner's Equity), the left side of the equation must also increase by the same amount, $25,000.

7. a. Incorrect.
   b. Incorrect.
   c. **Correct**. The payment of a credit of $6,000 decreases the asset, Cash, and decreases the liability, Accounts Payable.
   d. Incorrect.

8. a. Incorrect.
   b. Incorrect.
   c. Incorrect.
   d. **Correct**. The amount of net income for the year is $40,000. It is computed as ending owner's equity $135,000 ($355,000 − $220,000) less beginning owner's equity $100,000 ($290,000 − $190,000) equals the change in owner's equity, $35,000. The change in owner's equity of $35,000 plus withdrawals of $30,000 less the additional investment of $25,000 equals the net income for the year, $40,000.

9. a. **Correct**. The amount of net income of $11,000 is determined by subtracting expenses, $59,000, from the revenues, $70,000. The owner's withdrawals, $25,000, do not affect the determination of net income.
   b. Incorrect.
   c. Incorrect.
   d. Incorrect.

10. a. **Correct**. The statement of cash flows does not contain a section for cash flows from marketing activities.
   b. Incorrect. The statement of cash flows contains a section for investing activities.
   c. Incorrect. The statement of cash flows contains a section for financing activities.
   d. Incorrect. The statement of cash flows contains a section for cash flows from operating activities.

True/False

1. T
2. F Accountants and their staffs who provide services on a fee basis are said to be employed in public accounting, not private accounting.
3. F Managerial accounting uses both financial accounting and estimated data to aid management in running day-to-day operations.
4. F The concept that expenses incurred in generating revenue should be matched against the revenue in determining net income or net loss is the matching concept, not the cost concept.
5. F The operating activities section, not the financing activities section, of the statement of cash flows includes cash transactions that enter into the determination of net income.
6. F The debts of a business are called its accounts payable, not accounts receivable.
7. F A partnership is owned by two or more individuals.
8. T
9. F A summary of the changes in the owner's equity of a business entity that have occurred during a specific period of time, such as a month or a year, is called the statement of owner's equity, not the statement of cash flows.
10. F A claim against a customer for sales made on credit is an account receivable, not an account payable.

Exercise 1-1

	A	L	OE			A	L	OE
1.	+	0	+	**6.**		+,−	0	0
2.	+	+	0	**7.**		+,−	0	0
3.	+	0	+	**8.**		−	−	0
4.	+	0	+	**9.**		−	−	0
5.	−	0	−	**10.**		−	0	−

Problem 1-1

	Assets					=	Liabilities	+	Owner's Equity	
	Cash	+	Supplies	+	Land		Accounts Payable		Ed Casey, Capital	
(1)	$40,000								$40,000	I
(2)	_____		+$2,000		_____		+$2,000		_____	
Bal.	$40,000		$2,000				$2,000		$40,000	
(3)	−14,000		_____		$14,000		_____		_____	
Bal.	$26,000		$2,000		$14,000		$2,000		$40,000	
(4)	− 1,800		_____		_____		−1,800		_____	
Bal.	$24,200		$2,000		$14,000		$ 200		$40,000	
(5)	− 2,000		_____		_____		_____		− 2,000	D
Bal.	$22,200		$2,000		$14,000		$ 200		$38,000	
(6)	− 2,800		_____		_____		_____		− 2,800	E
Bal.	$19,400		$2,000		$14,000		$ 200		$35,200	
(7)	_____		_____		_____		+ 900		− 900	E
Bal.	$19,400		$2,000		$14,000		$1,100		$34,300	
(8)	+10,000		_____		_____		_____		+10,000	I
Bal.	$29,400		$2,000		$14,000		$1,100		$44,300	
(9)	+ 500		_____		_____		_____		+ 500	R
Bal.	$29,900		$2,000		$14,000		$1,100		$44,800	
(10)	_____		− 600		_____		_____		− 600	E
Bal.	$29,900		$1,400		$14,000		$1,100		$44,200	

Problem 1-2

(1)

Tom's Painting Service
Income Statement
For Year Ended December 31, 20--

Sales		$27,450
Operating expenses:		
Supplies expense	$5,450	
Advertising expense	4,825	
Truck rental expense...	1,525	
Utilities expense	700	
Misc. expense	1,400	13,900
Net income..		$13,550

(2)

Tom's Painting Service
Statement of Owner's Equity
For Year Ended December 31, 20--

Investment, Jan. 1, 20--..		$ 4,000
Additional investment by owner...	$ 2,000	
Income for the year...	13,550	
Less withdrawal	(1,000)	
Increase in owner's equity		14,550
Tom Wallace, capital, Dec. 31, 20--.......................................		$18,550

(3)

Tom's Painting Service
Balance Sheet
December 31, 20--

Assets		Liabilities	
Cash...	$10,050	Accounts payable..........................	$ 4,450
Accounts receivable......................	8,950	**Owner's Equity**	
Supplies	4,000	Tom Wallace, capital.....................	18,550
Total assets..................................	$23,000	Total liability & owner's equity........	$23,000

CHAPTER 2

Fill In the Blank—Part A

1. account	12. debit
2. chart of accounts	13. credit
3. revenue	14. journal
4. T account	15. journalizing
5. debits	16. double-entry
6. debit	accounting
7. credit	17. posting
8. debit	18. two-column journal
9. credit	19. materiality
10. liability	20. transposition
11. credit	

Fill In the Blank—Part B

1. ledger	11. debit
2. assets	12. debit
3. liabilities	13. credit
4. owner's equity	14. horizontal
5. expenses	15. liability
6. credits	16. asset
7. balance	17. debit
8. journalizing	18. credit
9. drawing	19. trial balance
10. unearned revenue	20. slide

Multiple Choice

1. a. Incorrect.
   b. **Correct**. The receipt of cash from customers in payment of their accounts would be recorded by a debit to Cash and a credit to Accounts Receivable.
   c. Incorrect.
   d. Incorrect.

2. a. Incorrect. The third step in recording a transaction in a two-column journal is to list the account to be credited.
   b. Incorrect. The fourth step in recording a transaction in a two-column journal is to list the amount to be credited.
   c. Incorrect. The second step in recording a transaction in a two-column journal is to list the amount to be debited.
   d. **Correct**. The first step in recording a transaction in a two-column journal is to list the account to be debited.

3. a. Incorrect. Cash is debited when the owner invests cash.
   b. **Correct**. The drawing account of a sole proprietorship is debited when the owner withdraws cash.
   c. Incorrect. Accounts Payable is debited when a liability is paid.
   d. Incorrect. An expense account is debited when an expense is paid.

4. a. Incorrect.
   b. Incorrect.
   c. **Correct**. The equality of debits and credits in the ledger should be verified at the end of each accounting period by preparing a trial balance.
   d. Incorrect.

5. a. **Correct**. Incorrectly computing an account balance will cause an inequality in the trial balance totals.
   b. Incorrect. A failure to record a transaction will not cause an inequality in the trial balance totals.
   c. Incorrect. Recording the same transaction more than once will not cause an inequality in the trial balance totals.
   d. Incorrect. Posting a transaction to the wrong account will not cause an inequality in the trial balance totals.

6. a. Incorrect.
   b. **Correct**. Since cash is an asset, credits to Cash result in a decrease in assets.
   c. Incorrect.
   d. Incorrect.

7. a. Incorrect.
   b. **Correct**. Under the rules of double-entry accounting, debits to expense accounts signify a decrease in owner's capital.
   c. Incorrect.
   d. Incorrect.

8. a. Incorrect.
   b. Incorrect.
   c. Incorrect.
   d. **Correct**. Under the rules of double-entry accounting, when rent is prepaid for several months in advance, the debit is to Prepaid Rent, an asset account.

9. a. Incorrect.
   b. Incorrect.
   c. **Correct**. Under the rules of double-entry accounting, when an asset is purchased on account, the credit is to Accounts Payable, a liability account.
   d. Incorrect.

10. a. Incorrect.
   b. **Correct**. Under the rules of double-entry accounting, when a payment is made to a supplier for goods previously purchased on account, the debit is to Accounts Payable, a liability account.
   c. Incorrect.
   d. Incorrect.

True/False

1. F Amounts entered on the left side of an account, regardless of the account title, are called debits or charges to the account, not credits.
2. T
3. T
4. F The balance sheet accounts, not the income statement accounts, are listed first in the chart of accounts.
5. T
6. F Every business transaction affects a minimum of two accounts, not one account.
7. F The process of recording a transaction in a journal is called journalizing, not posting.
8. F The group of accounts for a business entity is called its ledger, not a journal.
9. T
10. F A recording error caused by the erroneous rearrangement of digits, such as writing $627 as $672, is called a transposition, not a slide.

Exercise 2-1

Transaction	Account Debited		Account Credited	
	Type	Effect	Type	Effect
(1)	asset	+	capital	+
(2)	asset	+	liability	+
(3)	asset	+	liability	+
(4)	asset	+	revenue	+
(5)	liability	−	asset	−
(6)	expense	+	liability	+
(7)	asset	+	asset	−
(8)	drawing	+	asset	−

Problem 2-1

(1)
June	1	Cash	11	5,000	
		Equipment......................................	18	14,500	
		Vehicles	19	21,000	
		Joan Star, Capital......................	31		40,500
	16	Equipment......................................	18	5,500	
		Accounts Payable	21		5,500
	28	Supplies..	12	500	
		Accounts Payable	21		500
	30	Accounts Payable............................	21	2,100	
		Cash...	11		2,100

(2)

ACCOUNT *Cash*   ACCOUNT NO. 11

DATE	ITEM	POST. REF.	DEBIT	CREDIT	BALANCE DEBIT	BALANCE CREDIT
20--						
June 1		1	5,000		5,000	
30		1		2,100	2,900	

ACCOUNT *Supplies*   ACCOUNT NO. 12

DATE	ITEM	POST. REF.	DEBIT	CREDIT	BALANCE DEBIT	BALANCE CREDIT
20--						
June 28		1	500		500	

ACCOUNT *Equipment*   ACCOUNT NO. 18

DATE	ITEM	POST. REF.	DEBIT	CREDIT	BALANCE DEBIT	BALANCE CREDIT
20--						
June 1		1	14,500		14,500	
16		1	5,500		20,000	

ACCOUNT *Vehicles*   ACCOUNT NO. 19

DATE	ITEM	POST. REF.	DEBIT	CREDIT	BALANCE DEBIT	BALANCE CREDIT
20--						
June 1		1	21,000		21,000	

ACCOUNT *Accounts Payable*   ACCOUNT NO. 21

DATE	ITEM	POST. REF.	DEBIT	CREDIT	BALANCE DEBIT	BALANCE CREDIT
20--						
June 16		1		5,500		5,500
28		1		500		6,000
30		1	2,100			3,900

ACCOUNT *Joan Star, Capital*   ACCOUNT NO. 31

DATE	ITEM	POST. REF.	DEBIT	CREDIT	BALANCE DEBIT	BALANCE CREDIT
20--						
June 1		1		40,500		40,500

(3)

Star Service Company
Trial Balance
June 30, 20--

Cash	2,900	
Supplies	500	
Equipment	20,000	
Vehicles	21,000	
Accounts Payable		3,900
Joan Star, Capital		40,500
	44,400	44,400

Problem 2-2

(1)

	Cash			
(a)	20,000	(b)		2,500
(d)	19,600	(c)		1,000
		(e)		1,100
		(g)		2,600
		(h)		5,000
		(i)		800
		(k)		240
		(l)		1,700
		(m)		2,000
		(n)		5,000
		(o)		500

	Office Supplies	
(c)	1,000	
(f)	200	

	Prepaid Insurance	
(l)	1,700	

	Library	
(n)	5,000	

	Office Equipment	
(a)	13,200	

	Auto	
(g)	13,000	

	Accounts Payable			
(k)	240	(f)		200
(m)	2,000	(g)		10,400
		(j)		240

	Judy Turner, Capital		
		(a)	33,200

	Judy Turner, Drawing	
(h)	5,000	

	Legal Fees		
		(d)	19,600

	Rent Expense	
(b)	2,500	

	Salary Expense	
(e)	1,100	

	Telephone Expense	
(j)	240	

	Auto Repairs & Maintenance Expense	
(i)	800	

	Janitor Expense	
(o)	500	

(2)

Judy Turner
Trial Balance
January 31, 20--

Cash	17,160	
Office Supplies	1,200	
Prepaid Insurance	1,700	
Library	5,000	
Office Equipment	13,200	
Auto	13,000	
Accounts Payable		8,600
Judy Turner, Capital		33,200
Judy Turner, Drawing	5,000	
Legal Fees		19,600
Rent Expense	2,500	
Salary Expense	1,100	
Telephone Expense	240	
Auto Repairs & Maintenance Expense	800	
Janitor Expense	500	
	61,400	61,400

Problem 2-3

(a)

Prepaid Insurance	1,000	
Prepaid Rent		1,000
To correct erroneous debit to prepaid rent.		

(b)

Accounts Receivable	200	
Accounts Payable		200
To correct erroneous credit to accounts receivable.		

(c)

Drawing	3,000	
Cash		3,000
To correct erroneous entry debiting cash and crediting drawing.		

CHAPTER 3

Fill In the Blank—Part A

1. accounting period
2. cash
3. revenue recognition
4. adjusting
5. deferred expenses
6. accrued expenses
7. advertising expense
8. accumulated depreciation—equipment
9. unearned fees
10. taxes payable
11. overstated
12. understated
13. understated
14. $10,700
15. $800
16. fixed assets
17. depreciation
18. book value
19. $88,700
20. adjusted

Fill In the Blank—Part B

1. accrual
2. matching
3. adjusting
4. deferred revenues
5. accrued revenues
6. depreciation
7. accumulated depreciation
8. understated
9. overstated
10. interest expense
11. prepaid rent
12. depreciation expense
13. fees earned
14. vertical
15. balance sheet
16. expense
17. overstated
18. overstated
19. $1,950
20. $800

Multiple Choice

1. a. Incorrect.
   b. **Correct.** Entries required at the end of an accounting period to bring the accounts up to date and to assure the proper matching of revenues and expenses are called adjusting entries.
   c. Incorrect.
   d. Incorrect. Correcting entries correct errors in the accounting records. Entries required at the end of an accounting period to bring the accounts up to date and to assure the proper matching of revenues and expenses are called adjusting entries.

2. a. **Correct.** The amount of accrued but unpaid expenses at the end of the fiscal period is both an expense and a liability.
   b. Incorrect. The amount of accrued but unpaid expenses at the end of the fiscal period is both an expense and a liability, not an asset.
   c. Incorrect. The amount of accrued but unpaid expenses at the end of the fiscal period is both an expense and a liability, not a deferral.
   d. Incorrect. The amount of accrued but unpaid expenses at the end of the fiscal period is both an expense and a liability, not a revenue.

3. a. Incorrect.
   b. Incorrect.
   c. **Correct.** If the effect of the debit portion of an adjusting entry is to increase the balance of an expense account, the effect of the credit portion of the entry is a decrease in the balance of an asset account.
   d. Incorrect.

4. a. Incorrect.
   b. Incorrect.
   c. Incorrect.
   d. **Correct.** If the effect of the credit portion of an adjusting entry is to increase the balance of a liability account, the effect of the debit portion of the entry is an increase in the balance of an expense account.

5. a. Incorrect.
   b. **Correct.** The balance in the prepaid rent account before adjustment at the end of the year is $12,000, which represents three months' rent paid on December 1. The adjusting entry required on December 31 debits Rent Expense, $4,000 and credits Prepaid Rent, $4,000.
   c. Incorrect.
   d. Incorrect.

6. a. **Correct.** At the end of the preceding fiscal year, the usual adjusting entry for accrued salaries owed to employees was omitted. The error was not corrected, and the accrued salaries were included in the first salary payment in the current fiscal year. As a result, Salary Expense was overstated and net income was understated for the current year.
   b. Incorrect. Salaries Payable is understated at the end of the preceding fiscal year, not the current year.
   c. Incorrect. Salary Expense was overstated and net income was understated for the current fiscal year, not the preceding year.
   d. Incorrect. Salary Expense and Salaries Payable were understated, rather than overstated, for the preceding year.

7. a. Incorrect.
   b. Incorrect.
   c. **Correct.** The decrease in usefulness of fixed assets as time passes is called depreciation.
   d. Incorrect.

8. a. **Correct.** The difference between the fixed asset account and the related accumulated depreciation account is called the book value of the asset.
   b. Incorrect.
   c. Incorrect.
   d. Incorrect.

9. a. Incorrect. Expenses will be understated, not overstated.
   b. Incorrect. Net income will be overstated, not understated.
   c. Incorrect. Assets will be overstated, not understated.
   d. **Correct**. If a $250 adjustment for depreciation is not recorded, owner's equity will be overstated.

10. a. **Correct**. The corrected net income is computed as $50,000 less the adjusting entry for supplies expense of $500 and accrued salaries of $1,300.
   b. Incorrect.
   c. Incorrect.
   d. Incorrect.

True/False

1. T
2. F When the reduction in prepaid expenses is not properly recorded, the asset accounts will be overstated, but the expense accounts will be understated, not overstated.
3. T
4. F If the adjusting entry to record accrued wages at the end of the year is omitted, net income and owner's equity will be overstated, but total assets will not be affected. Instead, liabilities will be understated.
5. T
6. T
7. T
8. F Expenses that have not been paid or revenues that have not been received are accruals, not deferrals.
9. T
10. F The amount of accrued revenue is recorded by debiting an asset account, not a liability account. The credit is to a revenue account.

Exercise 3-1

(1)

Cash		Prepaid Insurance		Insurance Expense	
	May 1 5,400	May 1 5,400	Dec. 31 1,200	Dec. 31 1,200	

(2) Unexpired insurance $4,200

(3) Insurance expense............................ $1,200

Exercise 3-2

(1)

Cash			Salary Expense			Salaries Payable		
	Oct. 7	250	Oct. 7	250			Oct. 31	50
	14	250	14	250				
	21	250	21	250				
	28	250	28	250				
			31	50				

(2) Salary expense................................. $1,050

(3) Salaries payable............................... $50

Exercise 3-3

Unearned Rent					Rent Revenue			
Dec. 31	500	Dec. 1	6,000				Dec. 31	500

Dec. 31	Unearned Rent..	500	
	Rent Revenue		500

Exercise 3-4

Interest Receivable			Interest Revenue		
Dec. 31	320			Dec. 31	320

Dec. 31	Interest Receivable	320	
	Interest Revenue		320

Problem 3-1

(1) **(a)** Salaries Expense 2,000
       Salaries Payable   2,000

(b) Rent Expense 726
       Prepaid Rent.....................................   726

(c) Supplies Expense 1,750
       Supplies..   1,750

(d) Depreciation Expense............................. 400
       Accumulated Depreciation   400

(e) Accounts Receivable 2,100
       Service Fees.....................................   2,100

(2)

Bob's Service Company
Adjusted Trial Balance
July 31, 20--

Cash..	9,218	
Accounts Receivable	9,377	
Supplies	1,000	
Prepaid Rent	7,986	
Tools & Equipment	21,829	
Accumulated Depreciation......................................		1,935
Accounts Payable		7,117
Salaries Payable...		2,000
Bob Jones, Capital..		37,417
Bob Jones, Drawing..	3,234	
Service Fees...		30,799
Salary Expense...	17,929	
Rent Expense	726	
Supplies Expense	1,750	
Depreciation Expense...	400	
Miscellaneous Expense	5,819	
	79,268	79,268

CHAPTER 4

Fill In the Blank—Part A

1. work sheet
2. note receivable
3. current liabilities
4. balance sheet
5. balance sheet
6. net income
7. net loss
8. income summary
9. owner's capital
10. income summary
11. owner's capital
12. post-closing
13. natural business year
14. accounting cycle
15. working capital

Fill In the Blank—Part B

1. current assets
2. property, plant, and equipment
3. long-term liabilities
4. income statement
5. income statement
6. net loss
7. net income
8. closing entries
9. income summary
10. owner's capital
11. income summary
12. owner's capital
13. fiscal year
14. solvency
15. current

Multiple Choice

1. a. Incorrect. Notes receivable are written claims against customers, not creditors.
   b. Incorrect. Notes receivable are written claims against customers, not owner's equity.
   c. **Correct**. Notes receivable are written claims against customers.
   d. Incorrect. Notes payable, not notes receivable, are written claims against assets.

2. a. Incorrect. A work sheet is completed by extending the adjusted trial balance amounts to the Income Statement and Balance Sheet columns as well as totaling the Adjustment columns and extending the work sheet adjustments to the Adjusted Trial Balance columns.
   b. Incorrect. A work sheet is completed by totaling the Adjustment columns as well as extending the adjusted trial balance amounts to the Income Statement and Balance Sheet columns and extending the work sheet adjustments to the Adjusted Trial Balance columns.
   c. Incorrect. A work sheet is completed by extending the work sheet adjustments to the Adjusted Trial Balance columns as well as totaling the Adjustment columns and extending the adjusted trial balance amounts to the Income Statement and Balance Sheet columns.
   d. **Correct**. A work sheet is completed by extending the adjusted trial balance amounts to the Income Statement and Balance Sheet columns, totaling the Adjustment columns, and extending the work sheet adjustments to the Adjusted Trial Balance columns.

3. a. **Correct**. If the Income Statement Credit column is greater than the Income Statement Debit column, a net income exists.
   b. Incorrect. If the Income Statement Credit column is greater than the Income Statement Debit column, a net income exists, not a net loss.
   c. Incorrect.
   d. Incorrect.

4. a. Incorrect. After all of the account balances have been extended to the Balance Sheet columns of the work sheet, the totals of the Debit and Credit columns are $377,750 and $387,750, respectively. The amount of net loss for the period is $10,000—the difference between the Balance Sheet Debit and Credit columns. Because the Balance Sheet Credit column is larger than the Debit column, a net loss has been incurred, rather than a net income.
   b. **Correct**. After all of the account balances have been extended to the Balance Sheet columns of the work sheet, the totals of the Debit and Credit columns are $377,750 and $387,750, respectively. The amount of net loss for the period is $10,000—the difference between the Debit and Credit columns. Because the Balance Sheet Credit column is larger than the Debit column, a net loss has been incurred.
   c. Incorrect. The net income or net loss is computed as the difference between the Balance Sheet Debit and Credit columns, not the total of the Debit column.
   d. Incorrect. The net income or net loss is computed as the difference between the Balance Sheet Debit and Credit column, not the total of the Credit column.

5. a. *Correct*. After all of the account balances have been extended to the Income Statement columns of the work sheet, the totals of the Debit and Credit columns are $62,300 and $67,600, respectively. The amount of the net income for the period is $5,300—the difference between the Debit and Credit columns. Because the Income Statement Credit column is larger than the Debit column, a net income has been incurred.

   b. Incorrect. After all of the account balances have been extended to the Income Statement columns of the work sheet, the totals of the Debit and Credit columns are $62,300 and $67,600, respectively. The amount of the net income for the period is $5,300—the difference between the Debit and Credit columns. Because the Income Statement Credit column is larger than the Debit column, a net income has been incurred, rather than a net loss.

   c. Incorrect. The net income or net loss is computed as the difference between the Income Statement Debit and Credit columns, not the total of the Debit column.

   d. Incorrect. The net income or net loss is computed as the difference between the Income Statement Debit and Credit columns, not the total of the Credit column.

6. a. Incorrect. Lisa Murray, Drawing should be closed to Lisa Murray, Capital at the end of the fiscal year, not to Income Summary.

   b. Incorrect. Accumulated Depreciation—Equipment is not closed at the end of the fiscal year.

   c. *Correct*. Sales should be closed to Income Summary at the end of the fiscal year.

   d. Incorrect. Accounts Payable is not closed at the end of the fiscal year.

7. a. Incorrect. Salaries Expense is closed at the end of the fiscal year to Income Summary.

   b. Incorrect. Sales is closed at the end of the fiscal year to Income Summary.

   c. *Correct*. Lisa Murray, Drawing should be closed to Lisa Murray, Capital at the end of the fiscal year.

   d. Incorrect. Accounts Receivable is not closed at the end of the fiscal year.

8. a. Incorrect. Salaries Expense is closed to Income Summary at the end of the period and does not appear in the post-closing trial balance.

   b. Incorrect. Lisa Murray, Drawing is closed to Lisa Murray, Capital at the end of the period and does not appear in the post-closing trial balance.

   c. Incorrect. Sales is closed to Income Summary at the end of the period and does not appear in the post-closing trial balance.

   d. *Correct*. Lisa Murray, Capital is not closed at the end of the period and does appear in the post-closing trial balance.

9. a. Incorrect. The maximum length of an accounting period is normally greater than 6 months.

   b. *Correct*. The maximum length of an accounting period is normally 1 year.

   c. Incorrect. The maximum length of an accounting period is normally less than 2 years.

   d. Incorrect. The maximum length of an accounting period is normally less than 3 years.

10. a. Incorrect.

   b. Incorrect.

   c. *Correct*. The complete sequence of accounting procedures for a fiscal period is frequently called the accounting cycle.

   d. Incorrect.

True/False

1. F The balance of Accumulated Depreciation—Equipment is extended to the Balance Sheet columns of the work sheet, not the Income Statement columns.

2. F The difference between the Debit and Credit columns of the Income Statement section of the work sheet is the same as the difference between the Debit and Credit columns of the Balance Sheet section. This difference is the net income or net loss for the period.

3. T

4. T

5. F The balances of the accounts reported in the balance sheet are carried from year to year and are called real or permanent accounts, not temporary accounts.

6. T

7. F If the Income Statement Debit column is greater than the Income Statement Credit column, the difference is a net loss, not a net income.

8. F A type of working paper frequently used by accountants prior to the preparation of financial statements is called a work sheet, not a post-closing trial balance. The post-closing trial balance is prepared after the closing entries have been recorded to verify the equality of the debit and credit balances.

9. T

10. T

Exercise 4-1

Aug.	31	Salary Expense...	1,500	
		Salaries Payable................................		1,500
	31	Rent Expense	560	
		Prepaid Rent.....................................		560
	31	Supplies Expense	700	
		Supplies..		700
	31	Depreciation Expense.............................	1,000	
		Accumulated Depreciation		1,000
	31	Accounts Receivable	3,200	
		Repair Fees......................................		3,200

Exercise 4-2

(1) 20--

Mar.	31	Service Fees...................................	50	19,225	
		Income Summary....................	45		19,225
	31	Income Summary	45	13,980	
		Salary Expense......................	58		8,550
		Supplies Expense	67		5,430

(2)

ACCOUNT	*Income Summary*				ACCOUNT NO.	*45*	
		POST.				BALANCE	
DATE	ITEM	REF.	DEBIT	CREDIT		DEBIT	CREDIT
20--							
Mar. 31		7		19,225			19,225
31		7	13,980				5,245

ACCOUNT	*Service Fees*				ACCOUNT NO.	*50*	
20--							
Mar. 15		5		4,850			4,850
31		6		14,375			19,225
31		7	19,225				–0–

ACCOUNT	*Salary Expense*				ACCOUNT NO.	*58*	
20--							
Mar. 31		5	8,550			8,550	
31		7		8,550		–0–	

ACCOUNT	*Supplies Expense*				ACCOUNT NO.	*67*	
20--							
Mar. 15		5	2,430			2,430	
25		6	1,720			4,150	
31		6	1,280			5,430	
31		7		5,430		–0–	

Problem 4-1

(1)

Castle Shop
Work Sheet
For Year Ended April 30, 20--

Account Title	Trial Balance Dr.	Cr.	Adjustments Dr.	Cr.	Adjusted Trial Balance Dr.	Cr.	Income Statement Dr.	Cr.	Balance Sheet Dr.	Cr.
Cash	10,056				10,056				10,056	
Accts. Rec.	7,938		(e) 3,000		10,938				10,938	
Supplies	3,000			(a) 1,200	1,800				1,800	
Prepaid Rent	9,504			(b) 792	8,712				8,712	
Tools & Equipment	23,814				23,814				23,814	
Acc. Depreciation		1,674		(c) 1,000		2,674				2,674
Accounts Payable		7,764				7,764				7,764
Unearned Fees		2,000	(f) 500			1,500				1,500
Castle, Capital		38,818				38,818				38,818
Castle, Drawing	3,528				3,528				3,528	
Service Fees		31,308		(e) 3,000		34,808		34,808		
				(f) 500						
Wages Expense	17,376		(d) 2,000		19,376		19,376			
Misc. Expense	6,348				6,348		6,348			
	81,564	81,564								
Wages Payable				(d) 2,000		2,000				2,000
Rent Expense			(b) 792		792		792			
Supplies Expense			(a) 1,200		1,200		1,200			
Depr. Expense			(c) 1,000		1,000		1,000			
			8,492	8,492	87,564	87,564	28,716	34,808	58,848	52,756
Net Income							6,092			6,092
							34,808	34,808	58,848	58,848

(2)

Castle Shop
Income Statement
For Year Ended April 30, 20--

Service fees		$34,808
Operating expenses:		
Wages expenses	$19,376	
Supplies expense	1,200	
Depreciation expense	1,000	
Rent expense	792	
Misc. expenses	6,348	
Total operating expenses		28,716
Net income		$ 6,092

Castle Shop
Statement of Owner's Equity
For Year Ended April 30, 20--

Capital, May 1, 20--		$38,818
Income for the year	$6,092	
Less drawing for the year	3,528	
Increase in owner's equity		2,564
Capital, April 30, 20--		$41,382

Castle Shop
Balance Sheet
April 30, 20--

Assets			Liabilities		
Current assets:			Current liabilities:		
Cash	$10,056		Accounts payable	$7,764	
Accounts receivable	10,938		Wages payable	2,000	
Supplies	1,800		Unearned fees	1,500	
Prepaid rent	8,712		Total liabilities		$11,264
Total current assets		$31,506			
Property, plant, and equipment:			Owner's Equity		
Tools & equipment	$23,814		Castle, capital		41,382
Less accumulated depreciation	2,674	21,140			
Total assets		$52,646	Total liabilities and owner's equity		$52,646

Problem 4-2

20--		Adjusting Entries		
Apr. 30	Supplies Expense		1,200	
	Supplies			1,200
30	Rent Expense		792	
	Prepaid Rent			792
30	Depreciation Expense		1,000	
	Accumulated Depreciation			1,000
30	Wages Expense		2,000	
	Wages Payable			2,000
30	Accounts Receivable		3,000	
	Service Fees			3,000
30	Unearned Fees		500	
	Service Fees			500

20--   Closing Entries
Apr. 30   Service Fees   34,808
               Income Summary   34,808

     30   Income Summary...   28,716
               Wages Expense   19,376
               Miscellaneous Expense...........................   6,348
               Supplies Expense....................................   1,200
               Depreciation Expense   1,000
               Rent Expense..   792

     30   Income Summary...   6,092
               Castle, Capital   6,092

     30   Castle, Capital...   3,528
               Castle, Drawing   3,528

CHAPTER 5

Fill In the Blank—Part A

1. cash payments
2. employee fraud
3. hardware
4. special
5. internal controls
6. purchases
7. general
8. cash payments
9. general
10. accounts receivable
11. cash
12. application
13. revenue
14. operating
15. general

Fill In the Blank—Part B

1. cash receipts
2. accounts receivable
3. accounting
4. accounts payable
5. cash payments
6. general
7. revenue
8. cash receipts
9. fees earned
10. accounts payable
11. elements
12. controlling
13. purchases
14. general
15. subsidiary

Multiple Choice

1. a. Incorrect. Installation is not a phase of installing or changing an accounting system.
   b. Incorrect. Verification is not a phase of installing or changing an accounting system.
   c. Incorrect. Management is not a phase of installing or changing an accounting system.
   d. *Correct*. The job of installing or changing an accounting system is made up of three phases: (1) analysis, (2) design, and (3) implementation.

2. a. Incorrect. Risk assessment is an element of the internal control framework.
   b. Incorrect. Control environment is an element of the internal control framework.
   c. *Correct*. Management is not an element of the internal control framework.
   d. Incorrect. Monitoring is an element of the internal control framework.

3. a. Incorrect. The total amounts in the "Accounts Payable Cr." column of the purchases journal are posted to the general ledger, not the individual amounts.
   b. Incorrect. Postings are not made to the general journal; rather, entries that do not fit in any of the special journals, such as the purchases journal, are recorded in the general journal.
   c. *Correct*. The individual amounts in the "Accounts Payable Cr." column of the purchases journal are posted to the appropriate account in the accounts payable subsidiary ledger.
   d. Incorrect. There is no such thing as an accounts payable journal.

4. a. Incorrect. The purchase of supplies on account would be recorded in the purchases journal.
   b. Incorrect. The receipt of cash for services rendered would be recorded in the cash receipts journal.
   c. *Correct*. The billing of fees earned on account would be recorded in the revenue journal.
   d. Incorrect. The payment of an account payable would be recorded in the cash payments journal.

5. a. **Correct**. The controlling account in the general ledger that summarizes the individual accounts with creditors in a subsidiary ledger is Accounts Payable.
   b. Incorrect.
   c. Incorrect. Accounts Receivable is the controlling account in the general ledger that summarizes the individual subsidiary ledger accounts for customers, not creditors.
   d. Incorrect.

6. a. Incorrect. Internal control policies and procedures do not necessarily provide reasonable assurance that a company will not be sued.
   b. Incorrect. Internal control policies and procedures do not necessarily provide reasonable assurance that a net income will be earned.
   c. Incorrect. Internal control policies and procedures do not necessarily provide reasonable assurance that management is competent.
   d. **Correct**. Internal control policies and procedures provide reasonable assurance that business information is accurate.

7. a. Incorrect.
   b. **Correct**. The controlling account for the customer's ledger is Accounts Receivable.
   c. Incorrect. Accounts Payable is the controlling account for the creditor's ledger, not the customer's ledger.
   d. Incorrect.

8. a. **Correct**. At regular intervals the amounts entered in the "Accounts Receivable Cr." column of the revenue journal are posted to the individual accounts receivable accounts.
   b. Incorrect. At the end of each month, the total of the "Accounts Receivable Cr." column of the revenue journal is posted to the Accounts Receivable controlling account. The individual accounts are posted more frequently.
   c. Incorrect. The Accounts Receivable control account is normally posted at the end of each month, while the individual accounts are posted more frequently.
   d. Incorrect. The adjusting entries are prepared and posted at the end of each month, while the individual accounts are posted more frequently.

9. a. Incorrect. Rotating duties among employees is a control procedure.
   b. Incorrect. Separating responsibilities for custody of assets and accounting for assets is a control procedure.
   c. **Correct**. Management's operating style is not a control procedure.
   d. Incorrect. Proofs and security measures is a control procedure.

10. a. Incorrect. The revenue journal is a special journal for recording services provided on account.
    b. **Correct**. The general journal is not a special journal, but instead it is an all-purpose journal for recording transactions that do not fit into any of the special journals.
    c. Incorrect. The cash receipts journal is a special journal for recording receipts of cash.
    d. Incorrect. The purchases journal is a special journal for recording purchases of items on account.

True/False

1. F   It is the goal of systems analysis, not systems design, to identify information needs and how the system should provide the information.
2. T
3. F   Transactions involving the payment of cash for any purpose usually are recorded in a cash payments journal, not a purchases journal. The purchases journal is used to record purchases of items on account.
4. F   When there are a large number of individual accounts with a common characteristic, it is common to place them in a separate ledger called a subsidiary ledger, not a detail ledger.
5. T
6. F   Acquisitions on account that are not provided for in special debit columns are recorded in the purchases journal in the final set of columns called "Other Accounts Dr.", not "Misc."

7. T
8. F At the end of each month, the total of the amount column of the revenue journal is posted as a debit to Accounts Receivable, not Cash. The credit is to Fees Earned.
9. T
10. T
11. T
12. F The cost of computer hardware and software has declined, thus making computerized accounting systems more affordable to small- and medium-size businesses.
13. T
14. T
15. F Regardless whether a business uses computers to process accounting data, the concepts and methods for a manual system *are* relevant.

Exercise 5-1

Feb.	1	purchases journal
	6	cash receipts journal
	8	general journal
	11	cash payments journal
	18	revenue (sales) journal
	28	cash receipts journal

Exercise 5-2

REVENUE JOURNAL

DATE	INVOICE NO.	ACCOUNT DEBITED	POST. REF.	ACCTS. REC. DR. FEES EARNED CR.
20--				
Oct. 3	2883	Blanders Co.		8,250
4	2884	Montana Co.		5,000

CASH RECEIPTS JOURNAL

DATE	ACCOUNT CREDITED	POST. REF.	OTHER ACCOUNTS CR.	ACCOUNTS REC. CR.	CASH DR.
20--					
Oct. 13	Blanders Co.			8,250	8,250
14	Montana Co.			5,000	5,000
25	Office Supplies		300		300
31	Fees Earned		39,600		39,600

GENERAL JOURNAL

DATE			
20--			
Oct. 8	Fees Earned..	1,000	
	Accounts Receivable—Blanders Co.		1,000

Exercise 5-3

PURCHASES JOURNAL

DATE	ACCOUNT CREDITED	POST. REF.	ACCOUNTS PAYABLE CR.	STORE SUPPLIES DR.	OFFICE SUPPLIES DR.	OTHER ACCOUNTS DR.
20--						
Mar. 2	Eastside Co.		1,250	1,250		
8	Bench Co.		600	600		
28	James & Co.		900	800	100	

CASH PAYMENTS JOURNAL

DATE	CK. NO.	ACCOUNT DEBITED	POST. REF.	OTHER ACCOUNTS DR.	ACCOUNTS PAY. DR.	CASH CR.
20--						
Mar. 16	230	Bench Co.			600	600
20	231	Office Supplies		250		250
27	232	Eastside Co.			950	950

GENERAL JOURNAL

20--				
Mar. 9	Accounts Payable—Eastside Co......................................		300	
	Store Supplies			300

Problem 5-1

(1)—(3)

REVENUE JOURNAL

DATE	INVOICE NO.	ACCOUNT DEBITED	POST. REF.	ACCTS. REC. DR. FEES EARNED CR.
20--				
Sept. 8	210	Robert Poon	✔	1,220
12	225	Jeff Lucas	✔	750
24	260	Pamela Stark	✔	860
30	290	Steve Kocan	✔	2,500
				5,330
				(113)(411)

(2) and **(3)**

GENERAL LEDGER ACCOUNTS RECEIVABLE LEDGER

Accounts Receivable 113	
Sept. 30 5,330	

Steve Kocan	
Sept. 30 2,500	

Jeff Lucas	
Sept. 12 750	

Fees Earned 411	
	Sept. 30 5,330

Robert Poon	
Sept. 8 1,220	

Pamela Stark	
Sept. 24 860	

(4)

Steve Kocan.................................	$2,500
Jeff Lucas.....................................	750
Robert Poon.................................	1,220
Pamela Stark	860
Total accounts receivable	$5,330

Problem 5-2

(1)—(3)

PURCHASES JOURNAL

DATE	ACCOUNT CREDITED	POST. REF.	ACCOUNTS PAYABLE CR.	STORE SUPPLIES DR.	OFFICE SUPPLIES. DR.	OTHER ACCOUNTS DR. ACCOUNT	POST. REF.	AMOUNT
20--								
Apr. 14	Mills Co.	✔	300	300				
16	Quick Co.	✔	175		175			
22	Mills Co.	✔	5,250			Store Equip.	121	5,250
30	Mills Co.	✔	280	280				
			6,005	580	175			5,250
			(211)	(115)	(116)			(✔)

(2) and (3)

GENERAL LEDGER

Store Supplies	115
Apr. 30	580

Store Equipment	121
Apr. 22	5,250

Office Supplies	116
Apr. 30	175

Accounts Payable	211
	Apr. 30	6,005

ACCTS. PAYABLE LEDGER

Mills Co.

Apr. 14	300
22	5,250
30	280

Quick Co.

Apr. 16	175

(4)

Mills Co.	$5,830
Quick Co.	175
Total accounts payable	$6,005

Problem 5-3

(1)

Store Supplies	3,650	Accounts Payable	15,890
Office Supplies	1,250		
Other Accounts	10,990		
Debit totals	15,890	Credit totals	15,890

(2)

PURCHASES JOURNAL

DATE	ACCOUNT CREDITED	POST. REF.	ACCOUNTS PAYABLE CR.	STORE SUPPLIES DR.	OFFICE SUPPLIES. DR.	OTHER ACCOUNTS DR. ACCOUNT	POST. REF.	AMOUNT
20--								
Oct. 29	Hartkemeyer Co.	✔	7,620			Store Equip.	121	7,620
31			15,890	3,650	1,250			10,990
			(211)	(115)	(116)			

GENERAL LEDGER

Store Supplies	115
Oct. 31	3,650

Office Supplies	116
Oct. 31	1,250

Store Equipment	121
Oct. 29	7,620

Accounts Payable	211
	Oct. 31	15,890

CHAPTER 6

Fill In the Blank—Part A

1. cost of merchandise sold
2. sales
3. operating expenses
4. merchandise inventory
5. periodic
6. invoice
7. purchases return or allowance
8. sales discounts
9. credit
10. FOB shipping point
11. $50
12. $60
13. $700
14. multiple-step
15. administrative
16. loss from operations
17. other
18. inventory shrinkage
19. $240,000
20. report

Fill In the Blank—Part B

1. gross profit
2. operating expenses
3. perpetual
4. physical inventory
5. purchases discounts
6. debit
7. sales return or allowance
8. trade discounts
9. FOB destination
10. $160
11. $15,100
12. $33
13. $9,900
14. $6,600
15. selling
16. income from operations
17. other income
18. single-step
19. $215,000
20. account

Multiple Choice

1. a. Incorrect. Cost of merchandise sold is not included in the owner's equity section of the balance sheet.
   b. Incorrect. Cost of merchandise sold is not included in the other income section of the income statement.
   c. *Correct*. The basic differences between the financial statements of a merchandising business and a service business include reporting cost of merchandise sold on the income statement and the balance sheet as a current asset.
   d. Incorrect. An owner's equity statement is prepared for both a merchandising business and a service business.

2. a. Incorrect. The sales discount should be deducted in determining the amount the seller will received.
   b. *Correct*. The seller will receive $58.80, computed as $60 less the sales discount of $1.20 ($60 × 2%).
   c. Incorrect.
   d. Incorrect. $1.20 is the amount of the sales discount, not the amount received by the seller.

3. a. Incorrect. A debit memorandum is issued by the buyer, not the seller.
   b. *Correct*. A credit memorandum is issued by the seller when a customer is allowed a reduction from the original price for defective goods.
   c. Incorrect.
   d. Incorrect.

4. a. *Correct*. When the seller prepays the transportation costs and the terms of sale are FOB shipping point, the seller records the payment of the transportation costs by debiting Accounts Receivable. This is because transportation costs are the responsibility of the buyer when the terms are FOB shipping point.
   b. Incorrect.
   c. Incorrect.
   d. Incorrect.

5. a. Incorrect.
   b. Incorrect.
   c. *Correct*. If the seller collects sales tax at the time of sale, the seller credits the tax to Sales Tax Payable.
   d. Incorrect.

6. a. Incorrect. Accounts Receivable normally appears in the chart of accounts of both a merchandising and a service business.
   b. Incorrect. Advertising Expense normally appears in the chart of accounts of both a merchandising and a service business.
   c. *Correct*. Sales Returns and Allowances appears in the chart of accounts for a merchandising business but not for a service business.
   d. Incorrect. Accumulated Depreciation normally appears in the chart of accounts of both a merchandising and a service business.

7. a. *Correct*. The excess of net revenue from sales over the cost of merchandise sold is gross profit.
   b. Incorrect. Operating profit, sometimes called income from operations, is gross profit less selling and administrative expenses.
   c. Incorrect.
   d. Incorrect.

8. a. Incorrect. Income from operations is computed by subtracting from gross profit both selling and administrative expenses.
   b. Incorrect. Income from operations is computed by subtracting from gross profit both selling and administrative (general) expenses.
   c. Incorrect. Income from operations is computed by subtracting from gross profit both selling and administrative expenses.
   d. *Correct*. Income from operations is computed by subtracting operating expenses from gross profit. Operating expenses include both selling and administrative expenses.

9. a. Incorrect.
   b. Incorrect.
   c. Incorrect.
   d. **Correct**. After all adjusting entries are posted, the balances of all asset, liability, revenue, and expense accounts correspond exactly to the amounts in the financial statements.

10. a. Incorrect. Sales appears as revenue from operations.
    b. **Correct**. In a multiple-step income statement of a merchandising business, interest revenue would appear as "other income."
    c. Incorrect. Sales discounts are deducted from sales in reporting revenue from sales.
    d. Incorrect. Sales returns and allowances are deducted from sales in reporting revenue from sales.

True/False

1. T
2. F In a perpetual inventory system, purchases of merchandise are recorded in the merchandise inventory account, not the purchases account.
3. T
4. F A discount offered the purchaser of goods as a means of encouraging payment before the end of the credit period is known as a purchases discount, not a bank discount.
5. T
6. F If the seller is to absorb the cost of delivering the goods, the terms are stated FOB (free on board) destination, not FOB shipping point.
7. F The liability for the sales tax is incurred at the time the seller sells the merchandise, not when the seller receives payment from the buyer.
8. T
9. T
10. F The work sheet procedures for a merchandising business are similar to, not significantly different from, those of a service business.
11. F The physical inventory taken at the end of the period is normally smaller, not larger, than the amount of the balance of the merchandise inventory account.
12. F Any merchandise inventory shrinkage is normally debited to the cost of merchandise sold account, not the merchandise inventory account.
13. F Expenses incurred directly and entirely in connection with the sale of merchandise are called selling expenses, not administrative expenses.
14. F Revenue from sources such as income from interest, rent, dividends, and gains resulting from the sale of fixed assets is classified as "other income," not income from operations.
15. T
16. T
17. T
18. F The traditional balance sheet arrangement of assets on the left-hand side with the liabilities and owner's equity on the right-hand side is called the account form, not the report form.
19. F After the adjusting and closing entries have been recorded and posted, the general ledger accounts that appear on the balance sheet *do* have balances. The general ledger accounts that appear in the income statement *do not* have balances. In addition, the owner's drawing account *does not* have a balance.
20. T

Exercise 6-1

(1)	Merchandise Inventory	5,000	
	Accounts Payable		5,000
(2)	Accounts Payable	5,000	
	Cash		4,900
	Merchandise Inventory		100

(3)	Merchandise Inventory	3,580	
	Accounts Payable		3,580
(4)	Accounts Payable	900	
	Merchandise Inventory		900
(5)	Accounts Payable	2,680	
	Cash		2,680

Exercise 6-2

(1)	Accounts Receivable	3,150	
	Sales		3,150
	Cost of Merchandise Sold	2,000	
	Merchandise Inventory		2,000
(2)	Cash	2,850	
	Sales		2,850
	Cost of Merchandise Sold	1,380	
	Merchandise Inventory		1,380
(3)	Cash	3,050	
	Credit Card Expense	100	
	Accounts Receivable		3,150
(4)	Accounts Receivable	4,500	
	Sales		4,500
	Accounts Receivable	150	
	Cash		150
	Cost of Merchandise Sold	3,100	
	Merchandise Inventory		3,100
(5)	Sales Returns and Allowances	400	
	Accounts Receivable		400
	Merchandise Inventory	275	
	Cost of Merchandise Sold		275
(6)	Cash	4,168	
	Sales Discounts	82	
	Accounts Receivable		4,250

Exercise 6-3

20--				
Jan.	3	Merchandise Inventory	25,000	
		Accounts Payable		25,000
	5	Accounts Payable	5,000	
		Merchandise Inventory		5,000
	12	Accounts Receivable	50,000	
		Sales		50,000
	12	Cost of Merchandise Sold	35,000	
		Merchandise Inventory		35,000
	13	Accounts Payable	20,000	
		Cash		19,600
		Merchandise Inventory		400

20--

Jan. 15	Sales Returns and Allowances	8,000	
	Accounts Receivable		8,000
15	Merchandise Inventory	5,600	
	Cost of Merchandise Sold		5,600
22	Cash	41,580	
	Sales Discounts	420	
	Accounts Receivable		42,000

Problem 6-1

20--

Sept. 3	Merchandise Inventory	8,500	
	Accounts Payable		8,500
4	Office Supplies	800	
	Cash		800
6	Accounts Receivable	4,000	
	Sales		4,000
6	Cost of Merchandise Sold	3,000	
	Merchandise Inventory		3,000
7	Accounts Payable	2,000	
	Merchandise Inventory		2,000
10	Merchandise Inventory	5,000	
	Cash		5,000
12	Accounts Receivable	5,500	
	Sales		5,500
12	Cost of Merchandise Sold	3,200	
	Merchandise Inventory		3,200
13	Accounts Payable	6,500	
	Cash		6,435
	Merchandise Inventory		65
16	Cash	3,920	
	Sales Discounts	80	
	Accounts Receivable		4,000
20	Cash	5,200	
	Credit Card Expense	300	
	Accounts Receivable		5,500
24	Accounts Receivable	3,000	
	Sales		3,000
24	Cost of Merchandise Sold	1,750	
	Merchandise Inventory		1,750
26	Cash	2,200	
	Sales		2,200
26	Cost of Merchandise Sold	1,400	
	Merchandise Inventory		1,400

20--
Sept. 30	Sales Returns and Allowances......................	1,000	
	Accounts Receivable.............................		1,000
30	Merchandise Inventory.................................	600	
	Cost of Merchandise Sold		600

Problem 6-2

(a)

Miller Co.
Income Statement
For Year Ended March 31, 20--

Revenue from sales:			
Sales..		$1,016,700	
Less: Sales returns and allowances..........................		13,010	
Net sales			$1,003,690
Cost of merchandise sold			681,060
Gross profit			$ 322,630
Operating expenses:			
Selling expenses:			
Sales salaries expense	$78,250		
Delivery expense..	42,100		
Advertising expense...	13,090		
Depr. expense—delivery equip.	9,050		
Misc. selling expense	13,950		
Total selling expenses		$ 156,440	
Administrative expenses:			
Office salaries expense.......................................	$55,800		
Insurance expense..	16,000		
Office supplies expense	9,100		
Misc. administrative expenses	6,870		
Total administrative expenses..........................		87,770	
Total operating expenses			244,210
Income from operations			$ 78,420
Other income:			
Interest revenue..			1,020
Net income..			$ 79,440

(b)

Miller Co.
Income Statement
For Year Ended March 31, 20--

Revenues:			
Net sales...		$1,003,690	
Interest revenue..		1,020	
Total revenues		$1,004,710	
Expenses:			
Cost of merchandise sold...	$681,060		
Selling expenses	156,440		
Administrative expenses	87,770		
Total expenses..		925,270	
Net income..		$ 79,440	

(c)

Cost of Merchandise Sold...	4,200	
Merchandise Inventory		4,200

Problem 6-3

Miller Co.
Statement of Owner's Equity
For Year Ended March 31, 20--

R. W. Miller, capital, April 1, 20--		$193,650
Net income for year	$79,440	
Less withdrawals	30,000	
Increase in owner's equity		49,440
R. W. Miller, capital, March 31, 20--		$243,090

Problem 6-4

Miller Co.
Balance Sheet
March 31, 20--

Assets

Current assets:		
Cash	$ 43,100	
Notes receivable	6,000	
Accounts receivable	107,780	
Interest receivable	520	
Merchandise inventory	115,800	
Office supplies	1,250	
Prepaid insurance	8,740	
Total current assets		$283,190
Property, plant, and equipment:		
Delivery equipment	$ 60,150	
Less accumulated depreciation	22,950	
Total property, plant, and equipment		37,200
Total assets		$320,390

Liabilities

Current liabilities:		
Accounts payable	$ 75,300	
Salaries payable	2,000	
Total current liabilities		$ 77,300

Owner's Equity

R. W. Miller, capital		243,090
Total liabilities and owner's equity		$320,390

CHAPTER 7

Fill In the Blank—Part A

1. cash
2. remittance advice
3. voucher
4. due
5. electronics fund transfer (EFT)
6. bank reconciliation
7. deducted from
8. deducted from
9. depositor's records
10. cash equivalents

Fill In the Blank—Part B

1. detective
2. change
3. Other income
4. voucher
5. receiving report
6. petty cash
7. added to
8. added to
9. deducted from
10. doomsday

Multiple Choice

1. a. Incorrect. Since the treasurer is responsible for the custody of cash, the remittance advices should not be sent to the treasurer.
   b. Incorrect. Since the cashier's department handles cash, the remittance advices should not be sent to the cashier's department.
   c. **Correct.** For good internal control over cash receipts, remittance advices should be separated from cash received by mail and sent directly to the accounting department.
   d. Incorrect. Voucher clerks do not use remittance advices in carrying out their responsibilities.

2. a. Incorrect. Vouchers are not prepared by the treasurer.
   b. Incorrect. Vouchers are not paid immediately after they are prepared; they are filed and paid by the due date.
   c. Incorrect. Paid vouchers are filed numerically, not by due date.
   d. **Correct.** An important characteristic of the voucher system is the requirement that a voucher be prepared for each major expenditure.

3. a. Incorrect. The drawer is the one who signs the check, ordering payment by the bank.
   b. **Correct.** The bank on which a check is drawn is known as the drawee.
   c. Incorrect. The payee is the party to whom payment is to be made.
   d. Incorrect. The creditor is the party to whom payment is owed.

4. a. **Correct.** In a bank reconciliation, deposits not recorded by the bank are added to the balance according to the bank statement.
   b. Incorrect.
   c. Incorrect.
   d. Incorrect.

5. a. Incorrect.
   b. **Correct.** The amount of the outstanding checks is included on the bank reconciliation as a deduction from the balance per bank statement.
   c. Incorrect.
   d. Incorrect.

6. a. Incorrect.
   b. **Correct.** The entry required in the depositor's accounts for receipts from cash sales of $7,500, recorded incorrectly as $5,700, is a debit to Cash and a credit to Sales for $1,800.
   c. Incorrect.
   d. Incorrect.

7. a. Incorrect.
   b. **Correct.** The entry required in the depositor's accounts for a credit memorandum for a short-term, non-interest-bearing note collected by the bank is a debit to Cash and a credit to Notes Receivable.
   c. Incorrect.
   d. Incorrect.

8. a. Incorrect.
   b. Incorrect.
   c. Incorrect.
   d. **Correct.** No entry is required in the depositor's accounts to record outstanding checks.

9. a. Incorrect. Journal entries based on the bank reconciliation are also required on the depositor's books for deductions from the balance according to the depositor's records.
   b. Incorrect. Journal entries based on the bank reconciliation are also required on the depositor's books for additions to the balance according to the depositor's records.
   c. **Correct.** Journal entries based on the bank reconciliation are required on the depositor's books for both additions to the balance according to the depositor's records and deductions from the balance according to the depositor's records.
   d. Incorrect. Journal entries based on the bank reconciliation are not required on the depositor's books for additions to and deductions from the balance according to the bank's records.

10. **a.** ***Correct***. The entry to record the replenishment of the petty cash fund includes a debit to various expense and asset accounts and a credit to Cash.
    b. Incorrect.
    c. Incorrect.
    d. Incorrect.

True/False

1. F There are three parties to a check, not four. The three parties are the drawer, the drawee, and the payee.
2. F The drawer is the one who signs the check, ordering payment by the bank, not the one to whose order the check is drawn. The drawee is the bank on which the check is drawn.
3. F In a bank reconciliation, checks issued that have not been paid by the bank are deducted from, not added to, the balance according to the bank statement.
4. T
5. T
6. F A debit balance in the cash short and over account at the end of the fiscal period represents a miscellaneous administrative expense not income.
7. F It is *not* common practice for businesses to require that every payment of cash be evidenced by a check signed by the owner. Some small payments of cash are often made out of a petty cash fund.
8. T
9. F When a petty cash fund is replenished, the accounts debited are determined by summarizing the petty cash receipts. Petty Cash is only debited when the fund is initially established or increased.
10. T

Exercise 7-1

(2)	Cash	1,920		
	Notes Receivable		1,800	
	Interest Revenue		120	
(3)	Miscellaneous Administrative Expense	28		
	Cash		28	
(6)	Accounts Payable—Charlie's Optical Supply	100		
	Cash		100	

Exercise 7-2

(1)	Petty Cash	400.00	
	Cash		400.00
(2)	Office Supplies	80.25	
	Miscellaneous Selling Expense	115.33	
	Miscellaneous Administrative Expense	78.05	
	Cash Short and Over		1.97
	Cash		271.66

Problem 7-1

(1)

Dumont Co.
Bank Reconciliation
September 30, 20--

Balance according to bank statement		$ 8,510
Add deposit not recorded...		1,900
		$10,410
Deduct outstanding checks:		
No. 255..	$325	
No. 280..	100	
No. 295..	700	1,125
Adjusted balance		$ 9,285
Balance according to depositor's records............................		$ 7,540
Add: Error in recording Check No. 289..................................	$270	
Error in a deposit	720	
Note and interest collected by bank	780	1,770
		$ 9,310
Deduct bank service charge		25
Adjusted balance		$ 9,285

(2)	Sept. 30	Cash...	1,745	
		Miscellaneous Administrative Expense................	25	
		Accounts Payable...		270
		Accounts Receivable.....................................		720
		Notes Receivable		700
		Interest Revenue		80

CHAPTER 8

Fill In the Blank—Part A

1. receivables
2. note receivable
3. allowance
4. aging of receivables
5. $7,150
6. $32,500
7. $309,000
8. October 10
9. dishonored
10. accounts receivable turnover

Fill In the Blank—Part B

1. account
2. uncollectible accounts
3. direct write-off
4. $310,000
5. $10,400
6. maturity value
7. $153,750
8. December 16
9. number of days' sales in receivables
10. promissory

Multiple Choice

1. a. **Correct**. When the allowance method is used in accounting for uncollectible accounts, any uncollectible account is written off against the allowance account. The entry is a debit to the allowance account and a credit to the accounts receivable account.
   b. Incorrect.
   c. Incorrect.
   d. Incorrect. When the direct write-off method is used in accounting for uncollectible accounts, any uncollectible account is written off against the uncollectible accounts expense account.

2. a. Incorrect. When the allowance method is used in accounting for uncollectible accounts, any uncollectible account is written off against the allowance account.
   b. Incorrect.
   c. Incorrect.
   d. **Correct**. When the direct write-off method is used in accounting for uncollectible accounts, any uncollectible account is written off against the uncollectible accounts expense account. The entry is a debit to the uncollectible accounts expense account and a credit to the accounts receivable account.

3. a. Incorrect.
  b. Incorrect.
  c. Incorrect.
  d. ***Correct***. The allowance for doubtful accounts is a contra asset account, normally with a credit balance.

4. a. Incorrect.
  b. ***Correct***. If the allowance account has a credit balance of $170 at the end of the year before adjustments and if the estimate of uncollectible accounts based on aging the receivables is $3,010, the amount of the adjusting entry for uncollectible accounts is $2,840 ($3,010 – $170).
  c. Incorrect.
  d. Incorrect.

5. a. Incorrect.
  b. Incorrect.
  c. ***Correct***. If the allowance account has a debit balance of $250 at the end of the year before adjustments and if the estimate of uncollectible accounts based on sales for the period is $2,200, the amount of the adjusting entry for uncollectible accounts is $2,200. The balance of the allowance account does not affect the amount of the adjusting entry when the estimate is based upon sales.
  d. Incorrect.

6. a. Incorrect.
  b. ***Correct***. After the accounts are adjusted and closed at the end of the fiscal year, Accounts Receivable has a balance of $430,000 and Allowance for Doubtful Accounts has a balance of $25,000. The expected realizable value of the accounts receivable is $405,000 ($430,000 – $25,000).
  c. Incorrect.
  d. Incorrect.

7. a. Incorrect. The payee is the one to whose order the note is payable.
  b. Incorrect.
  c. ***Correct***. On a promissory note, the one making the promise to pay is called the maker.
  d. Incorrect.

8. a. Incorrect.
  b. Incorrect.
  c. Incorrect.
  d. ***Correct***. The amount that is due on a note at the maturity or due date is called the maturity value.

9. a. Incorrect.
  b. ***Correct***. The due date of a 90-day note dated July 1 is September 29, determined as follows: 30 days in July; 31 days in August; and 29 days in September.
  c. Incorrect.
  d. Incorrect.

10. a. Incorrect.
  b. Incorrect.
  c. ***Correct***. The maturity value of a 60-day, 12% note for $15,000, dated May 1, is $15,300 computed as follows: [$15,000 + ($15,000 × 60/360 × 12%)].
  d. Incorrect.

True/False

1. T
2. T
3. F The direct write-off method of accounting for uncollectible receivables provides for uncollectible accounts in the year when the account is determined to be worthless (uncollectible), not the year of sale.
4. T
5. T
6. F Notes do not include all money claims against people, organizations, or other debtors. An account receivable is another example of a money claim against people, organizations, or other debtors.

7. T
8. T
9. F When a note is received from a customer on account, it is recorded by debiting Notes Receivable and crediting Accounts Receivable, not Sales.
10. T

Exercise 8-1

(1)	Mar. 31	Allowance for Doubtful Accounts	3,150	
		Accounts Receivable—Jane Eades................		3,150
(2)	May 8	Accounts Receivable—Jane Eades	3,150	
		Allowance for Doubtful Accounts.....................		3,150
	8	Cash	3,150	
		Accounts Receivable—Jane Eades................		3,150

Exercise 8-2

(1)	Aug. 31	Uncollectible Accounts Expense	550	
		Accounts Receivable—Don Shore.................		550
(2)	Oct. 8	Accounts Receivable—Don Shore	550	
		Uncollectible Accounts Expense		550
	8	Cash	550	
		Accounts Receivable—Don Shore.................		550

Exercise 8-3

1. $80   **5.** $75
2. $35   **6.** $270
3. $60   **7.** $210
4. $60

Exercise 8-4

Walton Company
Balance Sheet
December 31, 20--

Assets

Current assets:

Cash		$ 37,500
Notes receivable..		20,000
Accounts receivable	$35,000	
Less allowance for doubtful accounts	1,200	33,800
Interest receivable		9,900
Total current assets		$101,200

Problem 8-1

(1)	Uncollectible Accounts Expense.............................	24,000	
	Allowance for Doubtful Accounts		24,000
(2)	Uncollectible Accounts Expense.............................	5,955	
	Allowance for Doubtful Accounts		5,955
(3)	Allowance for Doubtful Accounts	3,500	
	Accounts Receivable—Bentley Co.....................		3,500

(4) Accounts Receivable—Apple Co. 1,235
      Allowance for Doubtful Accounts.......................... 1,235

    Cash.. 1,235
      Accounts Receivable—Apple Co......................... 1,235

Problem 8-2

(1) Notes Receivable.. 8,000.00
      Accounts Receivable—Dave Davidson............... 8,000.00

(2) Accounts Receivable—Dave Davidson...................... 8,160.00*
      Interest Revenue 160.00
      Notes Receivable 8,000.00

(3) Cash... 8,184.93
      Interest Revenue 24.93**
      Accounts Receivable—Dave Davidson............... 8,160.00

(4) Notes Receivable.. 3,000.00
      Accounts Receivable—Sue Smith....................... 3,000.00

(5) Accounts Receivable—Sue Smith 3,075.00
      Interest Revenue 75.00
      Notes Receivable 3,000.00

    * \$8,000 × 60/360 × 12% = \$160; \$8,000 + \$160 = <u>\$8,160</u>
    ** \$8,160 × 10/360 × 11% = <u>\$24.93</u>

CHAPTER 9

Fill In the Blank—Part A

1. physical inventory
2. understated
3. understated
4. last-in, first-out (lifo)
5. \$1,270
6. lifo
7. lower-of-cost-or-market (LCM)
8. \$15,000
9. gross profit
10. inventory turnover

Fill In the Blank—Part B

1. overstated
2. understated
3. first-in, first-out (fifo)
4. average cost
5. \$1,388
6. net realizable value
7. \$45
8. retail inventory
9. \$120,000
10. number of days' sales in inventory

Multiple Choice

1. a. Incorrect. If merchandise inventory at the end of the period is understated, gross profit will be understated, not overstated.
   b. Incorrect. If merchandise inventory at the end of the period is understated, owner's equity will be understated, not overstated.
   c. **Correct.** If merchandise inventory at the end of the period is understated, net income will be understated because cost of merchandise sold will be overstated.
   d. Incorrect. If merchandise inventory at the end of the period is understated, cost of merchandise sold will be overstated, not understated.

2. a. **Correct.** If merchandise inventory at the end of period 1 is overstated and at the end of period 2 is correct, gross profit in period 2 will be understated because cost of merchandise sold will be overstated in period 2.
   b. Incorrect. If merchandise inventory at the end of period 1 is overstated and at the end of period 2 is correct, assets at the end of period 2 will be correct, not overstated.
   c. Incorrect. If merchandise inventory at the end of period 1 is overstated and at the end of period 2 is correct, owner's equity at the end of period 2 will be correct, not understated.
   d. Incorrect. If merchandise inventory at the end of period 1 is overstated and at the end of period 2 is correct, cost of merchandise sold in period 2 will be overstated, not understated.

3. a. ***Correct***. The total cost of the 15 units on hand at the end of the period, as determined under a perpetual inventory system and the lifo costing method, is $80 [(5 units × $6) + (10 units × $5)].
   b. Incorrect.
   c. Incorrect.
   d. Incorrect.

4. a. Incorrect.
   b. Incorrect.
   c. Incorrect.
   d. ***Correct***. The total cost of the 15 units on hand at the end of the period, as determined under a perpetual inventory system and the fifo costing method, is $120 (15 units × $8).

5. a. ***Correct***. The total cost of the 15 units on hand at the end of the period, as determined under a periodic inventory system and the lifo costing method, is $80 [(5 units × $6) + (10 units × $5)].
   b. Incorrect.
   c. Incorrect.
   d. Incorrect.

6. a. Incorrect.
   b. Incorrect.
   c. Incorrect.
   d. ***Correct***. The total cost of the 15 units on hand at the end of the period, as determined under a periodic inventory system and the fifo costing method, is $120 (15 units × $8).

7. a. Incorrect.
   b. Incorrect.
   c. ***Correct***. The total cost of the 15 units on hand at the end of the period, as determined under a periodic inventory system and the average costing method, is $99 (15 units × $6.60).
   d. Incorrect.

8. a. Incorrect. During a period of rising prices, the fifo inventory costing method will result in the highest amount of net income.
   b. ***Correct***. During a period of rising prices, the lifo inventory costing method will result in the lowest amount of net income.
   c. Incorrect. During a period of rising prices, the average inventory costing method will result in an amount of net income that is higher than lifo and lower than fifo.
   d. Incorrect. The perpetual inventory system is not an inventory costing method.

9. a. Incorrect. The lower of cost or market method is permitted under both the periodic and the perpetual inventory systems.
   b. Incorrect.
   c. Incorrect.
   d. ***Correct***. If the replacement price of an item of inventory is lower than its cost, the use of the lower of cost or market method reduces gross profit for the period in which the decline occurred.

10. a. Incorrect.
   b. Incorrect.
   c. ***Correct***. When lifo is strictly applied to a perpetual inventory system, the unit cost prices assigned to the ending inventory will not necessarily be those associated with the earliest unit costs of the period if at any time during a period the number of units of a commodity sold exceeds the number previously purchased during the same period.
   d. Incorrect.

True/False

1. F If merchandise inventory at the end of the period is understated, gross profit will be understated, not overstated. This is because cost of merchandise sold will be overstated.
2. F The two principal systems of inventory accounting are periodic and perpetual. Physical is not an inventory system.

3. T

4. F If merchandise inventory at the end of the period is overstated, owner's equity at the end of the period will be overstated, not understated. This is because cost of merchandise sold will be understated, and thus net income and owner's equity will be overstated.

5. F During a period of rising prices, the inventory costing method that will result in the highest amount of net income is fifo, not lifo. This is because fifo will assign the highest costs to inventory, and thus, cost of merchandise sold will be lower than lifo.

6. T

7. T

8. F As used in the phrase "lower of cost or market," *market* is the cost to replace the merchandise on the inventory date, not the selling price.

9. F When the retail inventory method is used, inventory at retail is converted to cost by multiplying the inventory at retail by the ratio of cost to selling (retail) price for the merchandise available for sale. The denominator is the selling (retail) price for the merchandise available for sale, not the replacement cost of the merchandise available for sale.

10. T

Exercise 9-1

Sales	Cost of Merchandise Sold	Gross Profit
(1) Correct	**(1)** Overstated	**(1)** Understated
(2) N/A	**(2)** $5,000	**(2)** $5,000

Net Income	Merchandise Inventory (October 31, 2000)
(1) Understated	**(1)** Understated
(2) $5,000	**(2)** $5,000

Current Assets	Total Assets	Liabilities
(1) Understated	**(1)** Understated	**(1)** Correct
(2) $5,000	**(2)** $5,000	**(2)** N/A

Owner's Equity
(1) Understated
(2) $5,000

Exercise 9-2

Sales			$875,000
Cost of merchandise sold:			
Merchandise inventory, July 1, 1999		$130,000	
Purchases		$600,000	
Less: Purchases returns and allowances	$45,000		
Purchases discounts	10,000	55,000	
Net purchases		$545,000	
Add transportation in		7,500	
Cost of merchandise purchased.........................		552,500	
Merchandise available for sale....................................		$682,500	
Less merchandise inventory, June 30, 2000		125,000	
Cost of merchandise sold...			557,500
Gross profit			$317,500

Exercise 9-3

	Cost	Total Lower of Cost or Market
Commodity A	$3,750	$3,600
Commodity B	2,760	2,760
Commodity C	1,450	1,200
Commodity D	1,440	1,290
Total.............	$9,400	$8,850

Problem 9-1

(1)

Date Purchased	Units	Price	Total Cost
November 1	12	$58	$696
Total	12		$696

(2)

Date Purchased	Units	Price	Total Cost
January 10	2	$48	$ 96
February 15	5	54	270
November 1	5	58	290
Total	12		$656

(3)

Date Purchased	Units	Price	Total Cost
November 1	12	$58	$696
Total	12		$696

(4)

Date Purchased	Units	Price	Total Cost
January 10	10	$48	$480
February 15	2	54	108
Total	12		$588

(5) Average unit cost: $\dfrac{\$11,485}{210} = \$54.69$

12 units in inventory @ $54.69 = $656.28

Problem 9-2

	(1) Fifo	(2) Lifo	(3) Average Cost
Sales	$2,240,000	$2,240,000	$2,240,000
Ending inventory	145,600	100,000	118,920
Cost of merchandise sold	1,638,300	1,683,900	1,664,980
Gross profit	601,700	556,100	575,020

Computation of Ending Inventory

Fifo:	Date Purchased	Units	Price	Total Cost
	November 1	100	$69	$ 6,900
	December 1	1,900	73	138,700
	Total	2,000		$145,600
Lifo:	January 1	2,000	50	$100,000

Average Cost: $\dfrac{\$1,783,900}{30,000} = \$59.46$

$59.46 × 2,000 = $118,920

Problem 9-3

		Cost	Retail
(1)	Merchandise inventory, August 1	$118,500	$170,000
	Purchases in August (net)	299,125	472,500
	Merchandise available for sale	$417,625	$642,500

Ratio of cost to retail

$$\frac{\$417,625}{\$642,500} = 65\%$$

		Cost	Retail
	Sales in August (net)		479,000
	Merchandise inventory, August 31, at retail		$163,500
	Merchandise inventory, August 31, at estimated cost ($163,500 × 65%)...		$106,275

(2)	Merchandise inventory, August 1		$118,500
	Purchases in August (net)		299,125
	Merchandise available for sale		$417,625
	Sales in August (net)	$479,000	
	Less estimated gross profit ($479,000 × 30%)........................	143,700	
	Estimated cost of merchandise sold...		335,300
	Estimated merchandise inventory, August 31		$ 82,325

CHAPTER 10

Fill In the Blank—Part A

1. fixed
2. land
3. machine
4. residual
5. units-of-production
6. book
7. 25%
8. $11,250
9. $25,000
10. $12,600
11. capital
12. betterment
13. trade-in allowance
14. $65,000
15. capital
16. depletion
17. amortization
18. patents
19. Patents
20. trademark

Fill In the Blank—Part B

1. land
2. depreciation
3. straight-line
4. declining-balance
5. 20%
6. $14,000
7. $32,000
8. $16,800
9. accelerated
10. revenue
11. extraordinary repair
12. boot
13. $70,000
14. operating
15. intangible
16. goodwill
17. copyright
18. Accumulated Depletion
19. current operating expenses
20. fixed assets to long-term liabilities

Multiple Choice

1. a. Incorrect.
   b. Incorrect.
   c. **Correct**. If unwanted buildings are located on land acquired for a plant site, the cost of their removal, less any salvage recovered, should be charged to the land account.
   d. Incorrect.

2. a. **Correct**. The depreciation method used most often in the financial statements is the straight-line method.
   b. Incorrect. The declining-balance method is the third most used method for financial statements.
   c. Incorrect. The units-of-production method is the second most used method for financial statements.
   d. Incorrect. The MACRS method is used to compute depreciation for tax purposes.

3. a. *Correct*. The depreciation method that would provide the highest reported net income in the early years of an asset's life would be the straight-line method.
    b. Incorrect. The declining-balance depreciation method is an accelerated depreciation method that provides more depreciation in the early years of an asset's life.
    c. Incorrect. The 150% straight-line depreciation method is an accelerated depreciation method that provides more depreciation in the early years of an asset's life.
    d. Incorrect. Accelerated depreciation methods provide more depreciation in the early years of an asset's life.

4. a. Incorrect.
    b. Incorrect.
    c. Incorrect.
    d. *Correct*. Using the declining-balance method (at twice the straight-line rate), the amount of depreciation for the first year of use of the equipment is $6,000 ($15,000 × 40%).

5. a. Incorrect.
    b. *Correct*. The depreciation expense on the equipment in Year 3 using the straight-line method would be $5,900, computed as follows: depreciation in Years 1 and 2 is $3,600 per year [($20,000 – $2,000) / 5 years]; book value at the end of Year 2 is $12,800 ($20,000 – $3,600 – $3,600); remaining depreciation is computed as $5,900 [($12,800 – $1,000) / 2 years].
    c. Incorrect.
    d. Incorrect.

6. a. Incorrect.
    b. *Correct*. The cost of rebuilding the drill press should be charged to the appropriate accumulated depreciation account since the rebuilding of the drill press is an extraordinary repair.
    c. Incorrect.
    d. Incorrect.

7. a. Incorrect. $15,600 is the list price of the new equipment. It must be reduced by the unrecognized gain on the old equipment to determine the cost of the new equipment.
    b. Incorrect. $15,300 is the accumulated depreciation of the old equipment plus the cash (boot) given of $9,000. It is not the cost of the new equipment.
    c. *Correct*. The new equipment should be recorded at $13,700 determined as follows: book value of old equipment is $4,700 ($11,000 – $6,300); trade-in value allowed on the old equipment is $6,600 ($15,600 – $9,000); gain on trade-in of the old equipment of $1,900 ($6,600 – $4,700) is not recognized and instead reduces the cost of the new equipment; thus, the cost of the new equipment is $13,700 ($15,600 – $1,900). Alternatively, the cost of the new equipment is the cash (boot) given, $9,000, plus the book value of the old equipment, $4,700.
    d. Incorrect. $9,000 is the cash (boot) given. It must be added to the book value of the old equipment to determine the cost of the new equipment.

8. a. Incorrect.
    b. *Correct*. The new equipment should be recorded at $15,600, the price of the new equipment. A loss of $600 would also be recorded on the trade-in of the old equipment computed as follows: book value of the old equipment is $4,700 ($11,000 – $6,300); trade-in value allowed on the old equipment is $4,100 ($15,600 – $11,500); loss on trade-in of the old equipment is $600 ($4,700 – $4,100).
    c. Incorrect.
    d. Incorrect.

9. a. Incorrect.
    b. Incorrect.
    c. Incorrect. The lessee is the party to whom the rights to use the asset are granted by the lessor.
    d. *Correct*. The lessor legally owns the asset.

10. a. *Correct*. Mineral ore deposits are natural resources with tangible characteristics.
    b. Incorrect. Patents do not have tangible characteristics and are intangible assets.
    c. Incorrect. Copyright do not have tangible characteristics and are intangible assets.
    d. Incorrect. Goodwill do not have tangible characteristics and are intangible assets.

True/False

1. T
2. T
3. F In using the declining-balance method, the asset should not be depreciated below the asset's residual value, not below the net book value.
4. T
5. T
6. T
7. F A lease that transfers ownership of the leased asset to the lessee at the end of the lease term should be classified as a capital lease, not an operating lease.
8. F Long-lived assets that are without physical characteristics but useful in the operations of a business are classified as intangible assets, not fixed assets.
9. T
10. F Intangible assets are usually reported on the balance sheet in a separate section immediately following fixed assets, not in the current asset section.

Exercise 10-1

(a) Straight-line method   Depreciation
Year 1 .... $50,000
Year 2 .... $50,000

(b) Declining-balance method   Depreciation
Year 1 .... $105,000
Year 2 .... $78,750

Exercise 10-2

Dec. 31   Depreciation Expense—Equipment 20,800
                Accumulated Depreciation—Equipment   20,800

Exercise 10-3

Mar. 8   Accumulated Depreciation—Fixtures   2,500
              Cash   2,000
                  Fixtures   4,000
                  Gain on Disposal of Assets   500

Exercise 10-4

Dec. 31   Depletion Expense 240,000
                Accumulated Depletion—Mineral Rights   240,000

Exercise 10-5

Dec. 31   Amortization Expense—Patents 20,000
                Patents   20,000

Problem 10-1

Year	Depreciation Expense Straight-Line	Depreciation Expense Declining-Balance	Depreciation Expense Units-of-Production
20xA	$18,750	$40,000	$17,000
20xB	18,750	20,000	20,000
20xC	18,750	10,000	30,000
20xD	18,750	5,000	8,000
Total	$75,000	$75,000	$75,000

Problem 10-2

(1)	Dec. 31	Depreciation Expense—Automobile......................	5,000	
		Accumulated Depreciation—Automobile		5,000
	Dec. 31	Depreciation Expense—Automobile......................	5,000	
		Accumulated Depreciation—Automobile		5,000
(2)	Dec. 31	Depreciation Expense—Automobile......................	10,000	
		Accumulated Depreciation—Automobile		10,000
	Dec. 31	Depreciation Expense—Automobile......................	2,500	
		Accumulated Depreciation—Automobile		2,500
(3)	Dec. 31	Depreciation Expense—Automobile......................	7,000	
		Accumulated Depreciation—Automobile		7,000
	Dec. 31	Depreciation Expense—Automobile......................	5,600	
		Accumulated Depreciation—Automobile		5,600

Problem 10-3

(a)	Apr. 30	Accumulated Depreciation—Truck........................	12,000	
		Truck	20,200	
		Truck...		15,000
		Cash..		17,200
(b)	Apr. 30	Accumulated Depreciation—Truck........................	12,000	
		Truck	20,700	
		Loss on Disposal of Fixed Assets	2,000	
		Truck...		15,000
		Cash..		19,700

CHAPTER 11

Fill In the Blank—Part A

1. $30,900
2. $84,600
3. gross
4. net pay
5. Federal Insurance Contributions Act (FICA)
6. employee's earnings record
7. paid
8. defined benefit
9. postretirement
10. quick

Fill In the Blank—Part B

1. $77,250
2. $232,000
3. discount
4. discount
5. net
6. payroll register
7. Medicare Tax
8. payroll
9. fringe
10. defined contribution

Multiple Choice

1. a. Incorrect.
   b. **Correct**. The interest charged by the bank, at the rate of 12%, on a 90-day, non-interest-bearing note payable for $75,000 is $2,250 ($75,000 × 12% × 90/360).
   c. Incorrect.
   d. Incorrect.

2. a. **Correct**. The cost of a product warranty should be included as an expense in the period of the sale of the product.
   b. Incorrect.
   c. Incorrect.
   d. Incorrect.

3. a. Incorrect. $440 is the employee's gross pay.
   b. Incorrect. $374 doesn't deduct the FICA or Medicare withholdings.
   c. **Correct**. The employee's net pay for the week is $341, computed as follows: gross pay is $440 [($8 × 40 hours) + ($12 × 10 hours)]; thus, net pay is [$440 − ($440 × 6%) − ($440 × 1.5%) − ($440 × 15%)].
   d. Incorrect.

4. a. Incorrect.
   b. Incorrect. The gross pay is the earnings before any deductions such as federal income tax withholding.
   c. Incorrect.
   d. **Correct**. The gross pay for the employee is $855, computed as [($18 × 40 hours) + ($27 × 5 hours)].

5. a. Incorrect.
   b. Incorrect.
   c. **Correct**. The employer's total FICA tax (social security and Medicare) for this payroll period is $102, computed as [($200 × 6%) + ($1,000 × 6%) + ($1,000 × 1.5%) + ($1,000 × 1.5%)].
   d. Incorrect. The FICA tax is limited to $200 on the first employee ($80,000 − $79,800) rather than the full $1,000.

6. a. Incorrect.
   b. Incorrect.
   c. Incorrect.
   d. **Correct**. Payroll taxes levied against employees become liabilities at the time the liability for the employee's wages is paid.

7. a. Incorrect. Vacations are a fringe benefit.
   b. Incorrect. Employee pension plans are a fringe benefit.
   c. Incorrect. Health insurance is a fringe benefit.
   d. **Correct**. FICA benefits are not considered a fringe benefit.

8. a. **Correct**. For proper matching of revenues and expenses, the estimated cost of fringe benefits must be recognized as an expense of the period the employee earns the benefit.
   b. Incorrect.
   c. Incorrect.
   d. Incorrect.

9. a. Incorrect. Number of hours worked is a variable input in a payroll system.
   b. Incorrect. Vacation credits is a variable input in a payroll system.
   c. **Correct**. Number of income tax withholding allowances is a constant in a payroll system, not a variable input.
   d. Incorrect. Number of days sick leave with pay is a variable input in a payroll system.

10. a. Incorrect. A payroll register is an aid in internal control, but it does not aid in indicating employee attendance.
    b. Incorrect. An employee earnings record is an aid in internal control, but it does not aid in indicating employee attendance.
    c. **Correct**. "In and Out" cards are an aid in internal control over payrolls that indicates employee attendance.
    d. Incorrect. Payroll checks are an aid in internal control, but they do not aid in indicating employee attendance.

True/False

1. T
2. F Both employers and employees are required to contribute to the Federal Insurance Contributions Act program.
3. F Not all states require that unemployment compensation taxes be withheld from employees' pay.
4. F Employers are subject to federal and state payroll taxes based on the amount paid to their employees, not the amount earned by their employees.

5. F The amounts withheld from employees' earnings do not have an effect on the firm's debits to the salary or wage expense accounts.

6. T

7. F The recording procedures when special payroll checks are used are the same as when the checks are drawn on the regular bank account.

8. T

9. T

10. F In order for revenues and expenses to be matched properly, a liability to cover the cost of a product warranty should be recorded in the period when the product is sold, not repaired.

11. T

12. T

13. F The net periodic pension cost of a defined benefit plan is debited to Pension Expense, the amount funded is credited to Cash, and any unfunded amount is credited to Unfunded Pension Liability, not Revenue.

14. T

15. F The rate used by a bank in discounting a note is called the discount rate, not the prime rate.

Exercise 11-1

(1) $770
(2) $60
(3) $45
(4) $727.50

Exercise 11-2

(1)	Dec. 31	Vacation Pay Expense	3,225	
		Vacation Pay Payable		3,225
(2)	Dec. 31	Product Warranty Expense	4,500	
		Product Warranty Payable		4,500
(3)	Dec. 31	Pension Expense	40,000	
		Cash		27,500
		Unfunded Accrued Pension Cost		12,500

Problem 11-1

(1)	Dec. 7	Sales Salaries Expense	34,000	
		Office Salaries Expense	16,000	
		Social Security Tax Payable		3,000
		Medicare Tax Payable		750
		Employees Income Tax Payable		7,500
		Union Dues Payable		900
		United Way Payable		450
		Salaries Payable		37,400
(2)	Dec. 7	Salaries Payable	37,400	
		Cash		37,400
(3)	Dec. 7	Payroll Taxes Expense	6,850	
		Social Security Tax Payable		3,000
		Medicare Tax Payable		750
		State Unemployment Tax Payable		2,700
		Federal Unemployment Tax Payable		400
(4)	Dec. 7	Payroll Taxes Expense	3,150	
		Social Security Tax Payable		2,400
		Medicare Tax Payable		750

Problem 11-2

				Employer's Taxes				
Employee	Annual Earnings	Social Security Tax	Medicare Tax	Social Security Tax	Medicare Tax	State Unemployment	Federal Unemployment	Total
Avery	$ 12,000	$ 720	$ 180	$ 720	$ 180	$ 378	$ 56	$ 1,334
Johnson	5,000	300	75	300	75	270	40	685
Jones	59,000	3,540	885	3,540	885	378	56	4,859
Smith	73,000	4,200	1,095	4,200	1,095	378	56	5,729
Wilson	141,000	4,800	2,115	4,800	2,115	378	56	7,349
Total	$290,000	$13,560	$4,350	$13,560	$4,350	$1,782	$264	$19,956

Problem 11-3

(1)	Accounts Payable—Mayday Co.	2,000	
	Notes Payable		2,000
(2)	Notes Payable	2,000	
	Interest Expense	60	
	Cash		2,060
(3)	Cash	8,000	
	Notes Payable		8,000
(4)	Notes Payable	8,000	
	Interest Expense	220	
	Notes Payable		8,220
(5)	Cash	5,910	
	Interest Expense	90	
	Notes Payable		6,000
(6)	Notes Payable	6,000	
	Cash		6,000

CHAPTER 12

Fill In the Blank—Part A

1. stock
2. stockholders' equity
3. retained earnings
4. $995,000
5. outstanding
6. common
7. nonparticipating
8. $100,000
9. premium
10. $160,000
11. treasury
12. none
13. dividend
14. $32,500
15. retained earnings

Fill In the Blank—Part B

1. stockholders
2. paid-in
3. deficit
4. stated
5. preferred
6. cumulative
7. $140,000
8. discount
9. $32,500 decrease
10. $895,000
11. stock split
12. $36
13. stock dividend
14. par
15. dividend yield

Multiple Choice

1. a. Incorrect. Ownership represented by shares of stock is a characteristic of the corporate form of organization.
   b. Incorrect. Separate legal existence is a characteristic of the corporate form of organization.
   c. ***Correct***. Unlimited liability of stockholders is not a characteristic of the corporate form of organization. Rather, stockholders of a corporation have limited liability that limits the liability to the amount invested.
   d. Incorrect. Earnings subject to the federal income tax is a characteristic of the corporate form of organization.

2. a. Incorrect. The stated value is the amount the board of directors assigns to no-par stock.
b. Incorrect. The premium is the amount by which the issue price of a stock exceeds its par.
c. Incorrect. The discount is the amount by which the par value of a stock exceeds its issue price.
d. **Correct**. The amount printed on a stock certificate is known as par value.

3. a. Incorrect.
b. Incorrect.
c. **Correct**. The amount of preferred dividends that must be declared in the current year before a dividend can be declared on common stock is $150,000, computed as $120,000 dividends in arrears [(5,000 shares × $6) × 4 years] plus the current year dividend of $30,000 (5,000 shares × $6).
d. Incorrect.

4. a. Incorrect.
b. **Correct**. When a corporation purchases its own stock, Treasury Stock is debited for the cost of the stock.
c. Incorrect.
d. Incorrect.

5. a. Incorrect. Retained Earnings is credited for the income of a period, not for the excess of proceeds from selling treasury stock over its cost.
b. Incorrect. Premium on Capital Stock is credited for the issuance of new stock at a price exceeding the par or stated value of the stock.
c. Incorrect. A corporation cannot have gains and losses from trading its stock.
d. **Correct**. The excess of the proceeds from selling treasury stock over its cost should be credited to Paid-In Capital from Sale of Treasury Stock.

6. a. Incorrect. The claims of preferred stockholders are satisfied after the claims of creditors upon liquidation of a corporation.
b. Incorrect. The claims of preferred stockholders are satisfied after the claims of creditors upon liquidation of a corporation.
c. Incorrect. The claims of common stockholders are satisfied last upon liquidation of a corporation
d. **Correct**. The claims of the creditors must first be satisfied upon liquidation of a corporation.

7. a. **Correct**. The amount transferred from the retained earnings account to paid-in capital accounts as a result of the stock dividend is $36,000, computed as [(12,000 shares × 5%) × $60].
b. Incorrect.
c. Incorrect. The amount transferred from the retained earnings account to paid-in capital accounts as a result of the stock dividend is based upon the market price of the stock, not the par value.
d. Incorrect.

8. a. Incorrect. 5,000 is the number of shares reacquired.
b. **Correct**. The number of shares outstanding is 55,000 shares, determined as the 60,000 shares issued minus the 5,000 shares reacquired.
c. Incorrect. 60,000 is the number of shares issued.
d. Incorrect. 100,000 is the number of shares authorized.

9. a. Incorrect. Donated Capital is credited for the fair value of assets donated to a corporation as an incentive to locate or remain in a community.
b. Incorrect. Retained Earnings is credited for the income of the period.
c. Incorrect. Treasury Stock is credited when reacquired shares are sold.
d. **Correct**. The entry to record the issuance of common stock at a price above par would include a credit to Paid-In Capital in Excess of Par—Common Stock.

10. a. Incorrect. The total stockholders' equity will decrease, not increase.
b. Incorrect. The total stockholders' equity will decrease, not increase.
c. Incorrect. The decrease is based upon the cost of the reacquired stock, not its par value.
d. **Correct**. The effect on total stockholders' equity of purchasing 10,000 shares of its own $20 par common stock for $35 per share is a decrease of $350,000 (10,000 shares × $35).

True/False

1. T
2. T
3. F   The two main sources of stockholders' equity are paid-in capital and retained earnings, not long-term debt.
4. F   The preferred stockholders have a greater chance of receiving regular dividends than do common stockholders, not vice versa.
5. T
6. T
7. F   Preferred stock for which dividend rights are limited to a certain amount is said to be nonparticipating, not noncumulative.
8. T
9. F   Sales of treasury stock result in a net increase, not decrease, in paid-in capital.
10. F   Expenditures incurred in organizing a corporation, such as legal fees, taxes, fees paid to the state, and promotional costs, are charged to an intangible asset account entitled Organization Costs, not Goodwill.
11. F   A commonly used method for accounting for the purchase and resale of treasury stock is the cost method, not the derivative method.
12. F   A major objective of a stock split is to reduce the market price per share of the stock. A stock split does not affect the amount of total stockholders' equity.
13. T
14. F   A liability for a dividend is normally recorded in the accounting records on the date of declaration, not the date of record.
15. T

Exercise 12-1

(1)	Cash	700,000	
	Common Stock		700,000
(2)	Cash	500,000	
	Common Stock		500,000
(3)	Cash	1,200,000	
	Common Stock		1,000,000
	Paid-In Capital in Excess of Par—Common Stock		200,000
(4)	Equipment	145,000	
	Common Stock		100,000
	Paid-In Capital in Excess of Par—Common Stock		45,000
(5)	Cash	300,000	
	Preferred Stock		250,000
	Paid-In Capital in Excess of Par—Preferred Stock		50,000

Exercise 12-2

(1)	Oct. 1	Treasury Stock	150,000	
		Cash		150,000
(2)	Oct. 31	Cash	65,600	
		Treasury Stock		60,000
		Paid-In Capital from Sale of Treasury Stock		5,600
(3)	Nov. 20	Cash	7,000	
		Paid-In Capital from Sale of Treasury Stock	500	
		Treasury Stock		7,500

Exercise 12-3

(1)	Feb. 20	Cash Dividends	60,000	
		Cash Dividends Payable..		60,000
(2)	Mar. 22	Cash Dividends Payable	60,000	
		Cash...		60,000
(3)	Dec. 15	Stock Dividends..	200,000	
		Stock Dividends Distributable................................		160,000
		Paid-In Capital in Excess of Par—Common Stock....		40,000
(4)	Jan. 14	Stock Dividends Distributable	160,000	
		Common Stock		160,000
(5)	Feb. 20	None		

Problem 12-1

(1)

Year	Total Dividends	Preferred Dividends		Common Dividends	
		Total	Per Share	Total	Per Share
1	$ 7,000	$7,000	$7	—0—	—0—
2	9,000	9,000	9	—0—	—0—
3	28,000	8,000	8	$20,000	$ 5
4	48,000	8,000	8	40,000	10

(2)

Year	Total Dividends	Preferred Dividends		Common Dividends	
		Total	Per Share	Total	Per Share
1	$ 7,000	$7,000	$7	—0—	—0—
2	9,000	8,000	8	$ 1,000	$ .25
3	28,000	8,000	8	20,000	5.00
4	48,000	8,000	8	40,000	10.00

Problem 12-2

		(1)	(2)	(3)
		Column A	Column B	Column C
		Before Any Dividend	After Cash Dividend	After Stock Dividend
a.	Total number of shares outstanding	100,000	100,000	105,000
b.	Total par value of shares outstanding	$2,500,000	$2,500,000	$2,625,000
c.	Total additional paid-in capital	$1,500,000	$1,500,000	$1,525,000
d.	Total retained earnings	$6,440,000	$6,290,000	$6,290,000
e.	Total stockholders' equity	$10,440,000	$10,290,000	$10,440,000
f.	Amount required to pay a $1.50 per share cash dividend next year	$150,000	$150,000	$157,500
g.	Percentage of total stock owned by Rafael..	1%	1%	1%
h.	Total number of shares owned by Rafael.	1,000	1,000	1,050
i.	Total par value of Rafael's shares	$25,000	$25,000	$26,250
j.	Total equity of Rafael's shares	$104,400	$102,900	$104,400

CHAPTER 13

Fill In the Blank—Part A

1. taxable
2. $150,000
3. discontinued
4. extraordinary items
5. loss from discontinued operations
6. earnings per share (eps)
7. prior-period adjustments
8. comprehensive
9. trading
10. temporary investments
11. equity
12. consolidation
13. subsidiary
14. pooling-of-interests
15. minority interest

Fill In the Blank—Part B

1. temporary
2. $25,000
3. extraordinary item
4. appropriation
5. stockholders' equity
6. equity
7. available-for-sale
8. unrealized
9. cost
10. merger
11. investments
12. parent
13. purchase
14. consolidated
15. price-earnings

Multiple Choice

1. a. **Correct**. The amount of income tax deferred to future years is $40,000 [($300,000 − $200,000) × 40%].
   b. Incorrect.
   c. Incorrect.
   d. Incorrect.

2. a. Incorrect. A method of recognizing revenue when the sale is made is used for financial statements, and a method of recognizing revenue at the time the cash is collected is used for tax reporting *does* result in a temporary difference.
   b. Incorrect. Warranty expense is recognized in the year of sale for financial statements and when paid for tax reporting *does* result in a temporary difference.
   c. Incorrect. An accelerated depreciation method is used for tax reporting, and the straight-line method is used for financial statements *does* result in a temporary difference.
   d. **Correct**. Interest income on municipal bonds is recognized for financial statements and not for tax reporting *does not* result in a temporary difference.

3. a. Incorrect. A correction of an error in the prior year's financial statements is a prior-period adjustment and would be reported in the statement of retained earnings.
   b. Incorrect. A gain resulting from the sale of fixed assets is not an extraordinary item, but it is reported as other income on the income statement.
   c. Incorrect. A loss on sale of temporary investments is not an extraordinary item, but it is reported as other income or loss on the income statement.
   d. **Correct**. A loss on condemnation of land is an extraordinary item on the income statement.

4. a. Incorrect. Earnings per share is not required to be presented on the face of the income statement for extraordinary items.
   b. Incorrect. Earnings per share is not required to be presented on the face of the income statement for discontinued operations.
   c. **Correct**. Earnings per share is required to be presented on the face of the income statement for income from continuing operations and net income.
   d. Incorrect.

5. a. Incorrect.
   b. **Correct**. All changes in stockholders' equity during a period except those resulting from investments by stockholders and dividends is the definition of comprehensive income.
   c. Incorrect.
   d. Incorrect.

6. a. Incorrect. Under the equity method, the receipt of cash dividends on a long-term investment in common stock is accounted for as a debit to Cash and a credit to the investment account, not Dividend Revenue.
   b. Incorrect.
   c. **Correct**. Under the cost method, the receipt of cash dividends on a long-term investment in common stock is accounted for as a debit to Cash and a credit to Dividend Revenue.
   d. Incorrect.

7. a. **Correct**. Under the equity method, the receipt of cash dividends on a long-term investment in common stock is accounted for as a debit to Cash and a credit to Investment in Spacek Inc.
   b. Incorrect.
   c. Incorrect. Under the cost method, the receipt of cash dividends on a long-term investment in common stock is accounted for as a debit to Cash and a credit to Dividend Revenue, not a credit to Investment in Spacek Inc.
   d. Incorrect.

8. a. Incorrect.
   b. **Correct**. The amount of net increase in the Investment in Subsidiary account for the year is $112,500, determined as [($200,000 × 75%) − ($50,000 × 75%)].
   c. Incorrect.
   d. Incorrect.

9. a. **Correct**. The amount of loss on the sale is $1,000, determined as [($96,000 / 800 shares) − $115] × 200 shares sold.
   b. Incorrect. A loss, not gain, was incurred on the sale.
   c. Incorrect.
   d. Incorrect.

10. a. Incorrect.
    b. Incorrect.
    c. **Correct**. The balance of the account Investment in Subsidiary would appear in the investments section of the parent company's balance sheet.
    d. Incorrect.

True/False

1. F   Income that is exempt from federal taxes, such as interest income on municipal bonds, is not an example of a temporary tax difference since it will not reverse or turn around in later years. Instead, such differences are sometimes called permanent differences.
2. T
3. T
4. T
5. F   Over the life of a business, temporary differences do not reduce the total amount of tax paid. Rather, temporary differences only affect when the taxes are paid.
6. F   An appropriation is a restriction of retained earnings. It is not a part of paid-in capital of the corporation.
7. T
8. T
9. F   Under the cost method of accounting for investments in stocks, the investor records its share of cash dividends as an increase in Dividend Revenue, not a decrease in the investment account. The cash account is also increased for the dividends received.
10. T
11. T
12. F   When two or more corporations transfer their assets and liabilities to a corporation that has been created for the purpose of the takeover, the combination is called a consolidation, not a merger. A merger is when one corporation acquires all the assets and liabilities of another corporation, which is then dissolved.

13. F When two or more corporations become affiliated by means of exchange of the voting stock of one corporation (the parent) for substantially all of the voting common stock of another corporation (the subsidiary), the transaction is termed a pooling of interests, not a purchase.

14. T

15. T

Exercise 13-1

(1)	Income Tax	220,000	
	Income Tax Payable...		128,000
	Deferred Income Tax Payable		92,000

(2)	Income Tax	200,000	
	Deferred Income Tax Payable.............................	40,000	
	Income Tax Payable..		240,000

Exercise 13-2

(1)	Income Tax	62,500	
	Cash...		62,500

(2)	Income Tax	30,000	
	Income Tax Payable..		30,000

Problem 13-1

Paid-in capital:

Preferred $10 stock, $100 par (10,000 shares authorized; 7,500 issued)	$ 750,000		
Excess over par	375,000	$1,125,000	
Common stock, $25 par (150,000 shares authorized; 100,000 issued)	$2,500,000		
Excess over par	500,000	3,000,000	
From sale of treasury stock...................................		4,000	
Total paid-in capital...		$4,129,000	
Retained earnings		1,000,000	
Total...		$5,129,000	
Deduct treasury common stock (1,000 shares at cost).....................		50,000	
Total stockholders' equity		$5,079,000	

Problem 13-2

(1)	(a)	Investment in Norris Inc. Stock	600,000	
		Cash..		600,000

	(b)	Cash (40,000 × $.75)	30,000	
		Investment in Norris Inc. Stock.............................		30,000

	(c)	Investment in Norris Inc. Stock ($900,000 × 25%)	225,000	
		Income of Norris Inc...		225,000

(2)	(a)	Investment in Kline Inc.	150,000	
		Cash..		150,000

	(b)	Cash	5,000	
		Dividend Revenue		5,000

	(c)	None		

Problem 13-3

Wess Corp.
Income Statement
For Year Ended March 31, 20--

Sales..	$2,500,000
Cost of merchandise sold..	1,800,000
Gross profit...	$ 700,000
Operating expenses..	100,000
Income from continuing operations before income tax................................	$ 600,000
Income tax..	176,000
Income from continuing operations...	$ 424,000
Loss on discontinued operations, net of applicable income tax of $20,000	(50,000)
Income before extraordinary item and cumulative effect of a change in accounting principle	$ 374,000
Extraordinary item:	
Loss from earthquake, net of applicable income tax of $48,000	(192,000)
Cumulative effect on prior years of changing to a different depreciation method, net of applicable income tax of $18,000	62,000
Net income	$ 244,000
Earnings per common share:	
Income from continuing operations..	$ 8.48
Loss on discontinued operations	(1.00)
Income before extraordinary item and cumulative effect of a change in accounting principle.......................................	$ 7.48
Extraordinary item...	(3.84)
Cumulative effect on prior years of changing to a different depreciation method...	1.24
Net income...	$ 4.88

CHAPTER 14

Fill In the Blank—Part A

1. bond indenture (or trust indenture)
2. callable
3. debenture bonds
4. contract (or coupon)
5. premium
6. future value
7. $909.09 ($1,000 × 0.90909)
8. $17,125 ($10,000 × 1.71252)
9. straight-line
10. effective interest rate
11. sinking fund
12. carrying amount
13. $388,000 ($400,000 − $12,000)
14. $2,030,000
15. $103,650 [($100,000 × 1.03) + $650]
16. Interest Revenue
17. Investment in Bonds
18. $2,000 (loss)
19. held-to-maturity security
20. 12.6 [(29,000,000 + 2,500,000) / 2,500,000]

Fill In the Blank—Part B

1. term
2. convertible
3. discount
4. $712.99 ($1,000 × .71299)
5. $67,803 ($12,000 × 5.65022)
6. annuity
7. $10,000 (gain)
8. Investments
9. Long-term liabilities
10. Long-term liabilities
11. Investments
12. $73,850 [($75,000 × .98) + $350]
13. $5,045,000
14. $240,000 ($4,000,000 × .12 × 6/12)
15. $28,000 ($280,000 / 10 periods)
16. $120,000 ($4,000,000 × .12 × 3/12)
17. remains the same
18. number of times interest charges earned
19. 8.33 [(60,500,000 + 8,250,000) / 8,250,000]
20. present value

Multiple Choice

1. a. ***Correct***. A bond that gives the bondholder a right to exchange the bond for other securities under certain conditions is called a convertible bond.
   b. Incorrect. A bond sinking fund is a special fund in which amounts are set aside for the payment of a bond issue at its maturity date.
   c. Incorrect. Term bonds refers to bonds of an issue that all mature at the same time.
   d. Incorrect. Bonds issued on the basis of the general credit of the corporation are called debenture bonds.

2. a. Incorrect.
   b. ***Correct***. The present value of $2,000 to be paid in one year at a current interest rate of 6% is $1,887 ($2,000 / 1.06).
   c. Incorrect. The present value must be less than the amount to be received at the end of one year.
   d. Incorrect. The present value must be less than the amount to be received at the end of one year.

3. a. Incorrect.
   b. ***Correct***. The entry to record the amortization of a discount on bonds payable is a debit to Interest Expense and a credit to Discount on Bonds Payable.
   c. Incorrect.
   d. Incorrect.

4. a. Incorrect.
   b. Incorrect.
   c. ***Correct***. Under the straight-line method of bond discount amortization, as a bond payable approaches maturity, the total yearly amount of interest expense will remain the same.
   d. Incorrect.

5. a. Incorrect. The cost of the bond is more than its face value, since it was purchased at a premium.
   b. Incorrect. The cost of the bond also includes the brokerage commission.
   c. ***Correct***. The total cost to be debited to the investment account is $1,048 [($1,000 × 1.04) + $8].
   d. Incorrect.

6. a. Incorrect.
   b. Incorrect.
   c. Incorrect.
   d. ***Correct***. The interest method of amortizing bond discount or premium is required by generally accepted accounting principles.

7. a. Incorrect.
   b. Incorrect. Investments in bonds or other debt securities that management intends to hold to their maturity are called held-to-maturity securities.
   c. Incorrect. Sinking-bond funds are special funds in which amounts are set aside for the payment of bond issues at their maturity dates.
   d. ***Correct***. Bonds that do not provide for any interest payments are called zero-coupon bonds.

8. a. Incorrect. The present value is the value today of an amount to be received at a future date.
   b. Incorrect. The estimated worth in the future of an amount of cash on hand today invested at a fixed rate of interest is the future value.
   c. ***Correct***. The principal of each bond is also called the face value.
   d. Incorrect.

9. a. ***Correct***. A special fund accumulated over the life of a bond issue and kept separate from other assets in order to provide for payment of bonds at maturity is called a sinking fund.
   b. Incorrect.
   c. Incorrect.
   d. Incorrect.

10. a. Incorrect.
b. **Correct**. Held-to-maturity securities are classified on the balance sheet as investments.
c. Incorrect.
d. Incorrect.

True/False

1. F The interest rate specified on the bond indenture is called the contract rate. It is not called the effective rate, which is sometimes called the market rate.
2. F If the market rate is lower than the contract rate, the bonds will sell at a premium, not a discount.
3. T
4. T
5. F Bonds that may be exchanged for other securities under certain conditions are called convertible bonds, not callable bonds. Callable bonds are bonds that a corporation reserves the right to redeem before their maturity.
6. F When cash is transferred to the sinking fund, it is recorded in an account called Sinking Fund Cash, not Sinking Fund Investments. When investments are purchased with the sinking fund cash, the investments are recorded in Sinking Fund Investments.
7. T
8. T
9. T
10. T

Exercise 14-1

(1)	June 1	Cash	500,000	
		Bonds Payable...		500,000
	Dec. 1	Interest Expense	30,000	
		Cash...		30,000
(2)	Apr. 1	Cash	942,645	
		Discount on Bonds Payable...	57,355	
		Bonds Payable...		1,000,000
	Oct. 1	Interest Expense	57,868	
		Discount on Bonds Payable ($57,355 / 20)...............		2,868
		Cash...		55,000
(3)	Mar. 1	Cash	743,625*	
		Premium on Bonds Payable		43,625
		Bonds Payable...		700,000

*$700,000 × .3769 (present value of $1 for 20 periods at 5%)   263,830
$38,500 × 12.4622 (present value of an annuity of $1 for 20 periods at 5%)   479,795
Total present value of bonds   743,625

	Sept. 1	Interest Expense	36,319	
		Premium on Bonds Payable ($43,625 / 20)	2,181	
		Cash...		38,500

Exercise 14-2

(1)	Bonds Payable...	5,000,000	
	Loss on Redemption of Bonds Payable	50,000	
	Cash		5,050,000
(2)	Bonds Payable...	5,000,000	
	Cash		4,900,000
	Gain on Redemption of Bonds Payable		100,000

Exercise 14-3

(1) Oct. 1   Investment in Elgin Inc. Bonds ($400,000 × .99) 396,000
Interest Revenue 10,000
　　　　Cash 406,000

(2) Dec. 31   Cash 20,000
Interest Revenue 20,000

(3) Dec. 31   Investment in Elgin Inc. Bonds 120
Interest Revenue 120

(4) Dec. 1   Cash 424,667
　　　　Investment in Elgin Inc. Bonds 397,040
　　　　Interest Revenue 16,667
　　　　Gain on Sale of Investments 10,960

Problem 14-1

(1) (a) Present value of $1 at compound interest of 5½% in 20
　　　　semiannual periods .... .3427
Face amount of bonds .... × $2,000,000 $ 685,400

Present value of annuity of $1 for 20 periods at 5½% 11.9504
Semiannual interest payments .... × $ 110,000   1,314,544

Proceeds of bonds (present value) $1,999,944

Note: The difference of $56 between the face value of the
bonds and the present value is due to rounding.

(b) There is no premium or discount on the bond issuance.

(2) (a) Present value of $1 at compound interest of 6% in 20
　　　　semiannual periods .... .3118
Face amount of bonds .... × $2,000,000 $ 623,600

Present value of annuity of $1 for 20 periods at 6% 11.4699
Semiannual interest payments .... × $ 110,000   1,261,689

Proceeds of bonds (present value) $1,885,289

(b) The discount is $114,711 on the bond issuance.

(3) (a) Present value of $1 at compound interest of 5% in 20
　　　　semiannual periods .... .3769
Face amount of bonds .... × $2,000,000 $ 753,800

Present value of annuity of $1 for 20 periods at 5% 12.4622
Semiannual interest payments .... × $ 110,000   1,370,842

Proceeds of bonds (present value) $2,124,642

(b) The premium is $124,642 on the bond issuance.

Problem 14-2

(1) Dec. 31   Cash 531,161
　　　　Bonds Payable 500,000
　　　　Premium on Bonds Payable 31,161

(2) June 30   Interest Expense ($27,500 − $1,558) 25,942
Premium on Bonds Payable ($31,161 / 20) 1,558
　　　　Cash 27,500

(3)	Dec. 31	Interest Expense ($27,500 – $1,558)	25,942	
		Premium on Bonds Payable ($31,161 / 20)	1,558	
		Cash		27,500
(4)	Dec. 31	Bonds Payable	250,000	
		Premium on Bonds Payable [($31,161 – $1,558 – $1,558) / 2]	14,023	
		Gain on Redemption of Bonds		6,523
		Cash		257,500

Problem 14-3

(1)	Jan. 1	Cash	885,295	
		Discount on Bonds Payable	114,705	
		Bonds Payable		1,000,000
(2)	June 30	Interest Expense ($50,000 + $5,735)	55,735	
		Discount on Bonds Payable ($114,705 / 20)		5,735
		Cash		50,000
(3)	Dec. 31	Interest Expense ($50,000 + $5,735)	55,735	
		Discount on Bonds Payable ($114,705 / 20)		5,735
		Cash		50,000
(4)	Dec. 31	Bonds Payable	500,000	
		Loss on Redemption of Bonds	41,618	
		Discount on Bonds Payable [($114,705 – $5,735 – $5,735) / 2]		51,618
		Cash		490,000

CHAPTER 15

Fill In the Blank—Part A

1.	statement of cash flows	10.	decreased
2.	direct indirect	11.	$34,250
		12.	$102,000
		13.	$195,000
3.	operating	14.	$60,000
4.	investing	15.	$49,500
5.	investing	16.	$1,040,000
6.	financing	17.	$330,000
7.	investing	18.	financing
8.	increased	19.	$60,000
9.	decreased	20.	cash flow per share

Fill In the Blank—Part B

1.	indirect	11.	added to
2.	operating	12.	$330,000
3.	direct	13.	$746,250
4.	financing	14.	$3,125,000
5.	financing	15.	$46,000
6.	operating	16.	$20,000
7.	financing	17.	retained earnings
8.	investing	18.	$51,000
9.	noncash	19.	operating
10.	deducted from	20.	free cash flow

Multiple Choice

1. a. Incorrect. The cash flows from financing activities is a major section of the statement of cash flows.
    b. **Correct.** The cash flows from selling activities is not a major section of the statement of cash flows.
    c. incorrect. The cash flows from operating activities is a major section of the statement of cash flows.
    d. Incorrect. The cash flows from investing activities is a major section of the statement of cash flows.

2. a. Incorrect. Noncash investing and financing activities are not reported within the statement of cash flows because cash is not affected by these transactions.
    b. **Correct.** Although noncash investing and financing activities do not affect cash, these transactions are disclosed in a separate schedule that accompanies the statement of cash flows. This helps users interpret major investing and financing transactions that involve stock swaps, asset swaps, and other noncash events.

c. Incorrect. Noncash investing and financing activities are not reported within the statement of retained earnings because this statement shows the events that influence retained earnings, such as net income and dividends.

d. Incorrect. Noncash investing and financing activities are not reported in the footnotes to the balance sheet.

3. a. Incorrect. Depreciation is added to net income in deriving cash flows from operating activities under the indirect method.

b. Incorrect. Decreases in current assets are added to net income in deriving cash flows from operating activities under the indirect method.

c. *Correct.* Decreases in current liabilities are subtracted from net income in deriving cash flows from operating activities under the indirect method. This is because expenses have been accrued but not paid. Thus, the expenses overstate the amount of cash that has been spent on operating activities.

d. Incorrect. A loss on sale of equipment is added to net income in deriving cash flows from operating activities under the indirect method.

4. a. Incorrect.

b. Incorrect.

c. Incorrect.

d. *Correct.* The cash paid for dividends is $40,000 declared plus the difference between the beginning and ending dividend payable ($12,000 − $10,000), or $40,000 + $12,000 − $10,000.

5. a. Incorrect. The increase in accrued expenses is deducted from operating expenses under the direct method.

b. Incorrect. The decrease in prepaid expenses is deducted from operating expenses under the direct method.

c. Incorrect. The increase in income taxes payable is deducted from operating expenses under the direct method.

d. *Correct.* The increase in prepaid expenses is added to operating expenses under the direct method. The increase in a prepaid expense causes cash to be paid before the expense is recorded; hence, the increase must be added to the expense to reflect the cash outflow.

6. a. Incorrect. The receipt of cash from the sale of land is a cash flow from an investing activity.

b. Incorrect. The receipt of cash from the collection of accounts receivable is a cash flow from operating activities.

c. *Correct.* The payment of cash for the acquisition of treasury stock is a cash flow from a financing activity.

d. Incorrect. The payment of cash for new machinery is a cash flow from an investing activity.

7. a. Incorrect. The retained earnings does not appear on the statement of cash flows.

b. *Correct.* Cash received from customers is the first line when preparing the statement of cash flows under the direct method.

c. Incorrect. The net income appears first when preparing the statement of cash flows under the indirect method.

d. Incorrect. Depreciation is added to net income in the statement of cash flows under the indirect method, but it does not even appear under the direct method.

8. a. *Correct.* The withdrawal of cash by the owner of a business is a financing activity, similar to a dividend.

b. Incorrect. The issuance of common stock to retire long-term debt is a transaction that exchanges long-term debt for capital stock, so it is a noncash investing and financing activity.

c. Incorrect. The acquisition of a manufacturing plant by issuing bonds exchanges a fixed asset for long-term debt, so it is a noncash investing and financing activity.

d. Incorrect. The issuance of common stock in exchange for convertible preferred stock exchanges two types of capital stock, so it is a noncash investing and financing activity.

9. a. ***Correct.*** The increase in inventories uses more cash than is shown by the cost of goods sold; thus, the increase in inventories must be added to cost of goods sold to reflect the payment of cash for merchandise.
   b. Incorrect. The increase in accounts payable uses less cash than is shown by the cost of goods sold; thus, the increase in accounts payable must be deducted from cost of goods sold to reflect the payment of cash for merchandise.
   c. Incorrect. The decrease in inventories uses less cash than is shown by the cost of goods sold; thus, the decrease in inventories must be deducted from cost of goods sold to reflect the payment of cash for merchandise.
   d. Incorrect. The decrease in accounts receivable does not impact the cash paid for merchandise, but it impacts the cash received from customers.

10. a. Incorrect.
    b. Incorrect.
    c. ***Correct.*** The cash paid for income taxes is part of the cash flow from operating activities under the direct method.
    d. Incorrect.

11. a. Incorrect. The loss should not be added to the book value of the land.
    b. Incorrect. The loss should not be deducted from net income on the statement of cash flows.
    c. ***Correct.*** The loss should be deducted from the book value of the land in determining the cash flow from investing activities.
    d. Incorrect. The loss should not be deducted from net income on the statement of cash flows.

True/False

1. T
2. T
3. T
4. F Only cash receipts and payments from operations are evaluated under the direct method; thus, depreciation is not analyzed under the direct method.
5. F Increases in current liabilities are added to net income under the indirect method because expense accruals exceed cash payments when current liabilities increase.
6. T
7. T
8. T
9. F Both the direct and indirect methods report the same cash flows from operating activities; thus, neither method is more accurate than the other.
10. T

Exercise 15-1

	Cash Flows From			Schedule of Noncash Investing and Financing Activities
Item	Operating Activities	Investing Activities	Financing Activities	
1. Decrease in prepaid expenses	✔			
2. Retirement of bonds			✔	
3. Proceeds from sale of investments		✔		
4. Increase in inventories	✔			
5. Issuance of common stock			✔	
6. Purchase of equipment		✔		

Item	Cash Flows From			Schedule of Noncash Investing and Financing Activities
	Operating Activities	Investing Activities	Financing Activities	
7. Cash dividends paid			✔	
8. Acquisition of building in exchange for bonds				✔
9. Amortization of patents	✔			
10. Amortization of discount on bonds payable	✔			

Exercise 15-2

Cash flows from operating activities:		
Net income, per income statement		$150,000
Add: Depreciation	$45,000	
Decrease in prepaid expenses	2,625	
Increase in accounts payable	17,000	64,625
		$214,625
Deduct: Increase in trade receivables	$10,000	
Increase in inventories	15,625	
Decrease in salaries payable	3,000	28,625
Net cash flow from operating activities		$186,000

Exercise 15-3

Cash flows from operating activities:		
Cash received from customers		$520,000
Deduct: Cash payments for merchandise	$128,625	
Cash payments for operating expenses	160,375	
Cash payments for income tax	45,000	334,000
Net cash flow from operating activities		$186,000

Supporting calculations:

Sales (reported on income statement)	$530,000
Less increase in trade receivables	(10,000)
Cash received from customers	$520,000
Cost of merchandise sold	$130,000
Plus increase in inventories	15,625
Less increase in accounts payable	(17,000)
Cash payments for merchandise	$128,625
Operating expenses (other than depreciation)	$160,000
Less decrease in prepaid expenses	(2,625)
Plus decrease in salaries payable	3,000
Cash payments for operating expenses	$160,375

Problem 15-1

Stellar Inc.
Statement of Cash Flows
For Year Ended December 31, 2004

Cash flows from operating activities:			
Net income, per income statement		$114,000	
Add: Depreciation	$48,000		
Decrease in inventories	6,000		
Decrease in prepaid expenses	2,400		
Increase in accounts payable	7,200	63,600	
		$177,600	
Deduct: Increase in trade receivables	$12,000		
Gain on sale of land	18,000	30,000	
Net cash flow from operating activities			$147,600
Cash flows from investing activities:			
Cash received from land sold		$ 54,000	
Less cash paid for purchase of equipment		96,000	
Net cash flow used for investing activities			(42,000)
Cash flows from financing activities:			
Cash used to retire bonds payable		$ 60,000	
Cash paid for dividends		27,600*	
Net cash flow used for financing activities			(87,600)
Increase in cash			$ 18,000
Cash, January 1, 2004			66,000
Cash, December 31, 2004			$ 84,000

*30,000 + 21,600 − 24,000

Schedule of Noncash Investing and Financing Activities:

Acquisition of land by issuance of common stock	$ 20,000

Problem 15-2

Stellar Inc.
Statement of Cash Flows
For Year Ended December 31, 2004

Cash flows from operating activities:			
Cash received from customers		$563,000	
Deduct: Cash payments for merchandise	$211,800		
Cash payments for operating expenses	169,600		
Cash payments for income tax	34,000	415,400	
Net cash flow from operating activities			$147,600
Cash flows from investing activities:			
Cash received from land sold		$ 54,000	
Less cash paid for purchase of equipment		96,000	
Net cash flow used for investing activities			(42,000)
Cash flows from financing activities:			
Cash used to retire bonds payable		$ 60,000	
Cash paid for dividends		27,600*	
Net cash flow used for financing activities			(87,600)
Increase in cash			$ 18,000
Cash, January 1, 2004			66,000
Cash, December 31, 2004			$ 84,000

*30,000 + 21,600 − 24,000

Schedule of Noncash Investing and Financing Activities:
Acquisition of land by issuance of common stock .... $ 20,000

Schedule Reconciling Net Income with Cash Flows from Operating Activities:

Net income, per income statement		$114,000
Add: Depreciation	$48,000	
Decrease in inventories	6,000	
Decrease in prepaid expenses	2,400	
Increase in accounts payable	7,200	63,600
		$177,600
Deduct: Increase in trade receivables	$12,000	
Gain on sale of land	18,000	30,000
Net cash flow provided by operating activities		$147,600

Supporting calculations:

Sales (reported on income statement)	$575,000
Less increase in trade receivables	(12,000)
Cash received	$563,000
Cost of merchandise sold	$225,000
Less decrease in inventories	(6,000)
Less increase in accounts payable	(7,200)
Cash payments for merchandise	$211,800
Operating expenses (other than depreciation)	$172,000
Less decrease in prepaid expenses	(2,400)
Cash payments for operating expenses	$169,600

CHAPTER 16

Fill In the Blank—Part A

1. vertical analysis
2. profitability analysis
3. current position analysis
4. solvency
5. common-size
6. current
7. net sales to assets
8. acid-test
9. earnings per share on common stock
10. working capital
11. accounts receivable turnover
12. inventory turnover
13. liabilities to stockholders' equity
14. preferred dividends are earned
15. income from operations
16. stockholders' equity
17. dividends
18. independent audit
19. fixed assets to long-term liabilities
20. net sales

Fill In the Blank—Part B

1. horizontal analysis
2. dividend yield
3. independent auditors'
4. number of days' sales in receivables
5. number of days' sales in inventory
6. interest charges earned
7. rate earned on total assets
8. rate earned on stockholders' equity
9. leverage
10. price-earnings
11. management report
12. quick assets
13. common-size
14. solvency analysis
15. bankers'
16. number of days' sales in inventory
17. earnings per share (on common stock)
18. common-size
19. receivables
20. management report

Multiple Choice

1. a. Incorrect.
   b. Incorrect. Horizontal statements are one type of statement that uses both relative comparisons and dollar amounts.
   c. Incorrect. Vertical statements are one type of statement that uses both relative comparisons and dollar amounts.
   d. **Correct.** In common-size statements, all items are expressed in percentages.

2. a. Incorrect. The rate of return on total assets is a profitability ratio.
   b. Incorrect. The price-earnings ratio is a profitability ratio.
   c. **Correct.** The accounts receivable turnover is a measure of solvency (short-term).
   d. Incorrect. The ratio of net sales to assets is a profitability ratio.

3. a. Incorrect.
   b. Incorrect.
   c. **Correct.** $4,000,000 / [$250,000 + $345,000) / 2]
   d. Incorrect.

4. a. Incorrect.
   b. **Correct.** $6,500,000 / [($175,000 + $297,000) / 2]
   c. Incorrect.
   d. Incorrect.

5. a. Incorrect. The financial highlights section provides an overview of the previous period's performance.
   b. Incorrect. The president's letter usually provides a brief explanation for the previous year's results.
   c. Incorrect. The independent auditor's report attests to the fairness of the financial statements.
   d. **Correct.** The management discussion and analysis provides an in-depth discussion of prior results and statements regarding future prospects and business risks.

6. a. Incorrect. The working capital ratio provides a measure of the short-term, debt-paying ability.
   b. Incorrect. The acid-test ratio provides a measure of the short-term, debt-paying ability.
   c. Incorrect. The receivables to inventory ratio is not an interpretable financial ratio.
   d. **Correct.** The number of days' sales in receivables is a measure of the efficiency in collecting receivables.

7. a. Incorrect.
   b. Incorrect.
   c. **Correct.** ($510,000 + $30,000) / $30,000
   d. Incorrect.

8. a. **Correct.** ($27,000 + $23,000 + $90,000) / $70,000
   b. Incorrect.
   c. Incorrect.
   d. Incorrect.

9. a. Incorrect.
   b. **Correct.** In a vertical analysis balance sheet, items are expressed as a percentage of total assets.
   c. Incorrect.
   d. Incorrect.

10. a. Incorrect.
   b. Incorrect.
   c. **Correct.** ($460,000 − $50,000) / 50,000 shares
   d. Incorrect.

11. a. Incorrect. A high dividend yield is usually associated with low P/E companies, since most of the shareholder return is in the form of predictable dividends, rather than share appreciation.
   b. **Correct.** High P/E firms are usually associated with high growth companies.
   c. Incorrect. Debt position is not usually associated with the P/E ratio.
   d. Incorrect. Current position is not usually associated with the P/E ratio.

12. a. Incorrect.
   b. Incorrect.
   c. Incorrect.
   d. **Correct.** ($240,000 + $120,000) / $1,000,000

True/False

1. F This statement is true for a vertical analysis, not a horizontal analysis.
2. T
3. F The net sales to assets ratio is a profitability ratio that shows how effectively and efficiently assets are used to generate sales.
4. T
5. F The receivable turnover is determined by dividing the net sales on account by the average accounts receivable outstanding during the period.
6. T
7. F The rate earned on total assets is determined by adding interest expense to net income, then dividing this sum by average total assets during the period.
8. T
9. T
10. F Working capital is the excess of current assets over current liabilities.

Exercise 16-1

	2003	Percent	2002	Percent
Revenues	$450,000	100%	$389,000	100%
Costs and expenses:				
Cost of sales	$200,000	44%	$176,000	45%
Selling and administrative expenses	100,000	23%	73,000	19%
Interest expense	250	0%	396	0%
Total costs and expenses	$300,250	67%	$249,396	64%
Earnings before income taxes	$149,750	33%	$139,604	36%
Income taxes	35,321	8%	33,765	9%
Net earnings	$114,429	25%	$105,839	27%

Exercise 16-2

	2003	2002	Increase (Decrease) Amount	Percent
Current assets	$250,000	$219,500	$ 30,500	14%
Fixed assets	435,000	401,600	33,400	8%
Intangible assets	42,000	46,500	(4,500)	−10%
Current liabilities	88,000	80,000	8,000	10%
Long-term liabilities	225,000	250,000	(25,000)	−10%
Common stock	214,000	167,600	46,400	28%
Retained earnings	200,000	170,000	30,000	18%

Problem 16-1

Nordic Inc.
Comparative Income Statement
For the Years Ended December 31, 2003 and 2002

	2003	2002	Increase (Decrease) Amount	Increase (Decrease) Percent
Sales	$690,500	$585,000	$105,500	18.0%
Sales returns and allowances	25,500	23,000	2,500	10.9%
Net sales	$665,000	$562,000	$103,000	18.3%
Cost of goods sold	420,000	330,000	90,000	27.3%
Gross profit	$245,000	$232,000	$ 13,000	5.6%
Selling expenses	$ 43,000	$ 47,700	$ (4,700)	−9.9%
Administrative expenses	31,000	31,000	0	0.0%
Total operating expenses	$ 74,000	$ 78,700	$ (4,700)	−6.0%
Operating income	$171,000	$153,300	$ 17,700	11.5%
Other income	13,000	16,400	(3,400)	−20.7%
	$184,000	$169,700	$ 14,300	8.4%
Other expense	58,000	53,500	4,500	8.4%
Income before income taxes	$126,000	$116,200	$ 9,800	8.4%
Income taxes	34,000	32,400	1,600	4.9%
Net income	$ 92,000	$ 83,800	$ 8,200	9.8%

Nordic Inc.
Comparative Balance Sheet
December 31, 2003 and 2002

Assets	2003	2002	Increase (Decrease) Amount	Increase (Decrease) Percent
Cash	$ 76,000	$ 69,000	$ 7,000	10.1%
Marketable securities	98,900	130,000	(31,100)	−23.9%
Accounts receivable (net)	199,000	195,000	4,000	2.1%
Inventory	450,000	375,000	75,000	20.0%
Prepaid expenses	28,000	26,300	1,700	6.5%
Long-term investments	35,000	35,000	0	0.0%
Fixed assets (net)	871,000	835,000	36,000	4.3%
Intangible assets	18,000	22,800	(4,800)	−21.1%
Total assets	$1,775,900	$1,688,100	$ 87,800	5.2%
Liabilities				
Current liabilities	$ 129,000	$ 107,000	$ 22,000	20.6%
Long-term liabilities	420,000	440,000	(20,000)	−4.5%
Total liabilities	$ 549,000	$ 547,000	$ 2,000	0.4%
Stockholders' Equity				
Preferred 3% stock, $100 par	$ 102,000	$ 93,000	$ 9,000	9.7%
Common stock, $50 par	549,900	530,100	19,800	3.7%
Retained earnings	575,000	518,000	57,000	11.0%
Total stockholders' equity	$1,226,900	$1,141,100	$ 85,800	7.5%
Total liabilities and stockholders' equity	$1,775,900	$1,688,100	$ 87,800	5.2%

Problem 16-2

Voyageur Inc.
Comparative Balance Sheet
December 31, 2003 and 2002

	2003		2002	
Assets	Amount	Percent	Amount	Percent
Cash	$ 500,000	5.3%	$ 425,000	5.4%
Marketable securities	200,000	2.1%	185,000	2.4%
Accounts receivable (net)	680,000	7.3%	575,000	7.3%
Inventory	860,000	9.2%	740,000	9.4%
Prepaid expenses	104,000	1.1%	95,000	1.2%
Long-term investments	450,000	4.8%	410,000	5.2%
Fixed assets (net)	6,556,000	70.1%	5,420,000	69.0%
Total assets	$9,350,000	100.0%	$7,850,000	100.0%
Liabilities				
Current liabilities	$1,090,000	11.7%	$1,050,000	13.4%
Long-term liabilities	2,150,000	23.0%	2,050,000	26.1%
Total liabilities	$3,240,000	34.7%	$3,100,000	39.5%
Stockholders' Equity				
Preferred 5% stock, $100 par	$ 350,000	3.7%	$ 350,000	4.5%
Common stock, $10 par	2,550,000	27.3%	2,550,000	32.5%
Retained earnings	3,210,000	34.3%	1,850,000	23.5%
Total stockholders' equity	$6,110,000	65.3%	$4,750,000	60.5%
Total liabilities and stockholders' equity	$9,350,000	100.0%	$7,850,000	100.0%

Voyageur Inc.
Income Statement
For the Year Ended December 31, 2003

	Amount	Percent
Sales	$12,800,000	102.4%
Sales returns and allowances	300,000	2.4%
Net sales	$12,500,000	100.0%
Cost of goods sold	7,550,000	60.4%
Gross profit	$ 4,950,000	39.6%
Selling expenses	$ 1,550,000	12.4%
Administrative expenses	825,000	6.6%
Total operating expenses	$ 2,375,000	19.0%
Operating income	$ 2,575,000	20.6%
Other income	125,000	1.0%
	$ 2,700,000	21.6%
Other expense (interest)	150,000	1.2%
Income before income taxes	$ 2,550,000	20.4%
Income taxes	937,000	7.5%
Net income	$ 1,613,000	12.9%

Problem 16-3

		Calculation	Final Result
a.	Working capital	$2,344,000 − $1,090,000	1,254,000
b.	Current ratio	$\dfrac{\$2,344,000}{\$1,090,000}$	2.2
c.	Acid-test ratio	$\dfrac{\$1,380,000}{\$1,090,000}$	1.3
d.	Accounts receivable turnover	$\dfrac{\$12,500,000}{\left(\dfrac{\$680,000+\$575,000}{2}\right)}$	19.9
e.	Number of days' sales in receivables	$\dfrac{\$12,500,000}{365}=\$34,247 \qquad \dfrac{\$680,000}{\$34,247}$	19.9
f.	Inventory turnover	$\dfrac{\$7,550,000}{\left(\dfrac{\$860,000+\$740,000}{2}\right)}$	9.4
g.	Number of days' sales in inventory	$\dfrac{\$7,550,000}{365}=\$20,685 \qquad \dfrac{\$860,000}{\$20,685}$	41.6
h.	Ratio of fixed assets to long-term liabilities	$\dfrac{\$6,556,000}{\$2,150,000}$	3.0
i.	Ratio of liabilities to stockholders' equity	$\dfrac{\$3,240,000}{\$6,110,000}$	0.5
j.	Number of times interest charges earned	$\dfrac{\$2,550,000+\$150,000}{\$150,000}$	18.0
k.	Number of times preferred dividends earned	$\dfrac{\$1,613,000}{\$17,500}$	92.2
l.	Ratio of net sales to assets	$\dfrac{\$12,500,000}{\left(\dfrac{\$8,900,000+\$7,440,000}{2}\right)}$	1.5
m.	Rate earned on total assets	$\dfrac{\$1,613,000+\$150,000}{\left(\dfrac{\$9,350,000+\$7,850,000}{2}\right)}$	20.5%
n.	Rate earned on stockholders' equity	$\dfrac{\$1,613,000}{\left(\dfrac{\$6,110,000+\$4,750,000}{2}\right)}$	29.7%
o.	Rate earned on common stockholders' equity	$\dfrac{\$1,613,000-\$17,500}{\left(\dfrac{\$5,760,000+\$4,400,000}{2}\right)}$	31.4%
p.	Earnings per share on common stock	$\dfrac{\$1,613,000-\$17,500}{255,000}$	$6.26

		Calculation	Final Result
q.	Price-earnings ratio	$\dfrac{\$29.75}{\$6.26}$	4.8
r.	Dividends per share of common stock	$\dfrac{\$250,000}{255,000}$	$.98
s.	Dividend yield	$\dfrac{\left(\dfrac{\$250,000}{255,000 \text{ shares}}\right)}{\$29.75}$	3.3%